P9-DMU-848

LANDFORMS

GEOLOGY: LANDFORMS, MINERALS, AND ROCKS

LANDFORMS

EDITED BY JOHN P. RAFFERTY, ASSOCIATE EDITOR,
EARTH AND LIFE SCIENCES

Britannica
Educational Publishing

IN ASSOCIATION WITH

ROSEN
EDUCATIONAL SERVICES

Published in 2012 by Britannica Educational Publishing
(a trademark of Encyclopædia Britannica, Inc.)
in association with Rosen Educational Services, LLC
29 East 21st Street, New York, NY 10010.

Distributed exclusively by Rosen Educational Services.
For a listing of additional Britannica Educational Publishing titles, call toll free (800) 237-9932.

First Edition

Britannica Educational Publishing
Michael I. Levy: Executive Editor
J.E. Luebering: Senior Manager
Marilyn L. Barton: Senior Coordinator, Production Control
Steven Bosco: Director, Editorial Technologies
Lisa S. Braucher: Senior Producer and Data Editor
Yvette Charboneau: Senior Copy Editor
Kathy Nakamura: Manager, Media Acquisition
John P. Rafferty: Associate Editor, Earth and Life Sciences

Rosen Educational Services
Alexandra Hanson-Harding: Rosen Editor
Nelson Sá: Art Director
Cindy Reiman: Photography Manager
Matthew Cauli: Designer, Cover Design
Introduction by Monique Vescia

Library of Congress Cataloging-in-Publication Data

Landforms / edited by John P. Rafferty. — 1st ed.
    p. cm. — (Geology: landforms, minerals, and rocks)
Includes bibliographical references and index.
ISBN 978-1-61530-486-8 (library binding)
1. Geomorphology. 2. Landforms. I. Rafferty, John P., editor.
GB401.5.L36 2012
551.41—dc22

                                                                    2010044327

Manufactured in the United States of America

On the cover (front and back): Desert in the Algerian Sahara. *Shutterstock.com*
On the cover (front top), p. iii (from left): Wadi Rum Desert in southern Jordan; a boat in
calm waters among mountains in China; the Everest and Lhotse mountain peaks as viewed
from Nepal; a geological formation called "the submarine," in Ischigualasto Natural Park,
San Juan, Arg., which is a UNESCO World Heritage Site. *Shutterstock.com*

On pages 1, 45, 93, 125, 172, 193, 225, 255, 258, 261, 266: The Zagros Mountains rise above
pasturelands, southwestern Iran. *Fred J. Maroon/Photo Researchers*

CONTENTS

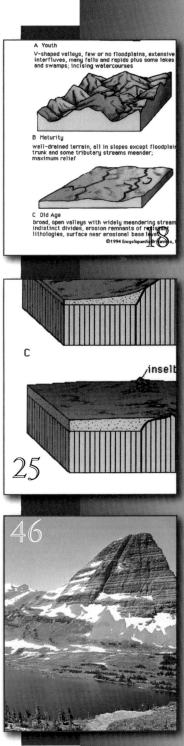

76

81

127

164

173

188

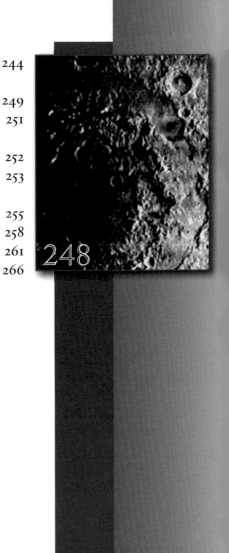

248

INTRODUCTION

When Ira Gershwin wrote his famous lyrics—"In time the Rockies may crumble, Gibraltar may tumble,"—for the classic song "Our Love is Here to Stay," he was talking about love, but he was thinking like a geomorphologist. Taken from the Greek *geo* for earth and *morph* for form, geomorphology is the study of landforms and the processes that affect them. A geomorphologist is, therefore, a scientist who studies landforms and the various natural processes that shape these physical features of a planet's surface. Mountain ranges, valleys, plateaus, caves, beaches, sea cliffs, fjords, and other landforms are distinctive features that give Earth its unique topography and supply the subject matter of this earth science.

When geomorphologists look at a landscape, they can envision it through a type of internal time-lapse photography. Through this exercise, mountains thrust up, only to settle down into heaps of debris; sea arches carved by ocean waves fall; and entire continents slide under the crust of another. Despite the appearance of permanence, everything on Earth is in the process of changing, and today's familiar landforms simply rest in just one particular phase of their continuing evolution.

In this volume, the study of landforms involves an adjustment to one's sense of time. Every landform, like every human being, has a life span. However, all of human existence represents only a tiny blip in comparison to the mind-bending span of geologic time. Geological processes, such as the creation of mountain ranges or the sculpting of river valleys, take many millennia to unfold. Some landforms, such as the stalagmites that form in the cool depths of a cave, grow by tiny increments, built up by the slow drip of minerals over hundreds of thousands

Mount Sir Donald in the Selkirk Mountains, British Columbia, and a segment of Trans-Canada Highway. Bob and Ira Spring/EB Inc.

of years. Other events occur far more quickly, driven by volcanic activity or the sudden collision of meteorites and comets that crater the planet's surface.

The study of landforms necessarily involves an understanding of the various processes that continue to mould Earth, the ocean floor, and other celestial bodies in the solar system. Most terrestrial landforms are shaped by a combination of tectonic forces—processes of volcanism, and crustal shortening, along with heating and thermal expansion—and what geologists call denudational processes, which are controlled by climate. Gravity also plays a part in the evolution of geological features. The shifting and collision of massive plates of rock that float on Earth's lithosphere and the movement of molten rock from volcanic activity create tectonic landforms such as mountains, plateaus, and rift valleys. Structural landforms, including sand dunes, subterranean caves, and fjords, are primarily the result of denudational processes. Over long spans of time, the movement of glaciers and the actions of wind and water wear away and carve out spaces in rock, sculpting various features on the planet's surface.

Human beings and other animals have a hand in the creation of landforms, as well. Human-engineered structures, such as the colossal Three Gorges Dam in China, and other biogenic landforms, such as dams made by beavers, have radically altered Earth's topography by flooding existing valleys and establishing new bodies of water. Creatures as tiny as termites can also construct landforms when they work together to build enormous termite mounds—some over 12 meters (forty feet tall)—such as those found in Africa and Australia.

Certain distinctive landforms, like towering mountains or deep canyons, have been regarded as sacred in many cultures, in part because they seem so mysterious. How did such incredible things come to be? Topographical features such as the Giant's Causeway in Northern Ireland

and Mount Fuji in Japan gave rise to myths and folk legends attributing their origins to supernatural forces. Since ancient times, people have searched for explanations for the presence of these natural wonders.

Some of the first gestures toward a geomorphic theory came about because people discovered marine fossils in unlikely places. In the fifth century BCE, the ancient Greek poet and philosopher Xenophanes of Colophon concluded that since seashells can be found on mountaintops, Earth's physical structure must change over time. Another fifth-century Greek, the historian Herodotus, noted that some rocks unearthed on land in Egypt contained marine fossils. He also theorized that the delta of the Nile River must have taken many millennia to form. One thousand years later, Leonardo da Vinci pondered the meaning of the presence of seashells on land, far from any ocean shore.

In the western world during the 18th and 19th centuries, theological beliefs about the Creation influenced the formulation of landform theories. Based on interpretations of the Bible, some calculations dated the age of Earth to 4004 BCE, a time far too recent to account for the presence of many landforms. This problem prompted the development of various catastrophic theories. Geologists such as Abraham Gottlob Werner argued that certain features of Earth's topography must have been created swiftly by violent forces. Others believed that the Great Flood described in the Bible, which supposedly deposited Noah's ark on Mount Ararat, accounted for the large-scale deposition of many rocks and widespread erosion as floodwaters receded.

Those who searched for scientific rather than theological explanations of landforms included the Scottish geologist James Hutton, considered the founder of modern geology. One of three major theories that dominated landform theory during the 18th and 19th centuries, Hutton's theory of uniformitarianism proposed that Earth's crust reached its current state as a result of geologic processes still occurring today. Hutton concluded that natural processes, such as erosion, deposition, sedimentation, and upthrusting, are cyclical and have happened many times in the planet's history.

Along with catastrophism and uniformitarianism, Sir Charles Lyell's concept of gradualism represented a significant contribution to early geomorphological science. In his groundbreaking book *Principles of Geology* (1830), Lyell argued against the catastrophic origins for landforms, maintaining instead that the planet's current physical appearance resulted from incremental changes taking place slowly over enormous spans of time. Ultimately, geologists would determine that both sudden and gradual processes occur in landform evolution.

Another theory that proved critical to the development of geomorphology was the concept of isostasy. Simply put, the concept posited that the elevations of continents and ocean floors correlate directly to the densities of the rock underneath them. For example, very high mountains must have very deep "roots" that extend down into Earth's mantle to balance the mass above sea level with an equivalent mass below. Observations made as early as 1735 laid the groundwork for isostatic theory, which was later refined in the mid-1880s by the work of two Englishmen, Sir George Biddell Airy and George Henry Pratt.

Gradually, additional theories gained traction. Among the most influential were those proposed by William Morris Davis, an American geologist and geographer whose concepts of erosion cycles and dynamic equilibrium dominated geomorphology until 1950. In 1899 Davis described a process he called the "geographical cycle." This cycle begins with an uplift of an area above sea level, after which the surface is worn down by the forces of gravity and running water. Davis classified landforms according to the categories of youth, maturity, and old age, depending on what evolutionary stage of the geographic cycle they had reached.

Once dismissed by many geologists as a purely accidental factor in landform development, continental glaciation is now recognized as a significant component in landform evolution. During the 1840s, a German-born mining engineer named Johann von Charpentier and the Swiss naturalist Louis Agassiz both published papers describing glacial movement as a geologic process. Through erosion and the deposition of sediment scoured from the rocks they pass over, glaciers have sculpted landforms such as the Matterhorn and other horns in the Swiss Alps, as well as less famous features called hanging valleys, paternoster lakes, and pingos.

Geologists have long observed that particular landforms tend to occur in areas subject to a specific type of climate. Such observations eventually lent support to the concept of climatic morphogenesis and the widespread acknowledgment that climate, in its wild extremes, plays a dynamic role in shaping Earth's physical appearance. Thus, extremely arid and humid climates can contribute to the evolution of unique landforms.

Another set of ideas that forced a wholesale reconsideration of geologic science was the concept of plate tectonics. The two principal tectonic actions recognized today are orogenesis—that is, the process of mountain-building, which is accomplished by the folding and faulting of the planet's crust—and epeirogenesis—that is, the uplift or depression of large areas to form continents or basins on the planet's surface. Theories of plate tectonics developed in the 1960s now form the foundations of geology and geomorphology. As a result, we know that the Himalayas, a range of massively high mountains in Nepal and Tibet, formed gradually over a period of 60 million years. Over many millions of years, the Indian Plate ploughed slowly and inexorably into and under the Asian Plate and part of the planet's crust was forced upward. Even today, India continues to slide under Tibet, and the Himalayan mountains grow 5 mm (0.2 inch) higher every year.

The complexity of the planet's topography has made it difficult for scientists to formulate a comprehensive theory that applies to Earth as a whole. Coastal areas are very different from mountainous terrains, and both have little in common with the weird formations that occur in karst landscapes and submarine caves. Geologists now agree that any modern unified theory must take into account a list of 24 factors. These factors include the recognition that some geological phenomena may take longer to occur than Earth is old (4.5 billion years); the acknowledgement that there is no such thing as an average terrestrial climate; and the understanding that meteorite and comet impacts can create massive landforms on a planet's surface.

Efforts to arrive at a single unified theory received a boost when geologists began to examine the solar system as a whole rather than focusing only on Earth. Any given planet is subject to two potential geomorphic factors:exogenic (originating from without) and endogenic (originating from within). The exogenic category includes solar debris, radiation, and other factors a planetary body is exposed to while orbiting its star. Endogenic factors arise because of the heat generated by the planet's molten core and the volcanism and tectonic movements resulting from the movement of heat. The particular morphogenesis, or structural formation, of a planetary body results from the interaction of these two factors. Consider the physical differences between Earth and Moon. Both exogenic and endogenic processes contributed to the evolution of these bodies. Powerful endogenic forces continue to transform the appearance of our planet, since Earth's core still generates tremendous heat and parts of its surface are in constant motion. In contrast, the much colder and less active Moon is mostly subject to exogenic forces.

Like Earth's landforms, geomorphology continues to evolve. While early work in the field was principally concerned with classifying various types of landforms, today's geomorphologists focus on the geologic processes and interactions that combine to shape Earth's topographical features. Scientists can now access and analyse images and other data gathered by satellites far above the planet's surface and leverage mathematical and computer models to better understand landform processes. Powerful new tools such as remote sensors and global positioning systems enable them to collect information with which they can map regions with greater accuracy.

The work of geomorphologists has many important practical applications as well. They are often called on to identify areas at risk from floods or landslides. They advise governments on the management or restoration of natural resources. Growing concerns about climate change, prompted by the accelerated melting of glaciers and the threat of rising sea levels, have raised the stakes for the practitioners of this relatively young science. Geomorphologists can help people better understand and prepare for the planet's transformation in the years to come.

Earth still guards some of its secrets. When the American geologist John Wesley Powell explored the Colorado River during the 19th century, he wondered why the watercourse seemed to have followed the path of highest resistance as it cut its way through the landscape. Modern geomorphology still cannot fully explain how certain plateaus such as those on the Iberian Peninsula and in north central Mexico came to be, and the exact origin of fjords also remains a matter of debate. Every landform tells a story about the various processes involved in its birth and evolution. It has taken geomorphologists a long time to begin to decipher the planet's language, and many mysteries remain to be solved.

CHAPTER 1
THE DEVELOPMENT OF LANDFORMS

A landform can be defined as any conspicuous topographic feature on Earth or a similar planetary body or satellite—topography being the configuration of a surface including its relief and the position of its natural and man-made features. Familiar examples are mountains (including volcanic cones), plateaus, and valleys. Comparable structures have been detected on Mars, Venus, the Moon, and certain satellites of Jupiter and Saturn. The term *landform* also can be applied to related features that occur on the floor of Earth's ocean basins, as, for example, seamounts, mid-oceanic ridges, and submarine canyons.

The distribution and structure of landforms reflect the geomorphic processes (relating to the surface features of Earth) that created them. Most landforms occurring at the surface of the terrestrial land masses result from the interaction of two fundamental types of processes over geologic time. These are (1) vertical tectonic movements, that is, upward folding and fault-creating movements in Earth's crust, and extrusion of magma (molten rock material) and (2) denudational processes, which include the weathering and erosion of rocks and the accumulation of the resulting sedimentary debris.

Relief features produced chiefly by uplift and subsidence (settling) of Earth's crust or by the upward movement of magma through volcanoes can be classified as tectonic landforms. They include rift valleys, plateaus,

BIOGENIC LANDFORMS

Any topographic feature that can be attributed to the activity of organisms is called a biogenic landform. Such features are diverse in both kind and scale. Organisms contribute to the genesis of most topography involving rock weathering, although the role they play is usually auxiliary, as demonstrated by bacterial and lichen activity, the effects of root wedging, and solutional erosion made possible by humic acid produced by rapid organic decay. The latter is responsible for much tropical karst.

On an entirely different level are features that constitute what may be termed micro topography. Some of these are produced by individual creatures or groups of such creatures. Examples include the cylindrical mud towers that stand 40–50 cm (16–20 inches) high atop crayfish burrows in the southern part of the United States; badger and bear den burrows; elephant waterholes on the veld (grasslands of Africa); and quarries and open-pit mines dug by humans. Other topographic features are attributable to colonial organisms. In various parts of the world such as the semiarid plains of the Western Sahara, colonies of termites build large conical mounds that reach a height of several metres. The interaction of corals, algae, and bryozoa is largely responsible for the framework of features known as organic reefs, which abound in tropical marine settings. Some of these reefs have given rise to entire insular land areas many kilometres in diameter. The largest example is the Great Barrier Reef of Australia, which covers an area of about 207,000 square km (about 80,000 square miles). Though nearly submerged today, it was an island during the Pleistocene glaciations.

With the possible exception of the Great Barrier Reef, all major biogenic landforms produced in recent times are attributable to the activities of humankind. The construction of modern superhighways involves some of the most extensive terrain changes on Earth, having in some cases resulted in the removal of mountains or at least large portions thereof. Many human effects are not necessarily tied to particular construction projects. On a subtler level, the removal of fluids from the ground, principally water and petroleum, has lowered water tables and reduced pore pressure so greatly that extensive areas have experienced subsidence, collapse, and shrinkage. Terrain changes due to groundwater removal are extremely severe in such regions as the southwestern United States or the area near Mexico City. To the foregoing human effects on topography must be added the bomb craters left by war that are very slowly being obliterated from Europe and Asia, and the erosional gullying of terrain where uncontrolled deforestation has been allowed. Finally, there are the engineering modifications of waterways and coasts practiced nowhere more intensively than in the United States and Europe. River flow patterns have been drastically altered, usually by channel straightening, and the construction of large dams has converted entire valleys, gorges, and canyons into lakes. In fact, dams are among the largest biogenic landforms produced.

mountains, and volcanic cones. Denudational features form other topographic features, such as pediments, sand dunes, subterranean caves, fjords, and beaches. These features, categorized as structural landforms, are attributable to the action of rivers, wind, groundwater solution, glaciers, sea waves, and other external agents as they erode rock and deposit it elsewhere.

Although tectonic and denudational processes account for the origin of most landform types, a few have been produced by other means. Impact craters, for one, are formed by collisions with asteroids, comets, and meteorites. Biogenic landforms, for another, are produced—as the term implies—by living organisms. They range from giant termite mounds and coral reefs to open-pit mines and dams created by humans.

Any conspicuous topographic feature on the largest land areas of Earth is called a continental landform. Mountains (including volcanic cones), plateaus, and valleys are familiar examples. Such structures are rendered unique by the tectonic mechanisms that generate them and by the climatically controlled denudational systems that modify them through time. The resulting topographic features tend to reflect both the tectonic and the denudational processes involved.

The most dramatic expression of tectonism is mountainous topography, which is either generated along continental margins (the edge of the continental crust where it meets with the ocean's crust) by collisions between the slablike plates that make up Earth's lithosphere or formed somewhat farther inland by rifting and faulting. The lithosphere is the outer part of the solid Earth, consisting of the crust and outermost layer of the mantle, and usually considered to be about 100 km (60 miles) in thickness. Far more subtle tectonic expressions are manifested by the vast continental regions of limited relief and elevation affected by gentle uplift, subsidence, tilting, and warping. Volcanism may modify any landscape by fissure-erupted flood basalts capable of creating regional lava plateaus or by vent eruptions that yield individual volcanoes. Once these features are created, the denudational processes act upon the tectonic "stage set" and are able to modify its features in a degree that reflects which forces are dominant through time.

The denudational processes, which involve rock weathering and both erosion and deposition of rock debris, are governed in character by climate, whose variations of heat and moisture create landscapes that are vegetated, desert, or glacial. Most regions have been exposed to repeated changes in climate rather than to a single enduring condition. Climates can change very slowly through continental drift, the large-scale horizontal movements of continents relative to one another during one or more episodes of geologic time, and much more rapidly through variations in such factors as solar radiation (electromagnetic radiation, including, among other things, X-rays, ultraviolet and radiation and light, emanating from the sun).

In most instances, a combination of the foregoing factors is responsible for any given landscape. In a few cases, tectonism (the process of deformation that produces in Earth's crust its continents and ocean basins), some special combination of denudational effects, or volcanism may control the entire landform suite. Where tectonism exists in the form of orogenic uplift, that is to say, the process of how mountains are formed by folding the crust of Earth, the high-elevation topography depends on the nature of denudation. In humid or glacial environments whose geomorphic agencies can exploit lithologic variations, the rocks are etched into mountainous relief like that of the Alps or the southern Andes. In arid orogenic settings (settings where mountains are formed), the effects of aggradation and planation—processes in which the land's surface becomes flatter and more uniform by the depositing of loose material such as rocks) often result in alluviated intermontane basins. These basins, filled with

Simien Mountains, rising above the Ethiopian Plateau in northwestern Ethiopia. Photo Almasy

clay, silt, sand, or gravel deposited by running water, merge with high plateaus that are interrupted or bordered by mountains such as the central Andes or those of Tibet and Colorado in the western United States.

In continental regions where mountainous uplifts are lacking, denudational processes operate on rocks that are only slightly deformed—if they are sedimentary—and only moderately elevated. This produces broad basins, ramps, swells, and plains. These are most thoroughly dissected in rain-and-river environments (sometimes attaining local mountainous relief on uplifts). Elsewhere, they may be broadly alluviated and pedimented where mainly arid, or widely scoured and aggraded where glacial. A pediment is a broad gently sloping bedrock surface with low relief that is situated at the base of a steeper slope and is usually thinly covered with alluvial gravel and sand.

Minor denudational landforms are superimposed on the major features already noted. Where aridity has dominated, they include pediments, pans, dune complexes, dry washes, alluvial veneers, bajadas, and fans. In humid regions, a type of landscape called ridge-ravine topography and integrated drainage networks with associated thick soils occur. Combinations of these features are widespread wherever arid and humid conditions have alternated, and either category may merge laterally with the complex suite of erosional and depositional landforms generated by continental glaciers at higher latitudes.

BASIC CONCEPTS AND CONSIDERATIONS

Landform evolution is an expression that implies progressive changes in topography from an initial designated morphology (structure) toward or to some altered form.

The changes can only occur in response to energy available to do work within the geomorphic system in question, and it necessarily follows that the evolution will cease when the energy is consumed or can no longer be effectively utilized to induce further change. The latter steady state, or dynamic equilibrium, situation will then continue with little topographic change until the prevailing conditions cease or are disrupted, so that a new evolutionary sequence can begin.

The English poet Alfred, Lord Tennyson once wrote:

The hills are shadows, and they flow
From form to form, and nothing stands;
They melt like mist, the solid lands,
Like clouds they shape themselves and go.

Tennyson's verse speaks well of the geomorphic necessities of time and landform change. Even the ancients were well aware of the ongoing effects of gravity, and it has long been realized that, given time and in the absence of opposing forces, gravity would pull Earth's surface roughness down to form a featureless subaqueous spheroid. Such an evolution would be simplicity in the extreme and may in fact foretell the eventual destiny of terrestrial landforms when internal processes that generate relief cease to operate some billions of years hence in response to growing entropy in the system.

Even now in regions where the uplifting and relief-creating mechanisms have been inoperative for several hundreds of millions of years, the lands have been reduced by denudation to low and often nearly featureless plains. Yet, it is clear that any modern theory of landform evolution must take into account the possibility of a periodic regeneration of continental elevations, particularly of large-scale relief features. For without such regeneration, there would be no continents or mountains even today, given their present rates of erosional destruction.

The history of landscape evolution theory is one of adapting concepts to new evidence of increasing complexity. This situation is quite apparent in the way thinkers and scientists have dealt with the processes within Earth that oppose gravity and re-create land elevation and roughness. The existence of such processes was implicit in the writings of Xenophanes of Colophon (c. 570–c. 478 BCE), Herodotus (c. 484–420? BCE), and Leonardo da Vinci (1452–1519). The culmination of ideas of continental renewal and relief genesis is found in the isostatic theory (i.e., a theory in which the general equilibrium in Earth's crust is maintained by a yielding flow of rock material beneath the surface that is under stress from gravity) formulated by John Henry Pratt and George Biddel Airy of England during the mid-1800s and in the concepts of plate tectonics put forth by Harry H. Hess and Robert S. Dietz of the United States during the early 1960s. Periodic resurrection of the surface roughness of Earth is an event that geologists continually plot, widely accept, and increasingly understand.

Over the years there have been many other ideas that have posed complications for geomorphic theory. Notable among these were notions of continental submergence by seas (proposed by Georges-Louis Leclerc, comte de Buffon, about 1750), which had implications of relative sea-level changes and sedimentary leveling of submerged areas.

Theoretical matters were complicated further by suggestions during the 19th century that iceberg rafting of gravel during Noah's Flood accounted for glacial "drift." Since that time, the Noachian Deluge theory has lost much of its geomorphic appeal. Yet, sedimentary deposits laid down in ancient inland seas are widely acknowledged to account for much continental bedrock, and they underlie and create vast structural plains in areas such as Australia.

The geomorphic implications of volcanism were already widely appreciated in the 1700s, though they were not well integrated into modern tectonic mechanisms until 1961. Climate, however, is another story. Glacial theory was introduced during the early 1800s and was seen by many to have climatic and geomorphic implications. Nonetheless, the most popular theory of landform evolution of the past century, that proposed by the American geologist and geographer William Morris Davis (c. 1899), relegated continental glaciation to accidental status and gave no real consideration to the geomorphic effects of non-glacial climates. Until about 1950 this Davisian view held sway in geomorphology. Since then, research has shown beyond question that a variety of climatic effects can have a profound influence on landscape, that climates change (often with great frequency and intensity), and that virtually none of these events can be termed accidental.

CONSTRAINTS ON MODERN LANDFORM THEORY

Rather than merely trace the hit-or-miss development of geomorphic ideas from their beginnings roughly two centuries ago, it seems preferable to cite here those conditions firmly determined by intensive research that must serve as constraints for any modern theory of landform evolution. A brief mention of the postulates of earlier theorists will then show immediately what they accomplished, ignored, failed to consider, or were ignorant of. In sum, a modern theory of landform evolution must contend with the following well-established factors:

- Continents consist of a craton (the stable interior portion of a continent characteristically composed of ancient crystalline basement rock) 1 billion to 3 billion or more years old, have been periodically submerged by epicontinental seas, and are in most cases locally covered with veneers of nearly flat-lying sedimentary rocks. A craton is a stable relatively immobile area of Earth's crust that forms the nuclear mass of a continent or the central basin of an ocean.

- Where orogenic events were involved less than 500 million years ago, mountainous elevations and relief containing deformed rocks exist on continents.

- Lowering of the land by denudational processes is accompanied by essentially continuous isostatic adjustment by load-compensating uplift.

- Mountainous relief of the continent-to-continent collision type (e.g., the Appalachian Mountains of eastern North America) can eventually be eliminated by erosion, whereas trench-type mountains (e.g., the Andes of western South America) probably cannot as long as the associated trench subduction system endures.

- Climates on lands vary through time in response to lateral continental drift of 0–12 cm (0–5 inches) per year. North America, for example, is moving northwest at a rate of about 3 cm (about 1 inch) per year. On the other hand, Antarctica is hardly moving and has been in a polar position undergoing glaciation for about 30 million years.

- Over most lands, climates also vary with atmospheric, oceanic, and solar factors in cycles lasting thousands of years (the Milankovitch solar radiation cycle, for example, has a duration of ±25,800 years).
- In select hydrographically favoured sites—that is, sites with favourable amounts of water—on time scales not influenced by continental drift (e.g., Antarctica), climates on continents or portions thereof can remain essentially constant for periods of millions of years.
- Since geomorphic processes under arid, humid, glacial, and possibly other climate conditions can induce particular landforms, areas subject to periodic climate change often show polygenetic landform associations, or, in other words, associations that have many distinct sources.
- Landforms exposed for millions of years to a constant environment may display a climax (steady-state) landform association that is essentially timeless and in which landform evolution through denudation is reduced to mere negative allotropic growth.
- Since volcanism is seemingly localized in accordance with mobile heat-dispersal patterns within Earth, eruptive effects may be imposed on any surficial geomorphic system at any stage of development.
- Similarly, mobile tectonic patterns involving rock deformation may be brought to bear on any surficial geomorphic system, with resulting relief, elevation, and topographic changes.
- Impacts on planetary surfaces by falling meteoroids, asteroids, and cometary bodies are

periodic but are capable of generating landforms of mountainous proportions.

- Surficial geomorphic agents of denudation
responsible for many, if not most, landforms
include mass wasting, running water, glacial
ice, and wind. They are not all of equal significance in every climatic setting, however.

- The geomorphic agents respond to various climates, changing in character and effect. They
also respond in some degree to altered conditions of elevation and relief.

- The behaviour of denudational agencies and
related geomorphic processes is neither constant nor linear in nature. Rates vary from
long-term, imperceptible, and gradual to brief,
rapid, and catastrophic.

- Changes produced by geomorphic agents vary
in magnitude but not directly with time—i.e.,
the same change involving the same energy
expenditure may be either slow or fast. (Studies
of river systems, for example, suggest that
greater changes in channel morphology occur
during brief infrequent floods than during protracted low-flow periods.)

- Perturbations in geomorphic processes or environments cause accelerated changes in most
landform configurations, soils, and deposits,
which eventually slow down as new equilibrium forms develop.

- A given landform or deposit is only stable in
association with its formative process and
environment, and in any subsequent alterna-
tive setting it begins to change toward a new
equilibrium morphology.

- In a denudational setting, slope as an influence over process rate may be subordinated to such factors as runoff volume, soil-moisture content, bedrock coherence, ground-cover type, channel roughness, channel cross section, weathering type, sediment calibre, and sediment quantity.
- When climate in a region changes, elimination of relict landforms (features or rocks remaining after other parts have disappeared) and deposits causes a disequilibrium phase, which is followed by a dynamic equilibrium phase as new geomorphic equilibria are established. The disequilibrium phase may range from a few score or hundred years for certain organic responses to many thousands of years for soil, hillslope, or drainage adjustments.
- Some landforms or deposits, once formed, strongly resist subsequent changes regardless of climatic history—e.g., entrenched meanders such as those that exist in parts of the Appalachians, chert felsenmeers (accumulations of rock blocks) like those in the southern Ozark region of the United States, and duricrusts of the type commonly found in Australia.
- No such thing as an "average" terrestrial climate seems to exist, and certainly a climatic "norm" for one continental configuration would differ from that for another—e.g., the supercontinent Pangaea of pre-Cretaceous times (more than 146 million years ago) differed climatically from its subsequent fragments for both the Cretaceous (approximately 146 million to 65.5 million years ago) and the present.

- Sea level has been found wanting as a stable limiting datum for erosional processes or as an influence on stream behaviour. Glacioeustatic fluctuations--changes relating to a worldwide change in sea level—on the order of 130–150 metres (about 425–500 feet) appear to have been commonplace during the continental glacial sequences of the Carboniferous (approximately 359 million to 299 million years ago) and Pleistocene (approximately 2.6 million to 11,700 years ago) and at other times, and periodic desiccation (drying up) of restricted ocean basins has occasionally permitted major rivers to deepen their courses thousands of metres below mean sea level.

- Earth and the solar system as a whole are at least 4.5 billion years old. This is long enough for some geomorphic phenomena to occur several times but probably not long enough for others to happen even once. Certainly it is doubtful if more than nine collision-type mountain systems can have been eroded away in one spot, even if it were possible for them to form there.

HISTORICAL SURVEY

Some of the more significant landform theories of the past 200 years or so are considered here, with particular attention to the degree to which they reflect the list of geomorphic constraints cited earlier. It should be noted that most early theorists operated within the chronological limitations imposed by theologians. During the 17th century, for example, Archbishop James Ussher of Ireland added up the ages of men cited in the Bible and concluded that the Creation had occurred in 4004 BCE. John

Lightfoot, an English divine and Hebraist, was so stimulated by this revelation that he additionally observed that the exact time was October 26 at 9:00 AM! This meant that all of Earth's surface features had to have been formed in less than 6,000 years. Given this time frame, geomorphologists could explain the genesis of landforms in only one way—on the basis of catastrophic events. Everything had to occur quickly and therefore violently.

LANDFORM THEORIES OF THE 18TH AND 19TH CENTURIES

Three theories guided the understanding of landform development during the 18th and 19th centuries. Proponents of catastrophism maintained that Earth's landforms were the product of abrupt cataclysms. It was later determined that catastrophes do explain the presence of and destruction of some landforms, but most evolve through processes described by uniformitarianism and gradualism.

CATASTROPHISM

During the late 18th and early 19th century, the leading proponent of this view was the German mineralogist Abraham Gottlob Werner. According to Werner, all of Earth's rocks were formed by rapid chemical precipitation from a "world ocean," which he then summarily disposed of in catastrophic fashion. Though not directed toward the genesis of landforms in any coherent fashion, his catastrophic philosophy of changes of Earth had two major consequences of geomorphic significance. First, it indirectly led to the formulation of an opposing, less extreme view by the Scottish scientist James Hutton in 1785. Second, it was in some measure correct: catastrophes do occur on Earth and they do change its landforms.

Asteroid impacts, Krakatoa-type volcanic explosions, hurricanes, floods, and tectonic erosion of mountain systems all occur, may be catastrophic, and can create and destroy landforms. Yet, not all change is catastrophic.

UNIFORMITARIANISM

The Huttonian proposal that Earth has largely achieved its present form through the past occurrence of processes still in operation has come to be known as the doctrine of uniformitarianism. This is a geologic rather than a simply geomorphic doctrine. It is, however, more nearly aimed at actual surficial changes that pertain to landforms than were Werner's notions. The idea championed by Hutton formed the basis of what is now often referred to as process geomorphology. In this area of study, research emphasis is placed on observing what can be accomplished by a contemporary geologic agency such as running water. Later, the role of moving ice, gravity, and wind in the molding of valleys and hillslopes came to be appreciated by study of these phenomena. Uniformitarianism also became the working principle for a growing number of geologic historians, notably William Smith and Sir Charles Lyell, in the 19th century. This was necessary as Lyell argued increasingly that geologic change was incremental and gradual. He needed a longer time scale if this approach was to work, and geologic historians were finding it for him.

GRADUALISM

Lyell's concept of gradualism and accompanying process observation on an expanded time scale resulted in firmly establishing the fact that much could be accomplished by small forces working constantly for long periods. That conclusion is consistent even with present-day thought. Lyell's almost total rejection of any geologic process that was abrupt and suggestive of catastrophe, however, was in itself an extreme posture. Research has shown that both gradual and rapid changes occur.

In the philosophical climate established by Hutton's uniformitarianism and Lyell's gradualism, geomorphologists of the 19th century realized many impressive accomplishments. Most notable among these were the studies of glacial phenomena in Europe by Johann von Charpentier and Louis Agassiz and the investigations of regional denudation in the American West by Grove K. Gilbert and Clarence E. Dutton, which emphasized the work of running water. The findings pertaining to glaciers still stand for the most part, and Gilbert's hydraulic studies laid the groundwork for modern ideas. Yet, neither he nor Dutton made comprehensive theoretical proposals of terrestrial morphogenesis of a scope that could match those of the aforementioned W.M. Davis.

DAVIS'S EROSION CYCLE THEORY

Beginning in 1899, Davis proposed that denudation of the land occurs in what he called "the geographical cycle." According to Davis, this cycle is initiated by an uplift of an area above sea level, followed by a wearing down of the surface through the action of running water and gravity until either the region is worn away (base leveled) or the events are interrupted by renewed uplift. It was further explained that such a cycle of erosion occurs under conditions of a rain-and-rivers environment (what present-day investigators would call a humid climate), which were assumed to reflect Earth's normal climate. The fact that Davis dismissed glacial phenomena as accidents of climate and viewed climatic areas as geographically fixed afforded his theory more latitude. Furthermore, Davis proposed the idea of a separate arid geographical cycle in 1905. In all cases,

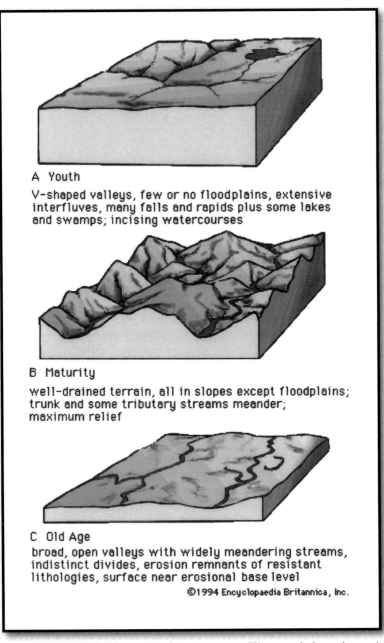

A Youth
V-shaped valleys, few or no floodplains, extensive interfluves, many falls and rapids plus some lakes and swamps; incising watercourses

B Maturity
well-drained terrain, all in slopes except floodplains; trunk and some tributary streams meander; maximum relief

C Old Age
broad, open valleys with widely meandering streams, indistinct divides, erosion remnants of resistant lithologies, surface near erosional base level

©1994 Encyclopaedia Britannica, Inc.

Davis's proposed landscape-development states. The morphology shown is meant to be an example of what could occur. It is not actually time-indicative. Adapted from H.F. Garner, *The Origin of Landscapes* (1974); Oxford University Press, Inc.

erosive power was presumed to be controlled primarily by slope; hence, the cyclic system was slowed down as the land was leveled and relief and elevation were diminished. The end point of a low-inclination, gently undulating, almost featureless plain was termed a peneplain, and it was said to be locally surmounted by erosionally resistant highs called monadnocks. A monadnock is an isolated hill of bedrock standing conspicuously above the general level of the surrounding area. Monadnocks are left as erosional remnants because of their more resistant rock composition; commonly they consist of quartzite or less jointed massive volcanic rocks. The peneplain as a whole was presumed to be graded to regional base level (in all likelihood mean sea level) by denudational agencies (e.g., running water), which were supposedly controlled by this datum.

The provisions of Davis's erosion cycle run counter to at least half of the 25 constraints on theories of landform evolution listed above. The Davisian erosion cycle theory is hurt by three factors in particular: (1) the presently understood need for continuous isostatic uplift during erosion, (2) the climatic variability displayed by most lands, and (3) the hydraulic behaviour of rivers noted by Gilbert that precludes valley alluviation under normal humid conditions and limits base-level influences over interior slopes.

The notion of an erosion cycle initiated by uplift is still possible within known constraints. Such a cycle is only possible under one particular climatic umbrella, however, and under much more limited geographic and hydrographic circumstances than Davis assumed. Moreover, the morphological sets of landforms selected by Davis as chronological "mile posts" for his cycle of landform change (i.e., stages of development) have been found to constitute special, generally polygenetic arrays of landscape features that reflect the interplay of several environments and that have little or no sequential time significance.

EROSION

The removal of surface material from Earth's crust, primarily soil and rock debris, and the transportation of this material by natural agencies from the point of removal is called erosion.

The broadest application of the term *erosion* embraces the general wearing down and molding of all landforms on Earth's surface, including the weathering of rock in its original position, the transport of weathered material, and erosion caused by wind action, fluvial processes, marine processes, and glacial processes. This broad definition is more correctly called denudation, or degradation, and includes mass-movement processes. A narrow and somewhat limiting definition of erosion excludes the transport of eroded material by natural agencies, but the exclusion of the transport phenomenon makes the distinction between erosion and weathering very vague. Erosion, therefore, includes the transportation of eroded or weathered material from the point of degradation, but not the deposition of material at a new site. The complementary actions of erosion and deposition or sedimentation operate through the geomorphic processes of wind, moving water, and ice to alter existing landforms and create new landforms.

Erosion will often occur after rock has been disintegrated or altered through weathering. Weathered rock material will be removed from its original site and transported away by a natural agent. With both processes often operating simultaneously, the best way to distinguish erosion from weathering is by observing the transportation of material.

Moving water is the most important natural erosional agent. The wastage of the sea coast, or coastal erosion, is brought about in the main by the action of sea waves but also, in part, by the disintegration or degradation of sea cliffs by atmospheric agents such as rain, frost, and tidal scour. Sea-wave erosion is accomplished primarily by hydraulic pressure, the impact of waves striking the shore, and by the abrasion of sand and pebbles agitated incessantly by the water.

In rivers and estuaries the erosion of banks is caused by the scouring action of the moving water, particularly in times of flood and, in the case of estuaries, also by the tidal flow on the ebb tide when river and tidewater combine in their erosive action. This scouring action of the moving water entrains and transports sediments within the river or stream load. These entrained sediments become instruments of erosion as they abrade one another in suspended transport or as they abrade other rock and soil as they are dragged along the river bottom.

Glacial erosion occurs in two principal ways: through abrasion as the ice grinds over the ground (much of the abrasive action being attributable to the debris embedded in the ice along its base) and by the plucking of rock from the glacier bed. In some arid tracts, the surface of sand dunes not held together by vegetation is subject to erosion by the drifting of blown sand. This eolian (wind) action also erodes material by sandblasting landforms with wind-blown debris.

Davis's contribution to the theory of landform evolution also includes the idea of process interruption as a means of accelerating change (rejuvenation) and the notion of process slowing in a late stage of process evolution as energy is consumed. The latter idea comes close to the present-day description of dynamic equilibrium, or attainment of a steady-state (climax) environment and parallels modern thinking on entropy relationships.

Davis proposed his scheme of landscape-development stages close on the heels of Charles Darwin's theory of organic evolution, and his landscape designations "youth," "maturity," and "old age" are blatantly anthropomorphic. Thus, it is quite understandable why they had, at the turn of the century, such appeal and acceptance in spite of their actual lack of chronological significance. Their continued use is less comprehensible.

The Geomorphic Concepts of Penck and King

The theoretical groundwork laid by Davis for geomorphic evolution was further developed in a rather special fashion

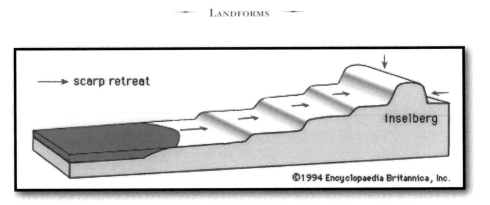

An escarpment is a long cliff or steep slope separating two comparatively level or more gently sloping surfaces and resulting from erosion or faulting. This diagram shows a cross section of an area undergoing erosion by escarpment retreat under Penck's Treppen *mechanism. Regional base level (± mean sea level) was presumed to provide a limiting downward erosional datum following each episode of uplift marked by stream incision and escarpment development. surfaces and resulting from erosion or faulting.* From H.F. Garner, *The Origin of Landscapes* (1974); Oxford University Press, Inc.

in 1924 by Walther Penck of Germany, and subsequently (1953) championed with variations by Lester C. King of South Africa. Both retained some Davisian devices, including peneplain, graded stream, and base-level control of erosion surfaces in Penck's case and the latter two in King's. Each thought that tectonic uplift punctuated the erosion cycle by initiating renewed stream incision, and each utilized the concept of parallel retreat of fluvial-structural escarpments to generate plains. King designated the planation process pedimentation, and his end point "pediplains" were surmounted by inselbergs (isolated hills standing above plains, the name being derived from the German term for "island mountains") rather than monadnocks. Because the resulting stair-stepped landscapes (*Treppen,* the German word for "steps") of scarps and flats were presumed to reflect tectonics and to be correlatable, the term *Tectonic Geomorphic School* has been applied to its advocates.

INSELBERGS

An inselberg (German: "island mountain") is an isolated hill that stands above well-developed plains and appears not unlike an island rising from the sea. The early German explorers of southern Africa were impressed by such features, and they dubbed the domed or castlelike highlands inselbergs. Spectacular examples include Uluru/Ayers Rock and the Olga Rocks (Kata Tjuta) in central Australia.

Inselbergs are relict features. They have maintained their relief as the adjacent surrounding landscape was lowered. C.R. Twidale of Australia demonstrated the role of subsurface weathering in shaping the flanking hillslopes and pediments of granitic inselbergs.

The occurrence of inselbergs implies immense variations in the rates of degradational activity on the land surface. These structures are one of several varieties of landform called paleoforms that can survive with little modification for tens of millions of years. In inselberg landscapes, the active erosional processes are confined to valley sides and valley floors.

The notion of geomorphologists that denudational landforms reflecting tectonic pulses were sufficiently synchronized on a global basis to be correlatable has suffered much from the development of the theory of plate tectonics. The separate notion that hillslopes, once developed, retreat laterally to produce a low-inclination surface worthy of a special name (pediment–pediplain) has found more support.

In retrospect, Penck's *Treppen* concept seems to suffer much of the same theoretical damage as Davis's geographical cycle, but it is generally less ingenious. Like Davis, Penck and King made no dynamic use of climatic influences, and in fact the latter went so far as to claim that climate makes no difference. Moreover, like Davis, neither King nor Penck acknowledged the isostatic implications for erosion established nearly a century earlier. King suggested that sheetfloods "mold" the surfaces of pediments and depicted sparsely vegetated regions where this might be possible under the label semiarid. More recent work suggests that sheetfloods may be a product, rather than a cause, of the "flat" terrain on which they occur. The so-called molding would appear to be the result of desert stream-flood processes operating to local base levels in the absence of appreciable plant cover, as will be discussed below.

There is an implied landform "chronology" for a geomorphic system tied to intermittent uplift, as suggested by Penck and King, though dating such events is not readily accomplished. Furthermore, King tied his planation method to a regional sea-level erosional datum that the aforementioned constraints throw into question. Perhaps the principal contribution of the Penck–King theoretical ensemble has to do with the concept of lateral escarpment retreat, as opposed to the wearing down of lands favoured by Davis. There are in fact landforms that are widely acknowledged to be pediments. They are planar in form, truncate a wide variety of bedrock types, and can most readily be explained by scarp retreat under non-vegetated conditions. Debate continues about how much or how little moisture best encourages this process. Yet, at least the general nature of the mechanism seems to have been identified (largely by detailed studies in the area of process geomorphology) and the hydraulic constraints established by Gilbert and others seem to be satisfied.

In essence, it has been found that runoff deposits sediment in deserts where its excess transport energy is dissipated by volume loss caused by infiltration and evaporation. Runoff upslope from the depositional base level established by the long-term locus of deposition cannot erode below the resulting deposit. Such overland flow must expend its energy against non-vegetated hillslopes, resulting in their backwearing.

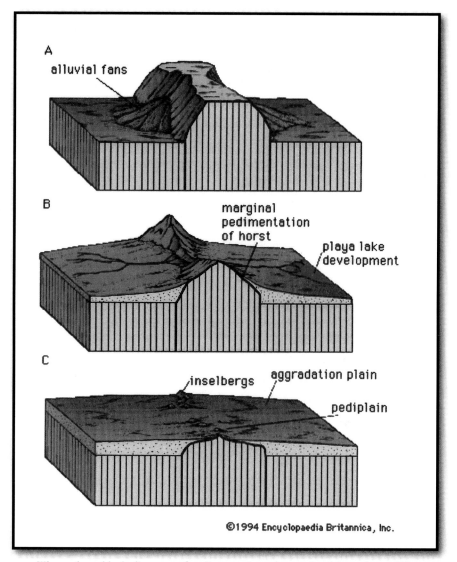

Three-phase block diagram of pedimentation of an upland in a desert. The process of scarp retreat and planation is accomplished by sheet wash on non-vegetated surfaces, but it cannot begin until a local base level of erosion-deposition is established. Streams dissecting the upland cannot cut below the level created where deposition of alluvium begins as runoff dissipates. The long-term locus of that deposition established the datum for lateral stream-bank and valley-wall recession at higher elevations. From H.F. Garner, The Origin of Landscapes (1974); Oxford University Press, Inc.

The pedimentation phenomenon must rank as one of the more astute geomorphic insights, regardless of the fact that the hydraulic and sedimentologic details involved were not established until later. Today, this form of land planation in association with alluvial aggradation in deserts, stream incision that establishes regional drainage networks and augments relief under humid conditions as described by Davis, and glacial scour and deposition as elucidated by Charpentier, Agassiz, and others stand as the three most widely established morphogenetic systems on Earth.

CLIMATIC MORPHOGENESIS

Notions that climate plays a major dynamic role in landform evolution were in evidence during the first decade of the 20th century but did not emerge in formalized theory until the mid-1900s. At that time German geographer Julius Büdel and several French geomorphologists, particularly Jean Tricart, André Cailleux, and Louis C. Peltier, began to employ the concept of a morphogenetic area— defined as a region in which a particular set of landforms is being generated under a particular climate. Only slowly, however, and mainly from studies in the tropics did it come to be appreciated how extreme the regional climate shifts between arid and humid have been on the different continents. Davis long ago understood how distinctive the geomorphic mechanisms of humid and arid lands were. It was, however, the new evidence of wide geographic mobility for such environments that forced the recognition of the morphogenetic, or geomorphic, system. Such a system is defined as a group of agencies and processes interacting under a particular environment to produce a landscape. Because morphogenetic areas and their systems can displace each other, it follows that they would leave behind relict landforms, soils, deposits, organisms, and so forth.

WEATHERING

Weathering is the disintegration or alteration of rock in its natural or original position at or near Earth's surface through physical, chemical, and biological processes induced or modified by wind, water, and climate.

During the weathering process the translocation of disintegrated or altered material occurs within the immediate vicinity of the rock exposure, but the rock mass remains in situ. Weathering is distinguished from erosion by the fact that the latter usually includes the transportation of the disintegrated rock and soil away from the site of the degradation. A broader application of erosion, however, includes weathering as a component of the general denudation of all landforms along with wind action and fluvial, marine, and glacial processes. The occurrence of weathering at or near Earth's surface also distinguishes it from the physical and chemical alteration of rock through metamorphism, which usually takes place deep in the crust at much higher temperatures.

Weathering involves physical, chemical, and biological processes acting separately or, more often, together to achieve the disintegration and decay of rock material. Physical weathering causes the disintegration of rock by mechanical processes and therefore depends on the application of force. Disintegration involves the breakdown of rock into its constituent minerals or particles with no decay of any rock-forming minerals. The principal sources of physical weathering are thermal expansion and contraction of rock, pressure release upon rock by erosion of overlaying materials, the alternate freezing and thawing of water between cracks and fissures within rock, crystal growth within rock, and the growth of plants and living organisms in rock. Rock alteration usually involves chemical weathering in which the mineral composition of the rock is changed, reorganized, or redistributed. The rock minerals are exposed to solution, carbonation, hydration, and oxidation by circulating waters. These effects on the mineral decomposition are added to the effects of living organisms and plants as nutrient extraction to alter rock.

Several factors control the type of weathering and the rate at which rock weathers. The mineralogical composition of a rock will determine the rate of alteration or disintegration. The texture of the rock will affect the type of weathering that is most likely to occur.

Fine-grain rock will usually be more susceptible to chemical alteration but less susceptible to physical disintegration. The pattern of joints, fractures, and fissures within rock may provide an avenue for water to penetrate. Thus, shattered and fractured rock masses are more likely to undergo weathering than are monolithic structures. Climate will also control the type and rate of weathering by affecting the likelihood of freeze–thaw cycles and chemical reactions. Chemical weathering is more likely to occur and to be more effective in humid tropical climates, and disintegration of rock from freeze–thaw cycles is more likely to take place and to be more effective in sub-Arctic climates.

The discovery of widespread climatic dynamism and the correlative recognition of plate-tectonic phenomena created a whole new theoretical situation for geomorphologists. Not a single theory of regional landform development existing in 1950 accounted for the constraints imposed by the new climatic and tectonic findings in any significant way.

Climates change and periodically impose one of the foregoing geomorphic systems on the relicts left by one of the others. In addition, areas of each climatic type export matter to adjacent morphogenetic areas and thereby modify the resulting landforms. For example, deserts export dust by eolian means, and the resulting deposits modify soil profiles in downwind regions, as in the eastern United States, or create actual depositional landforms of loess, as in Shansi Province of China on the lee of the Ordos Desert. River systems arising in humid lands develop their drainage networks therein and then may encroach on downslope deserts to create alluvial riverine plains where their flow will not maintain their sediment transport to some distant ocean. Alternatively, rivers form deltas following climate change when their sediment loads and flow are sufficient and the débouché (point of emergence) is protected. Glaciers produce their changes on ice-covered realms and then export their outwash deposits into whatever environment is downslope.

TECTONIC GEOMORPHOLOGY

In addition to the usual climatic imprints, orogenic tectonism (including volcanism) adds its obvious dimensions of elevation and slope to any surficial environment it encounters. It is now clear that orogenic realms in their early phases create gravitational opportunities for Earth sculpture that hardly exist elsewhere. The usual mechanisms for concomitantly gradualistic denudation by ice, wind, and running water are set aside in orogenic belts by relatively rapid uplifts of material ranging from nearly unconsolidated sediment to semicoherent but intensely deformed masses of metamorphic and igneous rocks. Under these conditions, masses of rock measured in thousands of cubic kilometres are torn loose by gravity and fall and/or slide, often moving hundreds of kilometres in a "geologic instant" to a lower resting place (in some cases lubricated by subaqueous avenues). The term "catastrophic" seems most appropriate for an occurrence of this type.

The sculpturing of Earth is thus seen as more than the mere gradual removal of weathered debris by mechanisms under the control of climatic regimes. The Kamchatka Peninsula in the far eastern part of Siberia is said to have more than 100 active volcanoes. Not surprisingly its terrain is dominated by volcanic landforms. The Afar Triangle at the foot of the Red Sea is shaped by newly formed faults that cut unweathered basaltic lava flows on a newly emergent seafloor in an almost totally tectonic landscape. In the Appalachians, south of the glaciated knobs, an ancient mountain system sheathed by thick saprolitic soils on its upper slopes exhibits ridge-ravine topography and may have been in a humid climatic nucleus for 100 million years. Yet, the same region retains water gaps and entrenched meanders that echo drainage patterns established long ago, probably on alluvial cover masses of Early Mesozoic age (roughly 225 million years old) following an arid-to-humid climate change at the end of the Jurassic Period (about 146 million years ago). In the same area, tropical soils and ridge-top lateritic deposits of Georgia and Alabama reflect weathering conditions established 150 million years ago when southeastern North America was still in the tropics before recent northwesterly continental drift.

CONSIDERATION OF UNIQUE LANDFORMS AND OTHER DISTINCTIVE TOPOGRAPHIC FEATURES

There are, of course, instances where special types of bedrock combine with particular weathering and erosion regimes to produce unique landforms and landscapes. Best known perhaps are the solutional effects expressed as karst topography. This is most pronounced in limestone terrain, such as that in Kentucky in the southeastern United States and the Karst plateau in Yugoslavia, as well as those in parts of northeast China and on islands like Puerto Rico and Jamaica. In tropical realms where silica is more soluble, similar landforms may develop on other varieties of sedimentary rock or on igneous or metamorphic types, as, for example, quartzite in the isolated plateau remnants of the Venezuelan Guiana Shield. The humid climatic conditions that promote solution production and dripstone formation are readily apparent in such tropical areas.

Granitic terrain in several parts of the world also gives rise to a distinctive array of landforms that include domed erosion residuals, often in patterns closely tied to joint spacing in bedrock as noted by the Australian geomorphologist C.R. Twidale. In regions where alternating humid and arid climates or human activity have led to erosional stripping of weathered zones, mammoth boulder piles of exhumed core stones exist. Such features are especially notable on the island of Hong Kong, in southern Brazil, in parts of India and Australia, and in the St. Francois Mountain region of Missouri in the United States.

THEORETICAL OVERVIEW OF LANDFORM DEVELOPMENT

The complexities of terrestrial surface change demand a theoretical overview that is both flexible and multifaceted. Oversimplified, sweeping landscape generalizations that apply to the whole Earth such as the postulates of Davis and King can hardly be employed when dealing with a planet where virtually every geomorphic element constitutes a potential interruption or complication to every other system. Nevertheless, there do seem to be certain kinds of activity that are repeated sporadically in both tectonic and climatic realms. These repetitions encourage the re-creation of particular suites of landforms and could be taken to imply a certain rationality to events. However, they probably are no more rational than eddies in a river that develop only where possible.

Matters of geographic and chronological scale also enter into the question of what is indeed geomorphically possible and repeatable. The interplay between density variations in matter and gravity dictates that Earth's core (once formed) must remain firmly fixed, and so too must the lighter substances that make up the lithosphere. Concentration of the least dense solids in the continents is involved in a complex process now associated with plate tectonics, and it is at this level that a discussion of landform evolution must begin.

Although the designers of the plate tectonics theoretical framework did not single out continents as landforms of a special kind, such is one of the basic consequences of that theoretical construct. Continents are first-order landforms, and there seemingly will be only one cycle of continental denudation in the history of Earth. It began with the earliest concentration of continental lithosphere at the surface, and it presumably will end, as suggested above, when the last endogenic forces (i.e., those within Earth) expire and gravity and entropy have their way as the internal systems of the planet run down. The details (in the context of this cycle's span of 8 billion to 10 billion years) hardly matter, since the results are inevitable—unless, of course, the Sun becomes a nova and disrupts things.

Second-order features on continents consist primarily of mountains and the relatively low-elevation areas that come into existence as the mountains rise. In the context of continental landforms, mountains and the geomorphic systems that act upon them are unique in that the uplift creates an excess of potential energy, one far above that of the remaining land area. Landform evolution in mountains is necessarily skewed by this special kind of excess energy. Davis seemed to sense this in his theorizing, but he did not understand the limits on slope as a denudational influence and the variety of climatic and tectonic factors at work.

OROGENIC AND EPEIROGENIC MORPHOGENESIS

Orogenies are mountain-building events that occur when two landmasses collide with one another. Orogenies tend to occur over relatively short time periods along linear belts and result in intensive deformation of the rock. They are also accompanied by folding and faulting of the strata. In contrast, epeirogenies are characterized by the broad regional upwarping of the cratonic (stable interior) portions of continents. Epeirogenies take place over broad, nonlinear areas. The process is relatively slow and results in only mild deformation.

Orogenic Geomorphic Systems

Such mountain-building systems evolve in the special contexts of type, setting, and style. The principal orogenic varieties recognized are (1) mountains of continent-continent collision type formed by lithospheric plate interaction along continental margins, (2) mountains of the collision type associated with oceanic trenches (sometimes developed along a single continental margin) with an adjacent plate-tectonic subduction system, and (3) rift-type mountains extending into continental interiors where transcurrent faults shear cratons and deform associated sediment veneers or where spreading zones develop to create fault-block (horst-graben) mountainous terrain. Geologic time is sufficient for several orogenic events of each type to have occurred, and different rules apply to the geomorphic evolution of any given type.

Mountains of the continent-continent collision type have special attributes that direct their geomorphic evolution. These distinctive characteristics are the following:

- The collision creating the mountains incorporates a finite volume of rock that is not augmented following the collision.
- The orogenic rock mass is subject to isostatic uplift during denudation; in general, sedimentary rock types are exposed first, followed by crystalline varieties.

- The collision that initiates such orogenesis ultimately adds rock to the adjacent craton, and in thickening the adjacent crust often initiates nearby cratonic tilting and/or uplift.
- Because such mountains develop between continents and are thus elevated in the midst of a consequent megacontinent (Pangaea in the case of the Appalachians), they are far from oceanic evaporation sources and therefore often undergo initial denudation under arid geomorphic systems in the manner of the present mountains of central Asia.
- As the climatic setting of such mountains is largely established tectonically, it may endure in the same climate for scores of millions of years and, as noted in 1901 by the American geomorphologist Douglas W. Johnson, a desert mountain range tends to bury itself in its own waste.
- Re-exposure of such mountains to nearby precipitation sources by plate adjustments may result in dramatic climate changes from arid to humid, so that perennial fluvial erosion is widely initiated on a relict arid, alluvial cover mass with resulting transverse drainage by superimposition. In illustration, one can compare the Appalachian Mountains of North America and the Zagros Mountains of Iran, as described by the American geomorphologist Theodore M. Oberlander in 1965.
- Because of their finite initial rock volume, mountains of the continent-continent collision type can be lowered by erosion, somewhat in the manner visualized by Davis. No such

structures more than 500 million years old show mountainous relief.

- Volcanic landforms are rarely a part of the topography during orogenesis of this mountain type.

Mountains of the collision type associated with oceanic trenches have their own distinct attributes that control evolution. These are as follows:

- The merging of a pair of lithospheric plates along a deep-sea trench initiates orogenesis tied to the subduction process (i.e., the sinking of one plate beneath another at convergent plate boundaries).

- Rock mass is added to the orogenic belt via subduction as long as the trench remains "operational."

- Denudation accompanies uplift and may reduce rock mass in the orogenic system in the long run, but whether the total mass is growing, shrinking, or static depends on the budget established by additions from subduction versus losses from erosion.

- Mountainous elevations tend to increase through much of the life of the orogenic system, since rock lost through erosion is generally removed locally and linearly by rivers and glaciers (the Andes exemplify the type bordering a continent, and they appear to be higher now than at any time since they began to form 150 million years ago).

- Because mountains of the trench-associated subduction type develop and endure adjacent

to an ocean on at least one side, they are subject to climatic variability tied to such factors as
latitudinal position, orientation with respect to
prevailing wind patterns, ocean surface temperatures, and progressively increasing elevations.

- Examples such as the Andes that border a continent can show alternating segments that are
highly volcanic.

- Andean types also may display highly contrast-
ing denudational systems under a variety of
climatic conditions on opposite sides as well as
along the length of the range.

- Although an erosion cycle resulting in overall
lowering of a trench-associated mountain system does not appear viable as long as the trench
endures, a complex steady-state mass situation
would seem to be one potential development
during this time.

- Occasionally orogenesis related to trench-
continent interaction may extend far inland;
the parts of the Andes exhibiting this trait display mechanical rock deformation but little
volcanism, and a similar genetic mechanism
has been suggested for the Rocky Mountains
of North America.

- During their early years, the Rocky Mountains
displayed volcanic phases accompanied by
upthrusting but now seem tectonically quiescent
and are apparently experiencing denudational
lowering.

Rift-type mountains are primarily of the block-fault
variety. They have the following set of special attributes:

- Block-fault mountains appear to originate where a spreading ridge of the plate-tectonic type develops.
- On continents, the spreading is expressed in high-angle faulting and may be accompanied by volcanism of tholeiitic basalt type.
- Rifting may be limited to linear zones, as in the Rift Valley system of East Africa, or may be more broadly expressed, as in the Basin and Range Province of the western United States.
- The extent of rifting may be limited to mere surficial fracturing of the continental crust, or it may extend to actual rupturing of a lithospheric plate and renewal of seafloor spreading, as occurred along the Atlantic seaboard of North America at the end of the Jurassic.
- Because block-fault mountains are of endogenic origin, they may occur in and experience a variety of denudational environments. The examples from Africa and North America cited above are in settings ranging from arid to humid. The highest such mountains show glacial effects.

CLIMATICALLY DOMINATED EPEIROGENIC REALMS

The epeirogenic portions of continents (i.e., those that have escaped orogenesis in the past 500 million years) experience denudation in a situation in which the slope factor, if at all tectonic in origin, is regional in expression and so gentle as to exert little influence beyond giving direction to flowing water or ice. It is these regions that variously exhibit veneers of sedimentary rock largely accumulated in epicontinental seas over the past 500 million years or that expose in shield areas the roots of worn-down mountain systems. In the absence of notable tectonism, it is not surprising to find that morphogenesis on stable cratons is dominated by climate. Vast expanses of cratons situated away from mountain belts either are occupied by temperate and tropical forests and grasslands or are seared by desert heat and wind. Only Antarctica currently supports a continental ice sheet, but both North America and Eurasia show they recently did so as well. It is in these epeirogenic regions that morphogenesis is most significantly punctuated by climate change. With few exceptions, the landforms are polygenetic. Many of the most recent glacial deposits scarcely show the incipient soil development begun under humid conditions only a few thousand years ago. Furthermore, broadly forested, humid regions still exhibit patches of cacti and alluvium left there when they were deserts. Therein, the notable slopes are denudational in origin; the steeper ones were usually developed by stream incision and the more gentle ones commonly were produced by alluviation and/or pedimentation.

A UNIFIED LANDFORM THEORY

Viewed in their entirety, the individual concepts that pertain to landform development so far discussed (catastrophism, uniformitarianism, gradualism, erosion cycle, dynamic equilibrium, disequilibrium, geomorphic system, morphogenetic area, tectonic geomorphology, and orogenic and epeirogenic morphogenesis) have to date been treated by theorists as independent conceptual constructs rather than as geomorphic elements of a unified comprehensive theory. There is a close parallel between this situation and the fable of the several blind men who decided what an elephant is by touching only individual parts of the animal. Each of their geomorphic concepts has a measure of validity, but the earliest ideas were formulated on the basis of very incomplete information. When considered in the context of the entire solar system, in which there is a group of planetary geomorphic entities, the theoretical pieces begin to fall into more distinctly rational positions. Although a degree of variability is imposed by planetary location and by early differentiation of cosmic material, randomness in the solar system is incomplete because of the directional factors imposed by gravity, radiation, and increasing entropy. For any given planet, there are two potential geomorphic factors: (1) exogenic impact phenomena from solar debris possibly modified by tidal disruption caused by nearby planetoids, or radiation phenomena tied mainly to the Sun resulting principally in climatic influences and biologic activity, and (2) endogenic phenomena related to internal heating and expressed as tectonism and volcanism, as on Earth. Morphogenesis occurs in accordance with interaction between planetary subsystems associated with the above factors.

BEHAVIOUR OF GEOMORPHIC SYSTEMS

Gravity-driven geomorphic systems are potentially cyclical in terms of the elimination of excess relief and elevation. They exhibit activity that graphs in a two-phase form—namely the initial disequilibrium occurring when free energy and relief are maximal (and the results are frequently catastrophic), and subsequent dynamic equilibrium where relief and elevation are nearly eliminated and free energy available to do work is so low that change is nearly imperceptible. The latter behaviour is clearly gradualistic. Such systems must be disturbed by outside forces in order for the cycle to be interrupted or reinitiated.

In the solar system the cycle of accretionary, gravity-propelled impact morphogenesis that creates cratered surfaces and high relief is in a distinctly waning phase. Such activity apparently reached a peak within the first one billion years after the planetary system was formed and is not likely to be renewed. Its expression is epitomized by the surface of objects such as the Moon and the planet Mercury, where the near absence of endogenic tectonic forces has left impact effects most intact. On Earth and a few other planets (or satellites), internal heating propels orogenesis and thereby periodically renews gravity-driven geomorphic cycles. As noted earlier, there will be only one continent-forming cycle in Earth's history.

Radiation-driven geomorphic systems are tied to the Sun's nuclear fusion processes and the fluctuations therein. Because of atmosphere and organisms, solar effects are most singularly manifested on Earth as morphogenetic areas characterized by a particular climate and associated processes. The geomorphic changes in such areas are cyclical largely with respect to the destruction of relict features exposed to the system as the morphogenic areas move and also with respect to the creation of landforms and deposits in morphological equilibrium with the new system. Changes in landforms, deposits, and processes also graph in two phases after the initiation of a system or after a perturbation in one. These landform changes are initially time-indicative, and unless morphogenesis has attained a dynamic equilibrium phase, the partially altered relict features may permit reconstruction of the events of landform evolution.

It will be noted from the above that there is a close relationship between process and form in the dynamic equilibrium phase of radiationally driven geomorphic systems. In morphogenetic areas in states of disequilibrium, form (strongly influenced by relict features) may show little or no consistency with process, which may have just been initiated. Relict features in the process of transformation, such as a desert or a glacial alluvial deposit in a valley being reworked by a perennial stream, thus constitute hybrid features. Compare with Davis's mature stream discussed above, the stream valley of which has a flat floor unlike that of a late-phase humid valley which has a V-shaped cross profile. Furthermore, the "hybrid" stream is not behaving as it would if there were no alluvium, and the alluvium is not the same after the stream has partially reworked it.

Occasionally, the sequence of geomorphic events may conspire to preserve a form that is foreign to the associated geomorphic system and processes. The sinuous paths of entrenched meanders that are cut into bedrock in such regions as the Appalachians express the granular surface and sediment-water volume relations that prevailed when the flow pattern was initiated in the Mesozoic rather than those of the present.

THE CONCEPT OF PERIODIC RANDOM DOMINANCE

On Earth, gravity- and radiation-driven geomorphic systems interact independently, so that their two types of activity can mingle under conditions of periodic random dominance. Thus, peak energy expenditures engendered by each type of system may or may not coincide geographically. Maximum rates of landform change occur where active orogenesis mingles with changing climates. Minimal change occurs where epeirogenic regions are occupied by morphogenic areas that are in states of dynamic equilibrium. In this arrangement of interacting geomorphic systems, there is clearly a place for both catastrophe and gradualism. There also is a place for cycles of erosion of several kinds and for dynamic equilibrium, either as an end phase of enduring climatic morphogenesis and/or as an end phase of relief and elevation reduction by denudation following orogenesis.

The concept of periodic random dominance as an aspect of landform evolution carries with it the implication of polygenetic landforms and landscapes where geomorphic system dominance fails to develop. Indeed, dominance becomes the special case because it is dependent on a particular juxtaposition of tectonic and/or climatic elements over a protracted interval in a given area. One estimate places polygenetic landforms over approximately 80 percent of Earth's land surface. Perhaps 20 percent is experiencing some type of geomorphic system dominance—less than 10 percent if Antarctica is omitted from the calculations.

PROCESS GEOMORPHOLOGY AND SYSTEMS EQUILIBRIA

Details of landform evolution within a given geomorphic system are matters of process behaviour and terrain response. In the context of geomorphic system dominance versus systemic alternation, two general situations exist: (1) those agencies operating in contact with relicts that they are modifying, often quite rapidly, and (2) those in contact with equilibrium features that they have created and have little or no ability to modify further. The principal surficial geomorphic agencies on Earth—wind, running water, glacial ice, and gravity—in any given geomorphic system induce processes that tend to evolve toward a situation of least work. Polygenetic terrain is usually some combination of hillslopes and "flats," and either topographic type may dominate in the latter part of a geomorphic cycle, depending on whether the system tends to generate relief or reduce it.

Natural geomorphic systems operating along Earth's surface are classified as open, since they are powered by external energy sources. Because the rates of both endogenetic and exogenetic energy input vary, the coordinate agencies experience changes analogous to power surges in an electrical system. Thus, rivers receiving excess run-off periodically flood. The atmosphere locally builds up excess heat, and the transfer of this heat is expressed in storms. Glaciers, normally the epitome of slowness, can acquire a mass-energy excess and consequently surge. In all instances, energy available for erosion, transportation, and deposition of sediment varies greatly over time. In addition, the interaction between solids, fluids, and gases results in turbulence, eddy formation, shearing and vortex activity, and periodic local stagnation.

In response to the foregoing situations, process associations within individual geomorphic systems exhibit typical systems phenomena, including "feedback," "threshold reactions," and evolution toward dynamic equilibrium (least-work) modes. Where a system is periodically perturbed, processes can pass back and forth between disequilibrium and steady-state conditions rather frequently.

The behaviour and apparent process direction of an individual agency may not reflect the evolution of the overall geomorphic system. For example, a 10,000-year-long episode leading to the formation of an alluvial fan may be seen to include numerous incidents of fan-head trenching that are separately destructive but subordinate to depositional events dominating the trend. Similarly, a river such as the Mississippi that is reworking a relict alluvial deposit in a valley may be seen to be depositing gravel on point bars on the insides of bends. The long-term consequence of the river's activity, however, will be to remove the entire alluvial deposit in its path, including the point bars, unless subject to systemic interruption. (Humankind has of course "short-circuited" the natural evolution of the Mississippi and that of many other rivers with engineering modifications.)

From the foregoing, it seems evident that the direction of landform evolution can only be grasped from the study of geomorphic process if the character and role of relict landforms and deposits are clearly understood. This is an obvious complication in the application of Hutton's doctrine of uniformitarianism.

The concept of periodic geomorphic system dominance provides the rational potential end point of landform evolution under a particular set of conditions. Ideally, it may yield either modified or unmodified tectonic landscapes. These in turn may be either orogenic or epeirogenic. Where modified, they may express marine effects and/or glacial, arid, or humid morphogenesis. Antithetically, where more common polygenetic morphogenesis occurs, some mixture of tectonic, marine, or climatic effects is superimposed on the setting, and a hybrid suite of landforms results.

CHAPTER 2
MOUNTAINS

A mountain is a landform that rises prominently above its surroundings, generally exhibiting steep slopes, a relatively confined summit area, and considerable local relief. Mountains generally are understood to be larger than hills, but the term has no standardized geological meaning. Very rarely do mountains occur individually. In most cases, they are found in elongated ranges or chains. When an array of such ranges is linked together, it constitutes a mountain belt.

A mountain belt is many tens to hundreds of kilometres wide and hundreds to thousands of kilometres long. It stands above the surrounding surface, which may be a coastal plain, as along the western Andes in northern Chile, or a high plateau, as within and along the Plateau of Tibet in southwest China. Mountain ranges or chains extend tens to hundreds of kilometres in length. Individual mountains are connected by ridges and separated by valleys. Within many mountain belts are plateaus, which stand high but contain little relief. Thus, for example, the Andes constitute a mountain belt that borders the entire west coast of South America; within it are both individual ranges, such as the Cordillera Blanca in which lies Peru's highest peak, Huascarán, and the high plateau, the Altiplano, in southern Peru and western Bolivia.

GEOMORPHIC CHARACTERISTICS

Mountainous terrains have certain unifying characteristics. Such terrains have higher elevations than do surrounding areas. Moreover, high relief exists within mountain belts and ranges. Individual mountains, mountain ranges, and mountain belts that have been created by different tectonic processes, however, are often characterized by different features.

Chains of active volcanoes, such as those occurring at island arcs, are commonly marked by individual high mountains separated by large expanses of low and gentle topography. In some chains, namely those associated with "hot spots," only the volcanoes at one end of the chain are active. Thus those volcanoes stand high, but with increasing distance away from them erosion has reduced the sizes of volcanic structures to an increasing degree.

The folding of layers of sedimentary rocks with thicknesses of hundreds of metres to a few kilometres often leaves long, parallel ridges and valleys termed fold belts, as, for example, in the Valley and Ridge Province of Pennsylvania in the eastern United States. The more

Bearhat Mountain above Hidden Lake on a crest of the Continental Divide in Glacier National Park, Montana. Ray Atkeson/EB Inc.

resistant rocks form ridges, and the valleys are underlain by weaker ones. These fold belts commonly include segments where layers of older rocks have been thrust or pushed up and over younger rocks. Such segments are known as fold and thrust belts. Typically their topography is not as regular as where folding is the most important process, but it is usually dominated by parallel ridges of resistant rock divided by valleys of weaker rock, as in the eastern flank of the Canadian Rocky Mountains or in the Jura Mountains of France and Switzerland.

Most fold and thrust belts are bounded on one side, or lie parallel to, a belt or terrain of crystalline rocks. These are metamorphic and igneous rocks that in most cases solidified at depths of several kilometres or more and that are more resistant to erosion than the sedimentary rocks deposited on top of them. These crystalline terrains typically contain the highest peaks in any mountain belt and include the highest belt in the world, the Himalayas, which was formed by the thrusting of crystalline rocks up onto the surface of Earth. The great heights exist because of the resistance of the rocks to erosion and because the rates of continuing uplift are the highest in these areas. The topography rarely is as regularly oriented as in fold and thrust belts.

In certain areas, blocks or isolated masses of rock have been elevated relative to adjacent areas to form block-fault mountains or ranges. In some places, block-fault ranges with an overall common orientation coalesce to define a mountain belt or chain, but in others the ranges may be isolated.

Block faulting can occur when blocks are thrust, or pushed, over neighbouring valleys, as has occurred in the Rocky Mountains of Colorado, Wyoming, and Utah in the western United States or as is now occurring in the Tien

Shan, an east–west range in western China and Central Asia. Within individual ranges, which are usually a few hundred kilometres long and several tens of kilometres wide, crystalline rocks commonly crop out. On a large scale, there is a clear orientation of such ranges, but within them the landforms are controlled more by the variations in erosion than by tectonic processes.

Block faulting also occurs where blocks are pulled apart, causing a subsidence of the intervening valley between diverging blocks. In this case, alternating basins and ranges form. The basins eventually fill with sediment, and the ranges—typically tens of kilometres long and from a few to 20–30 km (about 12–19 miles) wide—often tilt, with steep relief on one side and a gentle slope on the other. The uniformity of the gently tilted slope owes its existence to long periods of erosion and deposition before tilting, sometimes with a capping of resistant lava flows on this surface prior to tilting and faulting. Both the Tetons of Wyoming and the Sierra Nevada of California were formed by blocks being tilted up toward the east; major faults allowed the blocks on their east sides to drop steeply down several thousand metres and thereby created steep eastern slopes.

In some areas, a single block or a narrow zone of blocks has subsided between neighbouring blocks or plateaus that moved apart to form a rift valley between them. Mountains with steep inward slopes and gentle outward slopes often form on the margins of rift valleys. Less commonly, large areas that are pulled apart and subside leave between them an elevated block with steep slopes on both sides. An example of this kind of structure, called a horst, is the Ruwenzori in East Africa.

Finally, in certain areas, including those that once were plateaus or broad uplifted regions, erosion has left what are known as residual mountains. Many such mountains are isolated and not part of any discernible chain, as, for instance, Mount Katahdin in Maine in the northeastern United States. Some entire chains (e.g., the Appalachians in North America or the Urals in Russia), which were formed hundreds of millions of years ago, remain in spite of a long history of erosion. Most residual chains and individual mountains are characterized by low elevations; however, both gentle and precipitous relief can exist, depending on the degree of recent erosion.

TECTONIC PROCESSES THAT CREATE AND DESTROY MOUNTAIN BELTS AND THEIR COMPONENTS

Mountains and mountain belts exist because tectonic processes have created and maintained high elevations in the face of erosion, which works to destroy them. The

The volcano Chachani overlooks terraced fields in southern Peru. Chachani is the highest peak shown. Chip and Rosa Maria de la Cueva Peterson

topography of a mountain belt depends not only on the processes that create the elevated terrain but also on the forces that support this terrain and on the types of processes (erosional or tectonic) that destroy it. In fact, it is necessary to understand the forces that support elevated terrains before considering the other factors involved.

MECHANISMS THAT SUPPORT ELEVATED TERRAINS

Two properties of rocks contribute to the support of mountains, mountain belts, and plateaus, namely strength and density. If rocks had no strength, mountains would simply flow away. At a subtler level, the strength of the material beneath mountains can affect the scale of the topography.

In terms of strength, the lithosphere, the thickness of which is, as stated earlier, on average 100 km (60 miles), but can vary over the face of Earth from a few to more than 200 km (about 125 miles), is much stronger than the underlying layer, the asthenosphere. The strength of the lithosphere is derived from its temperature; thick lithosphere exists because the outer part of Earth is relatively cold. Cold, thick, and therefore strong lithosphere can support higher mountain ranges than can thin lithosphere, just as thick ice on a lake or river is better able to support larger people than thin ice.

In terms of chemical composition, and therefore density, Earth's crust is lighter than the underlying mantle. Beneath the oceans, the typical thickness of the crust is only 6 to 7 km (3.7 to 4.4 miles). Beneath the continental regions, the average thickness is about 35 km (about 22 miles), but it can reach 60 or 70 km (37 to 44 miles) beneath high mountain ranges and plateaus. Thus, most ranges and plateaus are buoyed up by thick crustal roots. To some extent the light crust floats on the heavier mantle, as icebergs float on the oceans.

It should be noted that the crust and lithosphere are defined by different properties and do not constitute the same layer. Moreover, variations in their thicknesses have different relationships to the overlying topography. Some mountain ranges and plateaus are buoyed up by a thick crust. The lithosphere beneath such areas, however, can be thin, and its strength does not play a significant role in supporting the range or plateau. Other ranges may overlie thick lithospheric plates, which are flexed down by the weight of the mountains. The crust beneath such ranges is likely to be thicker than normal but not as thick as it would be if the lithosphere were thin. Thus, the strength of the lithosphere supports these mountains and maintains the base of the crust at a higher level than would have been the case had the strong layer been absent. For instance, the Himalayas have been thrust onto the crust of the Indian shield, which is underlain by particularly cold, thick lithosphere that has been flexed down by the weight of the high range. The thickness of the crust is about 55 km (34 miles) beneath the high peaks, which stand more than 8,000 metres (about 26,250 feet) high. The thickest crustal segment of 70 km (44 miles), however, lies farther north beneath the Plateau of Tibet (or Tibetan Plateau), whose altitude is about 4,500 to 5,000 metres (about 14,760 to 16,400 feet) but whose lithosphere is much thinner than that beneath the Himalayas. The strong Indian lithosphere helps to support the Himalayas, but the buoyancy of the thick Tibetan crust maintains the high elevation of the plateau.

TECTONIC PROCESSES THAT PRODUCE HIGH ELEVATIONS

As noted above, individual mountains, mountain ranges, mountain belts, and plateaus exist because tectonic processes have elevated terrains faster than erosion could destroy them. High elevations are created by three major processes: these are volcanism, horizontal crustal shortening as manifested by folding and by faulting, and the heating and thermal expansion of large terrains.

VOLCANISM

Most, but not all, volcanoes consist of material that is thought to have melted in the mantle (at depths of tens of kilometres), which rose through the overlying crust and was erupted onto the surface. To a large extent, the physical characteristics of the erupted material determine the shape and height of a volcano. Material of low density can produce taller mountains than can denser material. Lavas with low viscosity, such as in Hawaii, flow easily and produce gentle slopes, but more viscous lavas mixed with explosively erupted solid blocks of rocks can form steeper volcanic cones, such as Mount Fuji in Japan, Mount Rainier in the northwestern United States, or Mount Kilimanjaro in Africa.

Many volcanoes are built on elevated terrains that owe their existence to the intrusion into the crust of magmas—i.e., molten rock presumably derived from the mantle. The extent to which this process is a major one in mountain belts is controversial. Many belts, such as the Andes, seem to be underlain, at least in part, by solidified magmas, but the volume of the intruded material and its exact source (melting of either the crust or the mantle) remain poorly understood.

CRUSTAL SHORTENING

In most mountain belts, terrains have been elevated as a result of crustal shortening by the thrusting of one block or slice of crust over another and/or by the folding of layers of rock. The topography of mountain ranges and mountain belts depends in part on the amount of displacement on such faults, on the angles at which faults dip, on the degree to which crustal shortening occurs by faulting or by folding, and on the types of rocks that are deformed and exposed to erosion. Most of the differences among mountain belts can be ascribed to some combination of these factors.

HEATING AND THERMAL EXPANSION

Rocks, like most materials, expand when they are heated. Some mountain ranges and plateaus are high simply because the crust and upper mantle beneath them are unusually hot. Most broad variations in the topography of the ocean floor, the mid-ocean ridges and rises, are due to horizontal variations in temperature in the outer 100 km (about 60 miles) of Earth. Hot areas stand higher—or at shallower depths in the ocean—than cold areas. Many plateaus, such as the Massif Central in south central France or the Ethiopian Plateau, are elevated significantly because the material beneath them has been heated.

TECTONIC PROCESSES THAT DESTROY ELEVATED TERRAINS

Besides erosion, which is the principal agent that destroys mountain belts, two tectonic processes help to reduce high elevations. Horizontal crustal extension and associated crustal thinning can reduce and eliminate crustal roots. When this happens, mountain belts widen and their mean elevation diminishes. Similarly, the cooling and associated thermal contraction of the outer part of Earth leads to a reduction of the average height of a mountain belt.

MAJOR TYPES OF MOUNTAIN BELTS

Mountain belts differ from one another in various respects, but they also have a number of similarities that enable Earth scientists to group them into certain distinct categories. Each of these categories is characterized by the principal process that created a representative belt. Moreover, within individual belts different tectonic processes can prevail and can be associated with quite different landforms and topography. Thus, for any category there are exceptions and special cases, as well as subdivisions.

Mountain Belts Associated with Volcanism

Volcanoes typically form in any of three tectonic settings. At the axes of the mid-ocean ridge system where lithospheric plates diverge, volcanism is common; yet, high-standing volcanoes (above sea level) rarely develop. At subduction zones where one plate of oceanic lithosphere plunges beneath another plate, long linear or arcuate chains of volcanoes and mountain belts associated with them are the norm. Volcanoes and associated landforms, as well as linear volcanic chains and ridges (e.g., the Hawaiian chain) also can exist far from plate boundaries.

Mid-Ocean Ridges and Rises

Where two lithospheric plates diverge, new material is intruded into the gap between the plates and accreted to each of them as they diverge. The vast majority of volcanic rocks ejected onto the surface of Earth are erupted at the mid-ocean ridges and rise where this process occurs. Thus, such submarine landforms comprise very long, narrow volcanic centres. Although volcanoes do form as isolated seamounts along the axes of mid-ocean ridges, they constitute only a small fraction of the erupted material. Moreover, areas along the ridges and rises where volcanism is particularly abundant are considered unusual; the excess amount of volcanic activity is generally attributed to "hot spots" in the mantle. Finally, most of the relief that defines the mid-ocean ridges and rises is not due to volcanism at all but rather to thermal expansion, as will be explained below.

VOLCANIC STRUCTURES ALONG SUBDUCTION ZONES

Linear or arcuate belts of volcanoes are commonly associated with subduction zones. Volcanoes typically lie 150 to 200 km (about 90 to 125 miles) landward of deep-sea trenches, such as those that border much of the Pacific Basin. The volcanoes overlie a zone of intense earthquake activity that begins at a shallow depth near such a trench and that dips beneath the volcanoes. They often form islands and define island arcs: these are arcuate chains of islands such as the Aleutians or the Lesser Antilles. Volcanoes usually are spaced a few to several tens of kilometres apart, and single volcanoes commonly define the width of such belts. Elsewhere, as in Japan, in the Cascade chain of the northwestern United States and southwestern Canada, or along much of the Andes, volcanoes have erupted on the margin of a continent. Nearly all features typical of an island arc, including the narrow belt of volcanoes, deep-sea trench, and intense earthquake activity, can be found at such continental margins.

The landscape of island chains of this kind is characteristically dominated by steep volcanic cones topped by small craters, and the relief between these volcanoes is low. A few such volcanoes have undergone massive eruptions and have expelled a large fraction of their interiors, as did Mount St. Helens in the northwestern United States in 1980. In the most intense eruptions of this sort, the remnants of the volcano collapse into the void at its centre, sometimes leaving a caldera (a very large crater with relatively low rims). Examples of such structures include those formed by Krakatoa in Indonesia in 1883 and by Thera (now called Santoríni) in the Aegean Sea a few thousand years ago.

RESIDUAL LANDFORMS

Residual landforms, which are also called relict landforms, evolve from the remains of an ancient landscape. (They have escaped burial or destruction to remain as part of the present landscape.) Residual landforms are often the result of changed climatic conditions, but they may be due to volcanism or to crustal uplift and downwarping. Examples of residual landforms are extinct volcanic cones, inactive stone rivers from climates on the fringe of glaciers, disconnected and abandoned parts of drainage systems, abandoned strandlines (or beachlines) from more humid climates, fixed sand dunes from drier climates, marine terraces from high sea levels, and plunging sea cliffs from lower sea levels. The percentage of residual landforms in a given landscape and the importance placed on relict landforms by different geomorphologists may vary tremendously.

The lavas erupted at these volcanoes are thought to be derived from the mantle in the wedge of asthenosphere above the lithospheric plate plunging into it. Water carried down in the interstices of the subducted rock and by hydrous minerals to which water is loosely bound chemically is expelled into the wedge of asthenosphere above the subduction zone. The introduction of water reduces the melting temperature of the rocks and allows material in the wedge to melt and rise to the surface.

LANDFORMS ASSOCIATED WITH HOT SPOT VOLCANISM

Some volcanic phenomena occur at large distances from plate boundaries (for example, on the Hawaiian Islands or at Yellowstone National Park in the western continental United States). Also, as noted above, volcanism is especially intense at some parts of the mid-ocean ridge system (as in Iceland or the Galápagos Islands in the eastern Pacific). Magmas erupted in these settings originate in the asthenosphere, perhaps at depths of several hundred kilometres or more at what are called hot spots in the mantle. Such sources of melting may be due to chemical differences rather than to heat. Active volcanoes are usually localized in a region with dimensions of 100 to 200 km (about 60 to 125 miles) or less.

A chain of extinct volcanoes or volcanic islands (and seamounts), like the Hawaiian chain, or a volcanic ridge, like Walvis Ridge between the islands of Tristan da Cunha and the east coast of Africa, can form where a lithospheric plate moves over a hot spot. The active volcanoes all lie at one end of the chain or ridge, and the ages of the islands or the ridge increase with their distance from those sites of volcanic activity. Older volcanoes are more eroded than younger ones and are often marked only by coral reefs that grow on the eroded and subsiding volcanic island.

Volcanic chains of this kind are not common in continental regions, in part because most continental masses move slowly over hot spots. Volcanic activity, however, can be particularly abundant when a plate moves so slowly with respect to a hot spot. Moreover, a long duration of volcanism often results in a warming of the lithosphere. This warming causes a localized thermal expansion and consequently a localized upwarping or doming of Earth's surface, as in the case of the Yellowstone area or the Massif Central in France. The resulting domes cover areas a few to several hundred kilometres in extent, and the mean elevations are rarely as much as 1,000 metres (3,280 feet) higher than the surrounding regions. Thus, except for the isolated volcanoes that lie on the upwarps, relief is gentle and due largely to erosion.

Some hot spots are associated with massive eruptions of lava and ash, primarily of basaltic composition, which cover vast areas as extensive as tens or hundreds of square kilometres. Such flood basalts, or traps, buried the Snake River Plain west of Yellowstone a few million years ago, the

Columbia River Valley some 20 million years ago, and central India (the Deccan traps) 60 million to 65 million years ago. Flood basalts create a remarkably flat surface that is later dissected into a network of sharply incised valleys.

Most volcanoes that cannot be ascribed either to a subduction zone or to seafloor spreading at mid-ocean ridges are attributed to hot spots. There are, however, some volcanoes, volcanic fields, and flood basalts that cannot yet be ascribed to hot spots with any certainty. Nevertheless, the landforms associated with such volcanic phenomena resemble those in other settings for which a simple cause can be offered.

MOUNTAIN BELTS ASSOCIATED WITH CRUSTAL SHORTENING

Most mountain belts of the world and nearly all of those in Europe, Asia, and North America have been built by horizontal crustal shortening and associated crustal thickening. The landforms associated with such belts depend on the rates, amounts, and types of crustal deformation that occur and on the types of rocks that are exposed to erosion. To some extent the deformation can be related to different tectonic settings. Large thrusted crystalline terrains and parallel fold and thrust belts are commonly associated with continental collisions in which two separate continents have approached each other and one has been thrust onto the other. Continental collisions are responsible for Alpine-, or Himalayan-, type mountain belts. Fold and thrust belts can also be associated with active continental margins or Andean-type margins, where oceanic lithosphere is subducted into the asthenosphere but where crustal shortening occurs landward of the volcanic arc on the overriding continental plate. Block-faulted ranges commonly form as intracontinental mountain ranges or belts, far from collision zones and subduction zones.

ALPINE- (OR HIMALAYAN-) TYPE BELTS

These belts are thought to have been created by the movement of one continent beneath another. In general, a thick layer of light, buoyant continental crust cannot be carried deep into the asthenosphere. Instead, the leading edge of the descending continent is scraped off, and the rest of the continent then plunges beneath the off-scraped slice. Eventually the convergence between the two plates carrying the continents comes to a halt, but usually not before several slices of continental material have been removed from the underthrusting continent and stacked on top of it.

The sedimentary rocks deposited on the continental crust and its margin long before the collision often constitute one or part of one of the off-scraped slices. They commonly are deformed into a fold and thrust belt as the basement under them continues to plunge beneath the overriding plate at the subduction zone. Layers of strong sedimentary rock detach from the underlying basement at weak layers that commonly consist of evaporites (salt, gypsum, or anhydrite) or of shale by a process called décollement (from the French word meaning "ungluing"). The stronger layers of sedimentary rock are then folded into linear, regularly spaced folds—alternating anticlines and synclines—and thrust on top of one another. The Valley and Ridge Province of Pennsylvania, which was formed during the collision of Africa and North America near the end of Paleozoic time (about 240 million years ago), is a classic example.

Convergence between two lithospheric plates can be rapid in such settings—10 to 100 mm (0.4 to 4 inches) per year—and the amount of displacement on the major thrust faults also can be large—tens to more than 100 km (about 60 miles). Thus, when a slice of crystalline rock from deep in the crust is scraped off the remainder of the continent and is underthrust by it, much of the slice is uplifted and pushed onto the relatively flat, ancient surface of the intact portion of the continent. Erosion generally removes the sedimentary cover of such slices and leaves expanses of crystalline rocks, as can be seen on Himalayan or Alpine peaks.

Faults along which a slice of continental crust is torn from the rest of the continent and thrust onto it are called ramp overthrusts. When the fault first forms, it dips at 10° to 30° (or more). Slip on this fault (i.e., the movement of one face of the fault relative to the other) brings the leading edge of the off-scraped slice of crust to Earth's surface, where it then slides along the surface. The intact continent is flexed down by the weight of the material thrust on top of it. As a consequence, its initially flat surface dips at a very gentle angle of only a few degrees. Accordingly, a ramp overthrust consists of two segments. The first segment, the ramp, dips relatively steeply; slip on it causes uplift of the overriding slice and of the crystalline rocks from deep in the crust to create high relief and the high range. The other segment, which was once the top surface of the continent, has been flexed down and dips at a gentle angle. Slip on it allows the overthrust slice to advance over the rest of the continent, where it plows the sedimentary layers in front of it into folds and smaller overthrusts.

When a major ramp overthrust is active and the intact continent is flexed down in front of the overriding mountain range, a foreland basin is formed by the flexure. Foreland basins usually exist as subsurface features that have been filled with debris eroded from the advancing overthrust slice of crust. These deposits, called molasse,

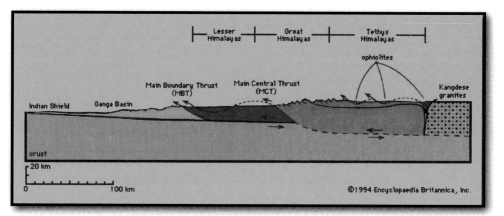

Simplified north–south cross section of the Himalayas, revealing a foreland basin (Ganga Basin), an overthrusting of crystalline terrains onto the Indian Plate, and a steeper thrust fault (a ramp) beneath the Great Himalayas. Encyclopædia Britannica, Inc.

can in turn be folded and thrust over one another shortly after they are deposited. Fold and thrust belts in such material, as found at the northern edge of the Alps or at the foot of most of the Himalayas, are often narrow, composed of only one or two parallel folds and faults. The topography associated with them generally consists of low, elongated hills of poorly consolidated sedimentary rock that is easily and rapidly eroded.

Collision zones are thus commonly identified by narrow belts of elevated crystalline terrain and parallel fold and thrust belts. The crystalline terrain has been thrust upward and toward the fold and thrust belt. Deformation is generally confined to shallow depths of only a few kilometres at such belts but penetrates deeply into Earth beneath the crystalline terrains. The rapid uplift of these resistant rocks creates a high range. A crystalline terrain often exhibits large folds in which the rocks appear to have flowed instead of having been bent. Folds of this sort have formed at depths where the rocks were hot and soft before they reached the relatively cold surface of Earth. The overthrusting of crystalline terrains onto intact continental crust can occur at rates of tens of millimetres per year, which is rapid for rates of slip on faults, and the crystalline rocks can be uplifted 10 to 20 km (about 6 to 12 miles) by slip on ramp overthrusts.

ANDEAN-TYPE BELTS

At some continental margins, oceanic lithosphere is subducted. At some of these sites, the landscape is dominated by volcanoes, such as along the Cascades of western North America or in Japan, but at others, such as along much of the Andes of South America, volcanoes constitute only a small or even negligible part of the relief. At Andean-type margins, the crust is typically thicker than normal, and high mountains can exist even in the absence of volcanoes. Some of the thickened crust is due to the intrusion of magma from the mantle, and some to crustal shortening.

Oceanic lithosphere is commonly subducted at active continental margins at rates of tens to more than 100 mm (4 inches) per year, but crustal shortening within the overriding plate typically occurs at rates of only a few millimetres annually. As at continent-continent collision zones, the crustal shortening occurs both by overthrusting of crystalline terrain onto intact continental crust, which in this case lies landward of the volcanic belt, and by the formation of a fold and thrust belt within sedimentary rock lying on the intact continent. The thrusting of crystalline terrain is probably facilitated by a heating and consequent weakening of the rocks near the volcanoes. The presence or absence of a parallel fold and thrust belt depends in part on the presence or absence of thick sedimentary rocks within which detachment of separate layers can take place.

Notwithstanding large variations in topography and in the style of deformation among Andean belts in general, the scales of deformation and uplift are less than those at collision zones. Overthrust crystalline terrains are smaller, and the crystalline rocks themselves have not been thrust up from depths as great as those at collision zones. Much of the Andes, for instance, consists of sedimentary rock that never was buried deeper than a few kilometres and therefore has not been metamorphosed (heated to high temperature or put under high pressure) or at most only has been mildly metamorphosed. Topography in the high parts of the Andes is typically much gentler than in the Himalayas. The most impressive relief is on the eastern flank of the Andes where rivers responding to a wet climate have cut deep canyons.

Fold and thrust belts can be very well developed at Andean margins. The eastern Cordillera of the Bolivian Andes is an extremely wide fold and thrust belt, but only along the eastern third of the cordillera do simple parallel folds control the topography. A cordillera (from old Spanish *cordilla,* "cord," or "little rope"), a system of mountain ranges that often consist of a number of more or less parallel chains. Farther west, both the greater role of thrust faulting in the evolution of the cordillera and the longer duration of erosion have diminished the role of folding. Except where rivers have cut deep canyons, relief is not exceptionally great. Similarly while oceanic lithosphere was underthrust beneath the west coast of Canada during the Mesozoic Era (251 million to 65.5 million years ago), the Canadian shield was underthrust more than 200 km (about 125 miles) beneath the Canadian Rocky Mountains, with crustal shortening occurring by décollement and by folding and thrust faulting within the sedimentary cover.

Thus Andean-type belts have a narrow belt of volcanoes and often a fold and thrust belt on their landward margin. The volcanoes of some belts are built on a high range that is more of a long, narrow plateau than a mountain range, for relief on it is not necessarily great.

INTRACONTINENTAL MOUNTAIN BELTS

In some regions, mountain belts have been formed by crustal shortening within a continental mass, rather than where two continents have collided. Some 40 million to 80 million years ago, the Rocky Mountains of Colorado, Utah, and Wyoming formed in this way, and today both the Tien Shan and the Atlas Mountains of northwestern Africa are actively forming within a continent. In general, intracontinental mountain belts are characterized by block faulting. Blocks, tens of kilometres wide and hundreds of kilometres long, are uplifted along faults that dip beneath them at angles of 25° to 45°. Because of the displacement on steep faults, crystalline rocks commonly crop out in the mountains. The edges of the ranges can be sharply defined. Fold and thrust belts are not common and are usually narrow where present.

At the edges of such ranges, sedimentary rocks are commonly tilted up, and, where resistant, they can form narrow, sharp-crested ridges called hogbacks that are parallel to the front of the ranges. A particularly prominent hogback lies along the east edge of the Front Range in eastern Colorado.

Intracontinental belts generally consist of elongated block-faulted ranges, which in some cases overlap but are not necessarily parallel to one another. Thus, in parts of the Tien Shan, two or three nearly parallel, sharply bounded ranges are separated from one another by parallel basins that are 10 to 30 km (about 6 to 19 miles) wide. The ranges of this great mountain system are being overthrust onto the basins, and one such basin, the Turfan Depression, has dropped below sea level. In contrast with the parallel ranges in the Tien Shan, the northwest-trending Wind River Range in Wyoming, the east–west trending Uinta

Mountains in Utah, and the north–south trending Front Range in Colorado are all part of the same intracontinental belt, the Rocky Mountains.

MAJOR MOUNTAIN BELTS OF THE WORLD

Most mountains and mountain ranges are parts of mountain belts that have formed where two lithospheric plates have converged and where, in most cases, they continue to converge. In effect, many mountain belts mark the boundaries of lithospheric plates, and these boundaries in turn intersect other such boundaries. Consequently, there exist very long mountain systems where a series of convergent plate boundaries continue from one to the next. A nearly continuous chain of volcanoes and mountain ranges surrounds most of the Pacific basin—the so-called Circum-Pacific System. A second nearly continuous chain of mountains can be traced from Morocco in North Africa through Europe, then across Turkey and Iran through the Himalayas to Southeast Asia; this chain, the Alpine-Himalayan (or Tethyan) System, has formed where the African, Arabian, and Indian plates have collided with the Eurasian Plate. Nearly all mountain ranges on Earth can be included in one of these two major systems and most that cannot are residual mountains, which originated from ancient continental collisions that occurred hundreds of millions of years ago.

THE CIRCUM-PACIFIC SYSTEM

A nearly continuous chain of volcanoes surrounds the Pacific Ocean. The chain passes along the west coast of North and South America, from the Aleutian Islands to the south of Japan, and from Indonesia to the Tonga

Islands, and to New Zealand. The Pacific basin is underlain by separate lithospheric plates that diverge from one another and that are being subducted beneath the margins of the basin at different rates. This Circum-Pacific chain of volcanoes (often called the Ring of Fire) and the mountain ranges associated with it owe their formation to the repeated subduction of oceanic lithosphere beneath the continents and the islands that surround the Pacific Ocean. Differences among the various segments of the Circum-Pacific chain arise from differences in the histories of subduction of the different plates.

THE ANDES

The Nazca Plate, which underlies most of the southeastern Pacific, is being subducted beneath most of the west coast of South America at a rapid rate of 80 to 100 mm (3 to 4 inches) per year. A nearly continuous chain of volcanoes lines the margin of South America, and the world's tallest volcano, Ojos del Salado (6,893 metres [about 22,620 feet]), is one of these peaks. The Andean range, however, is more than just a chain of volcanoes, and its highest peak, Mount Aconcagua (6,959 metres [about 22,830 feet]), the tallest outside Asia, is not volcanic. Crustal shortening and crustal thickening occur all along the eastern margin of the Andes by the westward underthrusting of the stable areas of Brazil and Argentina beneath the Andes at a rate of a few millimetres per year.

The southern part of the Andes in southern Chile and Argentina consists of a narrow range only 100 to 200 km (about 60 to 125 miles) wide. A chain of volcanoes follows the axis of the range, but crustal thickening due to crustal shortening is a principal cause of the high range, and many of the volcanoes are built on folded and faulted sedimentary rock.

An Aymara Indian poling a reed boat on Lake Titicaca, near the Bolivian shore. The Cordillera Real in the Bolivian Andes rises in the background. © Tony Morrison/South American Pictures

From northern Argentina to northern Peru and Ecuador, the Andes are much wider, with the widest segment across southern Bolivia. There, the mountain belt consists of two parallel ranges, the Cordillera Occidental (or Western Cordillera) and the Cordillera Oriental (or Eastern Cordillera), which surround the high plateau, the Altiplano.

The volcanic chain has been constructed on thick crust and forms the Cordillera Occidental. The Brazilian shield has been underthrust beneath the Cordillera Oriental, which comprises the western edge of a wide fold and thrust belt. This fold and thrust belt is marked by north–south trending folds and north–south trending ridges and valleys in northern Argentina and southeastern Bolivia. North of the latitude where the west coast of South America bends, the trend of the Andes, including that of both cordilleras, is northwesterly parallel to the coast of Peru. The fold and thrust belt east of the Cordillera Oriental is narrower than that farther south but is well defined by a few northwesterly trending ridges and valleys.

Lying between the two cordilleras in northern Argentina, western Bolivia, and southern Peru, the Altiplano stands at an average height of about 3,800 metres (about 12,470 feet). Within it lies Lake Titicaca, the highest navigable lake in the world. The Altiplano is a high arid basin that captures sediment eroded from the eastern and western cordilleras bounding it. Older rocks that crop out within it have been folded; thus crustal shortening probably has been an important factor in creating the high elevations and the thick crust that underlies this plateau.

In Colombia, the Andean chain diverges into three separate chains, each about 100 km (about 60 miles) wide. Volcanoes occur in the westernmost chain, but all three have undergone crustal shortening. For example, the easternmost of the three, which continues into Venezuela as the "Venezuelan Andes," is being underthrust from the northwest by the Maracaibo Basin and from the southeast by the Guiana Shield underlying southeastern Venezuela. Thus the Venezuelan Andes are an intracontinental mountain belt.

The divergence of the Andes into three chains in Colombia extends northward. The western chain continues into Panama and through Central America. The central chain continues toward the Caribbean. The Venezuelan Andes intersect an east–west trending chain along the north coast of South America in Venezuela.

THE CARIBBEAN CHAINS

The mountain range along the coast of Venezuela is a remnant of a phase when the Caribbean Sea was subducted southward beneath Venezuela and where rocks were folded along east–west axes. Right-lateral strike-slip faulting and rather slow mountain building occur there today, as much by slight vertical displacement on predominantly strike-slip faults as by slow obliquely oriented folding and thrust faulting and associated crustal shortening.

At the eastern end of the Caribbean Sea, the Lesser Antilles—volcanic islands that form a typical island arc—mark a zone where a part of the floor of the North Atlantic Ocean underthrusts that of the Caribbean Sea—namely, the Caribbean Plate. This plate has moved east relative to both North and South America at a rate of 10 to 20 mm (0.4 to 0.8 inch) per year for tens of millions of years. This displacement and the consequent overthrusting of the seafloor to the east are responsible for the volcanic arc that constitutes the Lesser Antilles as well as for the strike-slip displacement occurring in Venezuela.

Distant green mountains on the Caribbean island of Montserrat, Lesser Antilles. © Philip Coblentz—Digital Vision/Getty Images

Most of the major islands that define the northern margin of the Caribbean—Puerto Rico, Hispaniola, Cuba, and Jamaica—are mountainous, and these mountainous terrains, like that in northern Venezuela, are remnants of the period of convergence between North and South America and also of complicated deformation along the ancient margins of the Caribbean Plate. At present, crustal shortening occurs at only a very slow rate, if at all, on these islands.

At the western margin of the Caribbean Plate another small plate, the Cocos Plate, is being underthrust beneath Mexico and Central America. A belt of volcanoes extends from northern Panama to western Mexico, and virtually all of the highest mountains in this belt are volcanic. These volcanoes are built on thickened crust, and crustal shortening has occurred within the Central American Cordillera, but the principal tectonic process that has affected the landscape is volcanism.

THE NORTH AMERICAN CORDILLERA

A broad mountain belt extends north from Mexico to Alaska, and it reflects both a more diverse and a more complicated history of convergence between lithospheric plates than that presently occurring in the Andes or Central America.

Subduction of oceanic lithosphere presently occurs only beneath two segments of the coast of western North America. The subduction of a small plate, the Juan de Fuca Plate, beneath northern California, Oregon, Washington, and southern British Columbia is responsible for the Cascade chain of volcanoes, which includes Mount St. Helens. The very large Pacific Plate, which underlies most of the northern and western Pacific basin, moves north-northwest with respect to North America nearly parallel to the coast, and is subducted beneath southern Alaska and the Aleutians. The volcanic chain that forms the Aleutian Islands and continues into the Alaskan peninsula to the Wrangell Mountains is a consequence of this convergence and subduction.

Most of the North American Cordillera was built between about 170 million and 40 million years ago when lithospheric plates converged with North America at rapid rates of many tens to more than 100 mm (4 inches) per year. The Juan de Fuca Plate is the last remnant of one of these plates. The others have been subducted beneath western North America and have completely disappeared. Thus, in Mesozoic and Early Cenozoic times, an Andean margin similar to that which presently bounds the west coast of South America bounded western North America.

The Coast Ranges of central and northern California, Oregon, and Washington consist of folded and faulted slices of oceanic crust and its overlying sedimentary rocks. Much of the rock that constitutes these mountains was scraped off the oceanic lithosphere at the trench just west of the continent. The Olympic Mountains in northwestern Washington, for instance, consist largely of off-scraped seamounts. The rock of such coastal mountains was intensely deformed and metamorphosed before being elevated to produce the present range. Specifically, the hard basalt that makes up much of the oceanic crust has been metamorphosed into the easily deformed rock serpentinite, which contains the weak, fibrous mineral serpentine. The gentle relief of the Coast Ranges is due in part to the weakness of serpentinite, a characteristic that gives rise to frequent landslides and rapid erosion.

A belt of granite lies inland and forms a mountainous zone from the axis of Baja California (in Mexico), through southern California, along the Sierra Nevada in the states of California and Nevada, northwestward into Idaho, and then north-northwestward along the western margin of the Canadian Rocky Mountains to Alaska. This granite belt underlay the volcanoes that marked the subduction zone in Mesozoic and Early Cenozoic times. The intrusion of this granite was most intense between 170 million and 70 million years ago during the Mesozoic Era. The Sierra Nevada of California, which contains Mount Whitney, the highest peak in the contiguous United States, is composed almost entirely of this granite.

While subduction of oceanic lithosphere occurred beneath western North America, a major fold and thrust belt developed east of the granitic belt. During Mesozoic time, the Precambrian basement of Canada and North America was underthrust westward at least 200 km (about 125 miles) beneath the Andean margin, and the sedimentary rocks covering it were folded and thrust onto one another. Although present in the western United States, this fold and thrust belt is most clearly revealed in the Canadian Rockies along the border between the provinces of Alberta and British Columbia, particularly in Banff and Jasper national parks.

In sum, throughout the latter half of the Mesozoic, from about 170 million to 65.5 million years ago, the topography of western North America probably resembled that of western South America: a trench lay offshore; a belt of volcanoes underlain by granitic intrusions marked the western edge of a high range of mountains; and a fold and thrust belt lay east of the range. The tectonic history of western North America is more complicated, however, because during this period fragments of both continents and sub-oceanic plateaus were carried to the subduction zone and collided with North America. Most of the rock now found in westernmost Canada and Alaska consists of separate terrains of rock that were independently accreted to North America and that were subsequently deformed when the next such terrain collided with it. Moreover, tectonic processes occurring during the Cenozoic (since 65.5 million years ago) have been different from those that occurred earlier and have severely modified the landscape.

Beginning about 70 million to 80 million years ago, the locus of crustal shortening in the United States shifted from the fold and thrust belt, whose remnants now lie along the borders of western Utah and eastern Nevada and of western Wyoming and eastern Idaho, to eastern Utah, Colorado, and central Wyoming. Between about 70 million and 40 million years ago, thrust faulting on the margins of the Front Range in Colorado, the Laramie Mountains and the Wind River Range in Wyoming, and the Uinta Mountains in Utah, among others, allowed the uplift of blocks of Precambrian rock that are now exposed in the cores of these ranges. Together, these intracontinental ranges of block-faulted mountains form most of the Rocky Mountains of the United States.

During roughly the same period, volcanic rocks were erupted and deposited in parts of the Rockies, such as in southwestern Colorado in what are now the San Juan Mountains. The area that now forms the Colorado Plateau, in southern Utah and northern Arizona, underwent only very mild deformation in the form of small faults and folds and apparently lay at relatively low elevation. Sediment derived from the fold and thrust belt to its west and from the Rockies to its north and east was deposited on this relatively stable area. Thus, some 40 million years ago, a high range of mountains lay along the western margin of North America. This range consisted of a volcanic chain along most of its western edge and an eroded fold and thrust belt on its eastern edge. At the latitude of Wyoming, Colorado, and Utah, another belt of mountains, the present-day Rocky Mountains, lay farther east.

The topography of the western United States has been modified extensively by tectonic processes during the last

20 million years. Much of the mountainous terrain of Utah, Nevada, and California underwent large-scale crustal extension, beginning more than 40 million years ago but accelerating about 15 million years ago. The crustal extension approximately doubled the surface area of the region between central Utah and the Sierra Nevada, presumably with a reduction in the mean elevation of the mountains.

The present topography of the Basin and Range Province of North America is a direct manifestation of this crustal extension. The most prominent basins, such as Death Valley and Owens Valley in California, are small rift valleys that were formed during the last few million years. This phase of the crustal extension continues even today, with such basins becoming deeper and the surrounding ranges increasing in height. This condition is readily discernible in the case of Owens Valley and the Sierra Nevada. The occurrence of a major fault on the east side of the Sierras has allowed the valley to drop with respect to the mountain range, which has been tilted up toward the east.

Concurrent with this extension, the uppermost mantle beneath parts of the western United States has become hotter. The considerable height of the Colorado Plateau, for instance, appears to be the result of the warming of the underlying mantle during roughly the past 10 million years. Such mantle heating also seems to have been responsible, at least in part, for the present elevation of much of the North American Cordillera.

The one area where rapid subduction of oceanic lithosphere (more than 50 mm [2 inches] per year) has continued is southern Alaska, where the Pacific Plate is being underthrust beneath the coast. The St. Elias Mountains, the tallest in southeastern Alaska and the Yukon, appear to be the direct consequences of this convergence and rapid underthrusting. Deformation of the southern Alaskan crust extends northward several hundred kilometres to the Alaska Range, where the highest mountain in North America, Mount McKinley, is found.

North–south crustal shortening in southern Alaska occurs both by thrust faulting and by strike-slip faulting on nearly vertical, northwesterly trending planes. Mount McKinley lies adjacent to one such major strike-slip fault, the Denali Fault. The rocks that make up Mount McKinley have been displaced several tens of kilometres northwestward relative to the rocks north of the Denali Fault and a few kilometres upward. This small vertical component, compared with the large horizontal component, has created the high peak.

VOLCANOES AND ISLAND ARCS SURROUNDING THE NORTHWEST PACIFIC BASIN

A chain of volcanoes extends from mainland Alaska down the Alaska Peninsula along the Aleutian Islands and then southwestward down the peninsula of Kamchatka in northeastern Siberia and along the Kuril Islands to Japan. The Pacific Plate is being subducted beneath this long volcanic chain. Most of the relief is the result of volcanism. The Aleutians and Kurils are volcanic islands, and for the most part the volcanoes on the continental areas of the Alaska Peninsula, Kamchatka, and Japan are built up from sea level rather than on high ranges, as is the case with the Andes. For instance, Mount Fuji, a symmetrically shaped volcanic cone, rises from a low elevation to more than 4,000 metres (about 13,120 feet).

In the central part of the Japanese island of Honshu, the Circum-Pacific System diverges into two chains. One continues southward along the Izu, Bonin, and Mariana islands. These volcanic islands form island arcs where the Pacific Plate is subducted beneath the floor of the Philippine Sea to the west. Southwest of Honshu,

The summit of a partially submerged volcano forms the outline of Kraternaya Bay, Yankich Island, in the Kuril Islands of Russia. Michael V. Propp

the Ryukyu Islands are another island arc where the Philippine Sea floor is subducted beneath the Yellow Sea.

The Ryukyu island arc ends abruptly at the island of Taiwan, which is not part of the Ryukyu arc. Taiwan is a small mountainous island consisting of folded and thrusted sedimentary rocks on the southeastern margin of the Asian continent. The sedimentary rocks of Taiwan were deposited on that margin under tranquil conditions, much as sedimentary rocks have been deposited on the margins of the Atlantic Ocean. Then, in the last few million years a segment of the Asian continental margin encountered a subduction zone that dipped east-southeast. As that short segment of the margin began to be underthrust, the sedimentary rocks were scraped off its leading edge and thrust back on top of it. Thus, not only the mountains of Taiwan but also virtually the entire island consists of folded and thrust sedimentary rocks that have rapidly piled up on what had been a submerged continental shelf.

A couple of volcanic islands south of Taiwan mark the southward continuation of this subduction zone to Luzon, the large northern island of the Philippines. The mountainous landscape of the Philippine Islands is a consequence both of subduction of the South China Sea floor eastward beneath Luzon and of subduction of the Philippine Sea floor westward beneath the southern Philippine islands. Volcanism and, in Luzon, crustal shortening have built the major mountains.

A major system of island arcs extends across the Indonesian islands of Sumatra and Java and eastward almost to the island of New Guinea and then again eastward along the New Britain, Solomon, and New Hebrides (Vanuatu) chains. Virtually all of the high mountains of the Sunda, or Indonesian, arc are volcanoes, some of which are associated with particularly noteworthy eruptions. In 1883 the massive eruption of the volcano on the island of

Krakatoa, in the straits between Java and Sumatra, was followed by a collapse of its caldera, which caused a huge sea wave that was recorded all around the world. The eruption in 1815 of the Tambora Volcano on Sumbawa was perhaps the greatest in recorded history. Debris from this eruption darkened the skies for several months and caused a temporary global cooling that made 1816 "the year without a summer." The Sumbawa volcanic arc is associated with the northward subduction of the Indian Ocean floor beneath Indonesia. Similarly, the volcanic arcs of New Britain, the Solomon and New Hebrides islands, are associated with the northward subduction of the floor of the Solomon Sea and that of the Coral Sea beneath these island arcs.

A high range of mountains forms the backbone of the island of New Guinea between the Sunda and New Britain arcs. Whereas seafloor continues to be subducted beneath these arcs, the northern margin of the Australian continent has encountered the segment of the subduction zone between these arcs. The mountains of New Guinea consist of folded and faulted volcanic and sedimentary rocks. The volcanic rocks include both ancient seafloor and old island arcs that were thrust up and onto the northern margin of Australia. The sedimentary rock includes a full complement of Paleozoic, Mesozoic, and Cenozoic rock deposited in the tranquil conditions of an ancient continental shelf. Thrust faulting has elevated metamorphic rock to the crest of the high range where glaciers persist even at the Equator, while the sedimentary rock is being deformed in a fold and thrust belt along the southern margin of the range.

East of the New Hebrides Islands, the Circum-Pacific System is defined by the Tonga and Kermadec islands, volcanic islands associated with the westward subduction of the Pacific Plate. The subduction zone continues southward to the North Island of New Zealand, where volcanism is the principal tectonic process that has created mountains and relief. The mountains of the South Island of New Zealand, however, have been produced by different tectonic processes. Whereas the convergence between the Pacific Plate and the seafloor beneath the Tasman Sea manifests itself as subduction of the Pacific Plate at the Tonga-Kermadec-North Island zone, it results in crustal shortening across the South Island. The Southern Alps of New Zealand have resulted from this crustal shortening, which occurs by folding, by thrust faulting, and by vertical components of slip on predominantly strike-slip faults that trend southwest across the northern and western parts of the island. Rapid uplift, possibly as much as 10 mm (0.4 inch) per year, keeps pace with the rapid erosion of the easily eroded schists of the Southern Alps.

The Circum-Pacific System continues southwest of New Zealand along a submarine ridge, the Macquarie Ridge. In short, the Circum-Pacific System consists of a variety of mountain types and ranges where different tectonic processes occurring at different geologic times in the past have shaped the landscape. The grouping of these different belts into this single system is thus only a crude simplification.

THE ALPINE-HIMALAYAN, OR TETHYAN, SYSTEM

The interconnected system of mountain ranges and intermontane plateaus that lies between the stable areas of Africa, Arabia, and India on the south and Europe and Asia on the north owes its existence to the collisions of different continental fragments during the past 100 million years. Some 150 million years ago, India and much of what is now Iran and Afghanistan lay many thousands of kilometres south of their present positions. A vast ocean, called the Tethys Ocean, lay south of Europe and Asia and north of Africa, Arabia, and India. Much of the rock that now forms the mountain system, which includes the Alps and the Himalayas, was deposited on the margins of the Tethys Ocean.

As in the case for the Circum-Pacific System, the grouping of these different mountain ranges into a single system is an oversimplification. The various ranges (and plateaus) of the Alpine-Himalayan System formed at different times, at different rates, and between different lithospheric plates, and consist of different types of rocks.

THE HIMALAYAN CHAIN

The easternmost segment of the system begins at the western end of the Sunda island arc and continues into the arcuate chain of mountains that constitute the Himalayas, which contain the highest peaks on Earth. This chain was

The Dinaric Alps rising from the Dalmatian coast at Makarska, a resort town south of Split, Croatia. Leo de Wys Inc./Van Phillips

formed as the Indian subcontinent, a passenger on the same plate that currently underthrusts the Sunda arc, collided with the southern margin of Asia and subsequently penetrated some 2,000 km (about 1,250 miles) into the rest of Asia. As the leading edge of India, on which Paleozoic and Mesozoic sedimentary rocks had been deposited, plunged beneath southern Tibet, these rocks were scraped off the subcontinent and thrust back onto its more stable parts. With continued penetration of the Indian subcontinent, slices of the metamorphic basement of its leading edge were scraped off the rest of it and thrust onto one another, so that the rocks of the present-day Himalayan chain consist of slices of India's ancient northern continental margin.

Physiographically, this chain can be subdivided into three parallel belts: the Lesser Himalayas, the Great

The Plateau of Tibet looking toward the Himalayas and (right of centre) *Mount Everest.* Jill Singer—CLICK/Chicago

Himalayas, and the Tethys Himalayas. (Some authorities prefer a subdivision into four belts, the additional one designated the Outer, or Sub-Himalayas.) The Great Himalayas are defined by an arcuate chain of the highest peaks. To the south lie the Lesser Himalayas, a belt about 100 km (about 60 miles) wide with an average elevation of 1,000 to 2,000 metres (about 3,280 to 6,560 feet) that is dissected by the rivers emanating from the Great Himalayas and north of it. To the north, the Tethys Himalayas form the southern edge of the Tibetan Plateau.

The rocks of the Lesser Himalayas consist primarily of mildly metamorphosed sedimentary rock largely of Precambrian age. At present, the remainder of the Indian subcontinent underthrusts the Lesser Himalayas on a very gently dipping thrust fault, so that the rocks forming this belt are sliding over the ancient top surface of India. As a result, the uplift of the Lesser Himalayas seems to be relatively slow.

The rate of uplift in the Himalayas seems to be rapid in two parallel zones: (1) at the very front of the range where the ancient metamorphic and sedimentary rocks of the Lesser Himalayas have been thrust up and onto the young sediments, and (2) beneath the Great Himalayas. The thrust fault that carries the Himalayas onto the intact part of India is a ramp overthrust, with the steep part of the ramp dipping north beneath the Great Himalayas. Slip on this steep part allows the rapid uplift of the Great Himalayas, which in turn creates the high peaks and carries rock from deep in the crust to Earth's surface.

Most of the constituent rocks of the Great Himalayas are metamorphic; they once constituted the middle and lower crust of India's ancient northern margin but were subsequently scraped off and thrust up onto the surface. The very tops of many of the peaks, however, consist of Paleozoic sedimentary rocks, which dip northward. North of the Great Himalayas, in the Tethys Himalayas, these Paleozoic rocks and the Mesozoic sedimentary rocks deposited on them along the southern edge of the Tethys Ocean have been folded and faulted into east–west ridges.

Geologically, the northern margin of the Himalayas follows the Indus River in the west and the Brahmaputra River (also called Tsang-po or Yarlung Zangbo Jiang) in the east. The last remnants of the Tethys Ocean floor can be found in what some refer to as the Indus-Tsang-po Suture Zone, where a jumble of volcanic and sedimentary rocks have been folded and thrust over one another in a narrow zone parallel to these rivers. North of this suture, a belt of granites forms the backbone of the Trans-Himalayan range. These granites were intruded into the crust of the southern margin of Asia between 120 million and 50 million years ago, when the Tethys Ocean floor was being subducted beneath southern Asia and before India collided with it.

Since India collided with Eurasia, it has penetrated 2,000 km (about 1,250 miles) or more into the ancient Eurasian continent. The northern edge of India may have been subducted a few hundred kilometres beneath southern Tibet, but most of its penetration has been absorbed by crustal shortening north of the collision zone. The crust of the Tibetan Plateau appears to have been severely shortened; the thickness of its crust has approximately doubled. Although much of Asia underwent extensive deformation during phases of mountain building in Late Precambrian, Paleozoic, or Mesozoic times, the high altitudes of all of the mountain ranges surrounding the Tibetan Plateau, including the Pamir, Karakoram, Kunlun, Nan, Ch'i-lien (Qilian), and Lung-men (Longmen) mountains, have formed since India collided with Eurasia.

In some areas, blocks of crust undeformed since Precambrian time, such as beneath the Takla Makan (or Tarim Basin), have remained in that state, but have been displaced in response to India's penetration. The northward displacement of the Tarim Basin has caused intracontinental crustal shortening in the Tien Shan, the aforementioned east–west trending mountain range with peaks exceeding 7,000 metres (about 22,970 feet) in height that lies 1,000 to 2,000 km (about 620 to 1,250 miles) north of India's northern edge. The Tien Shan was the site of Late Paleozoic mountain building, but by the time India collided with Eurasia erosion had planed down the ancient Tien Shan to a featureless terrain buried in its own sediment. The present elevation therefore seems to be a consequence of India's penetration into Asia notwithstanding its great distance from India itself.

The penetration of India into Eurasia not only has caused crustal thickening in front of itself, but it also is squeezing parts of Asia eastward out of its northward path. One manifestation of this extrusion of material out of its path is the crustal shortening on the eastern margin of the Tibetan Plateau, where crustal thickening is actively occurring. The eastward displacement of crustal blocks along major strike-slip faults also seems to have caused rift systems to open in a northwest–southeast direction. The Baikal Rift Zone in Siberia and the Shansi Graben in northern China seem to have resulted from the east-southeastward extrusion of material out of India's path. Moreover, crustal thickening in the Tibetan Plateau has ceased, and now east–west extension of the plateau contributes to the eastward extrusion. The plateau is laced with northerly trending rift zones that are bounded by northerly trending tilted, block-faulted mountains. Thus, virtually all of the tectonic landforms of Asia seem to be attributable, directly or indirectly, to India's collision with Eurasia and its subsequent penetration into the continent.

The eastward extrusion has been facilitated by the lack of any major obstacle to the eastward displacement of South China. Minor westward displacement of material also has occurred in Afghanistan, but this process has been blocked by the collision of Arabia with southern Iran and Turkey, where to some extent the same processes have occurred as in eastern Asia.

THE ZAGROS AND BITLIS MOUNTAINS

The Arabian Peninsula, its northeastern edge covered by thick sedimentary rocks, has collided with Iran and Turkey at the Zagros and Bitlis sutures to form the Zagros and Bitlis mountains. Thick layers of salt in the Arabian shield's sedimentary rock have allowed the overlying layers to detach and fold, creating a particularly well-developed fold and thrust belt in the Zagros.

While these overlying sedimentary rocks have become detached and folded, the penetration of the Arabian shield into Iran and Turkey has built plateaus in front of it and mountain ranges on the north sides of the plateaus: these include the Kopet-Dag and Elburz ranges north of the central Iranian plateau and the Caucasus north of the Anatolian plateau. North–south crustal shortening is the principal process by which these ranges were built, but volcanism has contributed in some cases. Many of the high mountains in this area are volcanoes, including Mount Demavand, which towers over the city of Tehran, Mount Ararat on the border of Turkey and Armenia where Noah reputedly landed, and Mount Elbrus, the highest peak in the Caucasus. The penetration of the Arabian Peninsula into eastern Turkey also has induced a westward extrusion of Anatolia, the high central part of Turkey. Thus, the same processes active in eastern Asia have affected the landscape of the western portion but only on a smaller scale.

The Zagros Mountains rise above pasturelands, southwestern Iran. Fred J. Maroon/Photo Researchers

The evolution of the western segment of the Tethyan System is the most complicated, involving more than just a collision of the African continent with parts of Europe. In Early Jurassic time (about 180 million years ago), Africa, which then lay close to Europe, moved southeastward away from it. In doing so, it caused new ocean floor (Tethys) and new continental margins to form. Much of the rock in the Alps, for instance, was deposited on this newly formed margin of southern Europe. Later, during the Cretaceous (about 100 million years ago), the divergence of Africa and Europe ceased, and convergence between them began. Mountain ranges through northern Greece (the Pindus), the Yugoslav region (the Dinaric Alps), Romania, Hungary, the Czech Republic, and Slovakia (the Carpathians), and Austria, Switzerland, France, and Italy (the Alps) all formed as the Italian peninsula—a promontory on the African continent—moved first north-northeast toward Europe at 20 to 30 mm (0.8 to 1.2 inches) per year and later northwest at a slower rate of about 10 mm (0.4 inch) per year. The change in the direction of motion and the irregular shape of this promontory are two reasons why the tectonic evolutions of the different ranges of Europe are very different from each other. This is unlike the situation in the Himalayas, where the history of the belt is similar throughout the 2,500-km- (about 1,550-mile-) long range.

The best-studied of these ranges is the western Alps in Switzerland and France. The western end of the Tethys Ocean floor was subducted beneath northern Italy until about 45 million to 35 million years ago. At that time, southern Europe and northern Italy collided. As the southern margin of Europe began to be subducted beneath northern Italy, the sedimentary cover deposited on the

European margin of the Tethys Ocean was detached and scraped off the margin. Thick layers of relatively strong sedimentary rock (e.g., limestone and sandstone) that had been deposited on weak layers of salt (and in some cases shale) became detached and folded into huge nappes — enormous, flat layers of rock that seem to have been folded and sometimes dragged over one another like sheets of cloth pushed over a table or bed.

As northern Italy continued to override the coast of southern Europe, it not only pushed the sedimentary cover farther onto the European landmass, but it also scraped up bits and pieces of the deeper metamorphic rocks of Europe's basement. Moreover, as the crust thickened, the increase in pressure and temperature metamorphosed the deeply buried rocks. Although there are exceptions, the northern and western parts of the Alps thus are dominated by folded, unmetamorphosed sedimentary rock, and the southern part consists largely of metamorphic rock.

As Europe was flexed down under the weight of the Alps thrust onto it, a foreland basin formed just north of the Alps: this is the Molasse Basin of northern Switzerland and southern Germany. Continental convergence in the past 10 million years has caused folding and thrusting in the Jura Mountains of northwest Switzerland and France, and displacement on ramp overthrusts beneath the front of the Alps has elevated several crystalline massifs, including the Belledonne and Mont Blanc massifs in France and the Aare (or Aar) and Gotthard massifs in Switzerland. Moreover, with the elevation of the Alps above the Po plain of northern Italy, a southward overthrusting has carried the southern part of the Alps back onto the basin there as the Italian promontory has continued to penetrate into the rest of Europe.

The Apennines, which form the backbone of the Italian peninsula, were built by the folding and faulting of sedimentary rock deposited on the peninsula. The deformation in a direction nearly perpendicular to that of the Alps was due in part to a phase of the northeastward movement of Italy toward the Adriatic coast of the Balkan Peninsula and also to the rotation of Corsica and Sardinia away from southern France and toward Italy. Thus, while the crust of the Alps was being shortened in its north–south or northwest–southeast dimension, that of the Apennines was being shortened in its northeast–southwest dimension.

While the Alps, the Apennines, and the ranges of eastern Europe were being built, different processes created mountain ranges in parts of western Europe and destroyed others in eastern Europe. For instance, while the last remnant of the Tethys Ocean, the eastern Mediterranean Sea, continues to be subducted beneath Greece and Turkey, north–south crustal extension and associated crustal thinning occurs in the Aegean area and western Turkey. This crustal thinning has already lowered the surface of what may have been a high range or plateau to below the level of the Aegean Sea and is reducing the average elevation of western Turkey.

In contrast, the western Mediterranean Sea—between Italy, Spain, and North Africa—was formed during the past 30 million years and is not a remnant of the Tethys Ocean. Since that time and concurrently with the subduction of the Tethys lithosphere beneath southern Italy, Greece, and Turkey, fragments of crust have separated from southern Europe. As these fragments drifted across the ancient westernmost end of the Tethys Ocean, they opened the new western Mediterranean basin behind them.

The collisions of these fragments with parts of Italy and Africa have contributed to the building of mountain ranges in these areas. Corsica and Sardinia swung out from southern France, and the eastern margin of Corsica, which lies below sea level, collided with Italy. The Calabrian peninsula of southern Italy once lay against Sardinia, but its southward drift opened the Tyrrhenian Sea. The volcanoes of Italy, including Mount Vesuvius near Naples and Mount Etna on Sicily, were formed as a result of the subduction of the ancient oceanic lithosphere of the Tethys beneath the Calabrian arc, which only recently collided with the rest of Sicily and the southern part of the Italian peninsula. Small fragments farther west collided with North Africa, causing crustal shortening and mountain building across northern Tunisia, Algeria, and Morocco.

The convergence of another small fragment with Europe built the Pyrenees. The Iberian Peninsula lay against the western margin of France until about 90 million or 100 million years ago, when it began to rotate into its present position and opened the Bay of Biscay behind it. As the peninsula moved toward southern France, a combination of crustal shortening and strike-slip deformation along the Pyrenees built the narrow range that separates Spain and France.

RESIDUAL MOUNTAIN RANGES AND THERMALLY UPLIFTED BELTS

Although isolated mountains and mountainous terrains exist on all continents, most mountain belts not part of either the Circum-Pacific or the Alpine-Himalayan systems either are composed of residual mountains or owe their existences to localized thermally induced uplifts. Most such linear belts are residual ranges. The Appalachians in the eastern United States, for example, emerged as a result of a collision between Africa and North America in Late Paleozoic time before the present Atlantic Ocean formed. The well-developed Valley and Ridge Province in the states of Pennsylvania, West Virginia,

The Ahaggar Plateau rises from the barren landscape of the Sahara in southern Algeria. Geoff Renner/Robert Harding Picture Library

Virginia, and Kentucky has been eroded, but strong layers remain and define the ridges that once were limbs of folded layers. Similarly, the Ural Mountains were formed by the collision of Europe and Siberia in Late Paleozoic time. Much of the mountainous terrain in northeast Siberia was formed by collisions of continental fragments with the rest of Siberia in Mesozoic time.

Some high areas follow old mountain belts, but the present elevations are the result of recent uplift due to the heating of the lithosphere and to its thermal expansion. Strictly speaking, these belts are not residual mountain ranges. The mountainous topography of Norway and northern Sweden, for instance, follows an Early Paleozoic belt that marks the zone where Europe and North America (including Greenland) collided more than 400 million years ago, long before the present Atlantic Ocean formed. The present-day topography, however, probably exists because this area was heated when Greenland was rifted away from Europe some 55 million years ago when the North Atlantic Ocean began to form. Similarly, the mountains of eastern Australia, including the Snowy Mountains that contain the continent's highest peak, follow a Paleozoic belt; yet, the present topography seems to be the result of the warming of the lithosphere both when New Zealand separated from the east coast of Australia some 80 million to 90 million years ago and again when Australia drifted over a hot spot in the asthenosphere tens of millions of years ago.

Except for the chain of mountains across North Africa, virtually all mountains and high terrains on that continent and on Antarctica result from thermal processes. The high margins of the Red Sea and the Gulf of Aden on both Africa and Arabia are due to the heating of the lithosphere that occurred when these narrow bodies of water began to open 20 million–40 million years ago and to the existence of a hot spot in the asthenosphere beneath the Ethiopian Plateau. Most of the high plateaus of central and southern Africa, such as the Ahaggar, formed because of hot spots beneath them. The same can be said of the high plateau that surrounds the East African Rift System and of the high volcanoes, such as Mount Kilimanjaro and Mount Kenya, built on that plateau. Similarly, the Transantarctic Mountains probably are high because of recent heating of the lithosphere beneath them. At the end of the range are two volcanoes, Mount Erebus and Mount Terror, which probably owe their existence to a hot spot beneath them.

Most of the highlands of continents that are not characterized by chains of mountains have resulted from a heating of the lithosphere. The majority of them, however, are better described as plateaus than as mountain ranges.

CHAPTER 3
PLATEAUS AND VALLEYS

O ther continental landforms include plateaus and valleys. Although mountains tend to be more noticeable
due to their striking contrast with the surrounding landscape, the geographic extent of plateaus and valleys tend
to be larger features. Plateaus, in particular, are extensive
areas of flat uplands that are usually bounded by an escarpment on all sides. Some plateaus, however, are enclosed by
mountains. The essential criteria for plateaus are low relative relief and some altitude. These features are extensive,
and together with enclosed basins they cover about 45
percent of Earth's land surface. Valleys, on the other hand,
are elongate depressions on Earth's surface. They are most
commonly drained by rivers and may occur in a relatively
flat plain or between ranges of hills or mountains. Those
valleys produced by tectonic action are called rift valleys.
Very narrow, deep valleys of similar appearance are called
gorges. Both of these latter types are commonly cut in flat-
lying strata but may occur in other geological situations.

PLATEAUS

Although plateaus stand at higher elevation than surrounding terrain, they differ from mountain ranges in that
they are remarkably flat. Some plateaus, like the Altiplano
in southern Peru and western Bolivia, are integral parts
of mountain belts. Others, such as the Colorado Plateau
(across which the Colorado River has cut the Grand
Canyon), were produced by processes very different from
those that built neighbouring mountain ranges. Some

The Columbia Plateau is uniformly covered with basaltic lava flows and spans an area of about 259,000 sq km (100,000 square miles) in Idaho, Washington, and Oregon. Encyclopædia Britannica, Inc.

plateaus, as, for example, the Deccan Plateau of central India, occur far from mountain ranges. The differences among plateaus can be ascribed to the different geologic processes that have created them.

GEOMORPHIC CHARACTERISTICS

The high flat surface that defines a plateau can continue for hundreds or even thousands of kilometres, as in the case of the Tibetan Plateau. In spite of the paucity of roads, one can drive over most of this plateau, where elevations exceed 4,500 metres (14,760 feet), and encounter less relief than in some major cities of the world (e.g., San Francisco or Rio de Janeiro). Although ranges of hills and mountains rise above the rest of the plateau, their topography, too, is rather gentle.

Plateaus dissected by rivers have remarkably uniform maximum elevations, but their surfaces can be interrupted by deep canyons. In the case of some regions described as plateaus, the surface is so dissected that one does not see any flat terrain. Instead, such a plateau is defined by a uniform elevation of the highest ridges and mountains. The eastern part of the Tibetan Plateau, which constitutes the headwaters of many of the great rivers of Asia (e.g., Huang Ho, Yangtze, Mekong, Salween, and Irrawaddy), is dissected into deep canyons separated by narrow, steep ridges; the high uniform elevation that characterizes plateaus is only barely discernible in this area.

Formative Processes

The formation of a plateau requires one of the same three types of tectonic processes that create mountain ranges — volcanism, crustal shortening, and thermal expansion. The simplest of these is thermal expansion of the lithosphere (or the replacement of cold mantle lithosphere by hot asthenosphere).

When the lithosphere underlying a broad area is heated rapidly—e.g., by an upwelling of hot material in the underlying asthenosphere—the consequent warming and thermal expansion of the uppermost mantle causes an uplift of the overlying surface. If the uplifted surface had originally been low and without prominent relief, it is likely to remain relatively flat when uplifted to a relatively uniform elevation. The high plateaus of East Africa and Ethiopia were formed this way. As in parts of Africa, plateaus of this sort can be associated with volcanism and with rift valleys, but these features are not universal. Most of the high plateau in East Africa that holds Lake Victoria does not contain volcanic rock and is cut only by small, minor rift valleys.

Where the uplifted surface lay at a low elevation for a very long time and was covered by resistant sedimentary rock, the flatness of the plateau can be particularly marked. The rock underlying the Colorado Plateau has undergone only very mild deformation since Precambrian time, and layers of very resistant limestone and sandstone deposited during the Paleozoic form its top surface in many areas. The warming of the underlying lithosphere in late Cenozoic time caused this area to rise to its present elevation, and those resistant Paleozoic formations define the surfaces that make the remarkably flat horizons at the Grand Canyon.

The great heights of some plateaus, such as the Tibetan Plateau or the Altiplano, are due to crustal shortening. The geologic structure of plateaus of this kind is entirely different from that of the Colorado Plateau, for instance. Crustal shortening and crustal thickening, as described above, have created high mountains along what are now the margins of such plateaus. In most mountain ranges, streams and rivers transport eroded material from the mountains to the neighbouring plains. When drainage is internal and streams and rivers deposit their debris in the valleys between mountains, however, a plateau can form. The surface of this sort of plateau is defined by very flat, broad valleys surrounded by eroded hills and mountains. The rocks that make up the mountains and the basement of the valleys are often strongly deformed, but the young sediment deposited in the valleys usually lies flat. These plateaus generally survive erosion only in dry climates where erosion is slow. In many cases, the valleys, or basins, are occupied by flat dry lake beds. Thus, plateaus built by crustal shortening are really mountain ranges buried in their own debris.

A third type of plateau can form where extensive lava flows (called flood basalts or traps) and volcanic ash bury preexisting terrain, as exemplified by the Columbia Plateau in the northwestern United States. The volcanism involved in such situations is commonly associated with hot spots. The lavas and ash are generally carried long distances from their sources, so that the topography is not dominated by volcanoes or volcanic centres. The thickness of the volcanic rock can be tens to even hundreds of metres, and the top surface of flood basalts is typically very flat but often with sharply incised canyons and valleys.

The separation of plateaus into the above three types is not always easy because two or even all three of the processes involved frequently operate simultaneously. For instance, where the uppermost mantle is particularly hot, volcanism is common. The Ethiopian Plateau, on which Precambrian rocks crop out, stands high because the underlying lithosphere has been heated; however, Cenozoic volcanic rocks cover much of the plateau, especially those areas that are the flattest. Although the scale is different, there are active volcanoes and young lavas covering some broad basins on the northern part of the Tibetan Plateau. All three processes—thermal expansion, crustal shortening, and volcanism—may have contributed to the high, flat elevation of at least part of this plateau.

GEOGRAPHIC DISTRIBUTION

Plateaus of one type or another can be found on most continents. Those caused by thermal expansion of the lithosphere are usually associated with hot spots. The Yellowstone Plateau in the United States, the Massif Central in France, and the Ethiopian Plateau in Africa are prominent examples. Most hot spots are associated with the upwelling of hot material in the asthenosphere, and this hot upwelling not only heats the overlying lithosphere and melts holes through it to produce volcanoes but also uplifts the lithosphere. The relationship of such plateaus to hot spots insures both a wide distribution of plateaus and an absence of belts of plateaus or of interrelated plateaus.

Some plateaus, like the Colorado Plateau, the Ordos Plateau in northern China, or the East African Highlands, do not seem to be related to hot spots or to vigorous upwelling in the asthenosphere, but appear to be underlain by unusually hot material. The reason for localized heating beneath such areas is poorly understood, and thus an explanation for the distribution of plateaus of this type is not known.

Plateaus that were formed by crustal shortening and internal drainage lie within major mountain belts and generally in arid climates. They can be found in North Africa, Turkey, Iran, and Tibet, where the African, Arabian, and Indian continental masses have collided with the Eurasian continent. The Altiplano lies between the Cordillera Occidental composed of volcanoes and the Cordillera Oriental beneath which the Brazilian shield is being thrust. All these areas have undergone crustal shortening during Cenozoic time, and in each case the surface of the plateau includes both strongly deformed pre-Cenozoic rocks and very young, flat-lying sediment.

There are some plateaus whose origin is not known. Those of the Iberian Peninsula and north-central Mexico exhibit a topography that is largely high and relatively flat. Crustal shortening clearly occurred in Mexico during the Late Cretaceous and Early Cenozoic (between 100 million and 50 million years ago) and in some parts of Spain during the Cenozoic, but the high elevations in either case do not seem to be supported by thick crust. These areas are probably underlain by a hot uppermost mantle, but proof of this is still lacking.

Volcanic plateaus are commonly associated with eruptions that occurred during the Cenozoic or Mesozoic. Eruptions on the scale needed to produce volcanic plateaus are rare, and none seems to have taken place in recent time. The volcanic eruptions that produce lava plateaus tend to be associated with hot spots. For example, the basalts of the Deccan traps, which cover the Deccan Plateau in India, were erupted 60 million to 65 million years ago when India lay in the Southern Hemisphere, probably over the same hot spot that presently underlies the volcanic island of Réunion. The Serra Geral basalts that cap a plateau of the same name on the Atlantic coast of Brazil were erupted some 135 million years ago before Africa and South America separated from each other and when the future continental margins overlay the hot spot now beneath the volcanic island of Tristan da Cunha in the South Atlantic Ocean. In North America, the Columbia River basalts may have been ejected over the same hot spot that underlies the Yellowstone area today. Lava plateaus of the scale of these three are not common features on Earth.

VALLEYS

Wherever sufficient rainfall occurs, opportunity exists for the land surface to evolve to the familiar patterns of hills and valleys. There are, of course, hyperarid environments where fluvial activity is minimal. There also are geomorphological settings where the permeability of rocks or sediments induce so much infiltration that water is unable to concentrate on the land surface. Moreover, some landscapes may be so young that insufficient time has elapsed for modification by fluvial action. The role of fluvial action on landscape, including long-term evolutionary processes, is considered here in detail.

Probably the world's deepest subaerial (situated on or immediately adjacent to Earth's surface) valley is that of the Kāli Gandaki River in Nepal. Lying between two 8,000-metre (26,000-foot) Himalayan peaks, Dhaulāgiri and Annapūrna, the valley has a total relief of 6 km (about 4 miles). Because the Himalayas are one of Earth's most active areas of tectonic uplift, this valley well illustrates the principle that the most rapid downcutting occurs in areas of the most rapid uplift. The reason for this seeming paradox lies in the energetics of the processes of degradation that characterize valley formation. As will be discussed below, the steeper the gradient or slope of a stream, the greater its expenditure of power on the streambed. Thus, as uplift creates higher relief and steeper slopes, rivers achieve greater power for erosion. As a consequence, the most rapid processes of relief reduction can occur in areas of most rapid relief production.

Perhaps the most famous example of a canyon is the Grand Canyon of the Colorado River in northern Arizona. The Grand Canyon is about 1.6 km (1 mile) deep and 180 metres (590 feet) to 30 km (19 miles) wide and occurs along a 443-km- (275-mile-) long reach where the Colorado River incised into a broad upwarp of sedimentary rocks.

GEOMORPHIC CHARACTERISTICS

The relief of valleys and canyons is produced by the incising action of rivers. Hillslope processes are indeed critical in the development of valley sides, but it is rivers that lower the level of erosion through degradation. Rivers ultimately adjust to a baselevel, defined as the lowest point at which potential energy can be transformed to the kinetic energy of river flow. In most cases, the ultimate baselevel for rivers is sea level. Some rivers drain to enclosed basins below sea level, as, for example, the Jordan River, which flows to the Dead Sea in Israel and Jordan. Moreover, rivers may adjust to local baselevels, including zones of resistance to incision, lakes, and dams (both natural and artificial).

VALLEY LONGITUDINAL PROFILES

The longitudinal profile of a valley is the gradient through-out its length. Valleys formed by river action typically have a concave upward profile, steep in the headwaters and gentle in the lower reaches. The lower end of such a profile is adjusted to an effective lower limit of erosion defined by the baselevel.

In an ideal case of river adjustment to uniformly resis-tant materials, the longitudinal profile of a stream assumes a characteristic form that minimizes variations in trans-porting power. Power in a river derives from the rate of transfer of potential energy, dE/dt, which depends on the rate of fall in elevation of water, dy/dt, according to

$$\frac{dE}{dt} = mg\frac{dy}{dt}, \tag{1}$$

where E is energy, t is time, m is mass, g is the acceleration of gravity, and y is elevation. The rate of fall in elevation, in turn, can be expressed as follows:

$$\frac{dy}{dt} = \frac{dy}{dx}\frac{dx}{dt} = SV, \tag{2}$$

where S is the slope (fall in elevation, dy, with downstream horizontal distance, dx) and V is the flow velocity (change in horizontal distance, dx, with time, dt).

Combining equations 1 and 2 and using the fluid den-sity ρ (mass per unit volume of water), one obtains

$$\frac{dE}{dt} = \rho g(W \cdot D \cdot L)SV, \tag{3}$$

where W is channel width, D is channel depth, L is a unit length of stream, and the other parameters are as defined above. Because flow discharge Q is defined as

$$Q = W \cdot D \cdot V, \tag{4}$$

the power per unit length of flow, Ω, can be expressed as

$$\Omega = dE/dt/L = \rho g Q S. \tag{5}$$

It should be noted that in order to minimize variation in power, a river increasing its discharge in a downstream direction must decrease its slope. Thus, slope must be constantly decreasing downstream, explaining the concave upward character of the longitudinal profile.

The idealized concave upward longitudinal profile defined purely by energy considerations, noted above, only occurs where channel bed resistances and adequate adjustment time permit. Resistant zones of bedrock require greater power for a stream to incise at a given discharge Q than do less resistant zones. Therefore, by equation 5 the stream gradient S must be locally steeper at resistant zones. Similarly, a rapid base-level change, such as a fall of sea level, may not allow adequate time for the entire longitudinal profile to adjust. One indication of such effects on a longitudinal profile is a nick point, or abrupt change in slope of the profile.

VALLEY CROSS PROFILES

The cross profiles of valleys involve a combination of fluvial and hillslope processes. Although slopes and rivers are often studied separately by process geomorphologists, hills and valleys are the features that dominate landscapes. In upland areas cross profiles of valleys are often narrow and deep. Canyon morphologies are most common. Further downstream, valley floors are wider and often dominated by floodplains and terraces.

Types of Valleys

One of the few classifications of valleys is that used by the German climatic geomorphologists Herbert Louis and Julius Büdel. In areas of rapid uplift and intense fluvial action such as tropical mountains, *Kerbtal* (German for "notched valley") forms occur. These are characterized by steep, knife-edge ridges and valley slopes meeting in a V-shape. Where slopes are steep but a broad valley floor occurs, *Sohlenkerbtal* (meaning precisely a valley with such characteristics) is the prevailing form. Valleys of this kind develop under the influence of groundwater flow in Hawaii. Gutter-shaped valleys with convex sides and broad floors are called *Kehltal*; and broad, flat valleys of planation surfaces are termed *Fachmuldental*.

It is important to remember that the form of valleys reflects not only modern processes but also ancient ones. The entire valley or some landforms within it may be relict, with features inherited from past geologic periods during which occurred tectonic and climatic processes of intensities quite different from those prevailing today.

Hillslopes

Hillslopes constitute the flanks of valleys and the margins of eroding uplands. They are the major zones where rock and soil are loosened by weathering processes and then transported down gradient, often to a river channel.

Two major varieties of hillslopes occur in nature. On weathering-limited slopes, transport processes are so efficient that debris is removed more quickly than it can be generated by further weathering. Such hillslopes develop a faceted or angular morphology in which an upper free face, or cliff, contributes debris to a lower slope of accumulation. Slopes of this sort are especially common on bare rock where the profile of the slope is determined by the resistance of the rock, not by the erosional processes acting on it. One consequence of this is that many rock slopes retreat parallel to themselves in order to preserve the characteristic slope angle for a rock type of given strength. If the features of the rock change with depth into the slope, however, the characteristic angle of the slope will change. Rock slopes develop where weathering and soil erosion are slow (as in arid regions) and where rock resistance is high.

The second major variety of slope is transport limited. Transport-limited slopes occur where weathering processes are efficient at producing debris but where transport processes are inefficient at removing it from the slope. Such slopes lack free faces and faceted appearances, and they are generally covered with a soil mantle. The profile of this type of slope generally has a sigmoid appearance (c-shaped), with convex, straight, and concave

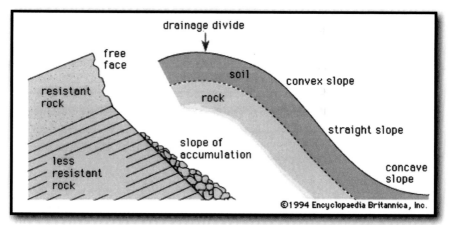

Comparison of idealized profiles for weathering-limited, faceted hillslopes (left) *and transport-limited, sigmoid hillslopes* (right). Encyclopaedia Britannica, Inc.

segments. The shape of the slope is an expression of the process acting upon it.

Convex slope segments commonly occur in the upper parts of soil-mantled slopes, as near the drainage divide. The noted American geomorphologist G.K. Gilbert elucidated the principles applying to convex slopes in his study of piles of mining-waste debris in California. The processes of soil creep (slow downslope movement of particles that occurs on every slope covered with loose, weathered material) and raindrop splash erode soil on the upper parts of slopes. Since soil eroded from the upper slope must pass each point below it, the volume of soil moved increases with distance from the divide. Since the transport rate for creep and rain splash is proportional to the slope angle, the slope angle must also increase from the divide, resulting in the slope convexity.

Straight slope segments are dominated by mass movement processes. Talus slopes are a type in which debris piles up to a characteristic angle of repose. When new debris is added to the slope, thereby locally increasing the angle, the slope adjusts by movement of the debris to reestablish the angle. Again, the result is a dynamic equilibrium in which the landform adjusts to processes acting upon it.

Concave slopes are especially common where overland-flow runoff transports sediment derived from upper slopes. Because the collection area for wash increases downslope and discharge Q is proportional to collection area, stream power can be maintained at lower slope angles. In addition, the size of particles being transported decreases downslope because of weathering and abrasion. Because the finer particles are easier to transport, slope angles can be reduced in the downslope direction. The result is a concave shape to the slope profile.

ORIGIN AND EVOLUTION

River valleys figure prominently in the evolutionary sequence of landscape development conceived by W.M. Davis. Unfortunately Davis's marvelous deductive scheme of progressive landscape change with time was somewhat abused by those who employed it merely for description and classification. By the mid-20th century, the focus of geomorphological research shifted from evolutionary sequences to studies of processes. Today, new procedures for radiometric dating have rekindled interest in long-term landscape evolution.

Valley development with time can be conceived of as a functional relationship, as follows:

$$v = f(c, r, l, p, t), \qquad (6)$$

where v is the valley morphology, c is the climate, r is relief factors including slope, l is lithology and rock structure, p is the type of process operating (surface runoff or spring sapping), and t is time.

Valley morphology can be described in numerous ways. A useful measure is drainage density Dd, which relates the length of valleys (or streams) L to the area A in which they occur:

$$Dd = \frac{\Sigma L}{A}. \qquad (7)$$

In many applications, A is defined as the drainage area in which a network of valleys is developed. There is a close relationship of drainage density to hillslope angles and local relief. For a given relief, higher drainage density results in short, steep valley-side slopes. For the same relief, a lower drainage density results in long, gentle slopes.

PROCESSES

Valley evolution can result from one or more processes: runoff is a process in which water moves over the surface of the ground, and sapping involves weathering and the movement of water underneath the ground. On the volcanic islands of Hawaii and on Mars, valley evolution involves other forces.

Runoff Processes

When rain falls on a land surface, part of it may infiltrate, depending on the rate of rainfall and the permeability of the substrate. The amount of rainfall that exceeds the infiltration capacity collects in pools and eventually flows over the land surface. This process of overland flow is quite inefficient because a large surface area greatly resists water movement. Depending on the substrate resistance and power of the flow, the tendency is to incise to form a channel. This transition from overland flow to channel flow is the first step toward a response to rainfall input. Eventually the dissection by channels leads to the differentiation of hills from valleys.

Not all the rainfall is transformed to overland flow and infiltration to groundwater. A portion is lost to evaporation and to transpiration by plants. What eventually flows off the landscape from surface and subsurface sources is the runoff R given by

$$R = P - ET \pm S, \tag{8}$$

where P is the precipitation and ET is the combination of evaporation and transpiration; S is a storage term for water held in plants, soils, and subsurface rocks. The overland flow component of runoff appears very quickly after storms, while the subsurface flow components appear much more slowly. In channels, all forms of runoff generate increased stream power because of increased discharge. This allows streams to incise, thereby deepening valleys, which may widen through hillslope processes.

Sapping

Sapping is a process of hillslope or scarp recession by the undermining of an overlying resistant material in the form of weathering or water flow occurring in an underlying less-resistant material. A variation of this process, spring sapping, occurs where groundwater (water that occurs below Earth's surface, where it occupies all or part of the void spaces in soils or geologic strata) outflow undermines slopes and, where appropriately concentrated, contributes to the development of valleys. The action of groundwater in sapping may be concentrated at valley heads, leading to headward growth. Both enhanced weathering and direct erosion by the concentrated fluid flow lead to slope undermining and collapse at sites of groundwater outflow.

A conceptual model of valley development by sapping can be envisioned with the initial condition of a water table (the upper level of an underground surface in which the soil or rocks are permanently saturated with water) having a regional slope toward a hydraulic sink provided by a depressed region. Water emerging along a spring line would then foster chemical weathering and thereby increase the porosity of the seepage zone, reducing the local rock tensile strength, or maximim load that a material can support without fracture, and rendering the weathering zone more susceptible to erosional undercutting of adjacent slopes. Local zones of heterogeneity in the rock will result in some zones achieving the critical conditions necessary for such undermining before other zones achieve them. Joints, faults, and folds serve this function. These critical zones then experience enhanced undermining. Once initiated, this process becomes self-enhancing because the lines of groundwater flow converge on the spring head. The increased flow accelerates chemical weathering, which leads to further piping at the same site.

The farther a spring head retreats, the greater the flow convergence that it generates, thereby increasing the rate of headward erosion. Headward sapping proceeds faster than valley widening because the valley head is the site of greatest flow convergence. Headward growth, however, may intersect other zones that are highly susceptible to sapping. A particularly favourable zone will result in a tributary that also experiences headward growth and that may generate tributaries of its own. Thus, sapping that occurs in a zone of jointing or faulting will develop a pattern aligned with those structures. It will, however, be organized by the hydraulic controls on the groundwater flow.

This process of sapping, headward retreat, and branching eventually forms a network of valleys. The developing network works to counteract the self-enhancing effect of flow concentration mentioned above. As spring heads migrate to the neighbourhood of one another, their demands for the available groundwater compete with each other. Eventually an equilibrium is achieved at some optimum drainage density.

Excellent examples of valleys formed by sapping are found in the massive sandstone terrains of the Colorado Plateau. Groundwater seepage from the sandstone contributes to local disintegration of the bedrock at the bases of cliffs, thereby undermining slopes and leading to backwearing. Because of structural concentration of water flow along joints and faults, valleys grow headward along zones of structural weakness. Canyons formed by sapping have prominent structural control vertical to overhanging walls, flat floors, elongate shape, low drainage density (leaving undissected uplands), relatively short tributaries to main trunk valleys, irregular variation in valley width as a function of valley length, and theatre-like valley heads. Many of the sapping valleys of the Colorado Plateau are probably relict features, since lowered water tables and/ or desiccating climatic conditions have in all likelihood resulted in reduced groundwater flow to the valley floors today. During wetter climatic episodes of the Quaternary (from about 2,600,000 years ago to the present), which probably coincided with periods of mountain glaciation, spring sapping activity would have been more pronounced. Under modern climatic conditions, the results of past spring-sapping processes are obscured by the modifying action of non-sapping morphogenetic processes.

Valley Evolution in Hawaii

The Hawaiian Islands comprise a chain of volcanic islands, with ages increasing progressively to the northwest from the island of Hawaii with its active volcanoes, Kilauea and Mauna Loa. In general, the dissection of the Hawaiian volcanoes also increases with age to the northwest, but the details of dissection are considerably influenced by climate, factors related to parent material, and changes in process. Nevertheless, a remarkable opportunity to study valley development with time is afforded by the phenomenon of the northwesterly movement of the Pacific Plate carrying a succession of volcanoes away from a stationary mantle plume (rising jet of partially molten rock material) located at the southern tip of Hawaii.

Rainfall is heaviest on the northeastern slopes of the volcanoes because of the prevailing trade winds. Although this results in generally higher drainage densities on the windward rather than leeward slopes of islands such as Hawaii, there are important exceptions. Mauna Loa, for example, lacks dissection on its northeastern flanks in spite of having the same amount of rainfall as highly dissected parts of Mauna Kea. Such is the case because the basaltic lava flows of the volcanoes are so permeable that drainage will not develop until a less permeable ash mantle is emplaced or until weathering reduces infiltration. Examples of both phenomena occur in Hawaii. Kilauea Volcano, the youngest of the Hawaiian shields, displays essentially no dissection except where ash from the 1790 Keanakakoi eruption was emplaced. The older Mauna Loa and Mauna Kea shields display V-shaped ravines only where their flanks were mantled by Pahala ash. Dissection is more pronounced on Mauna Kea, which is older than Mauna Loa. Kohala Volcano is the oldest shield on the island of Hawaii, having formed about 700,000 years ago. Deep weathering of its basalt has reduced infiltration sufficiently to promote high-density drainage on its northeastern slopes.

Valley initiation on the Hawaiian volcanoes thus depends on rainfall and infiltration capacity. When runoff valleys are initiated, their streams incise to form V-shaped ravines. The ravine systems eventually become sufficiently deep to expose deeper layers where groundwater activity and spring sapping become more important. The deepest incision produces U-shaped, theatre-headed valleys. Because the layered basalt flows are most permeable parallel to dip, there is efficient groundwater movement toward the sea. The regional water table on the islands is near sea level, with a slight bulge in the central parts of the islands that have a gentle seaward slope in all directions.

The U-shaped sapping valleys of the older Hawaiian volcanoes display enhanced weathering at the water table. This undermines the side slopes of the valleys, so that their steep-sided walls meet their floors at a sharp angle.

The valleys widened laterally as they were developed by headward growth of springs at the valley heads. Perennial flow was maintained by large springs.

Channels and Valleys on Mars

At least one other planetary body in the solar system besides Earth is dissected by valleys of fluvial origin—namely, Mars. The heavily cratered terrains of Mars are extensively dissected by interconnected, digitate networks of valleys. Many of the valleys are steep-walled and have theatre-like headward terminations, especially near the equatorial regions of the planet. Additional properties include common structural control of the networks, low drainage densities, and low junction angles with tributaries. This combination of features seems best explained by a sapping mechanism for much of the valley formation.

The valleys of Mars are for the most part extremely ancient. Very large numbers of craters are superimposed on the valleys, indicating that they formed about the time of the phase of heavy bombardment early in the history of the solar system.

Another variety of valley on Mars occurs at fairly high latitudes where temperatures are colder. These valleys have rounded, subdued wall topography, and their floors are covered with debris that appears to have been produced from the walls and flowed across the floors. Masses of similar debris surround isolated massifs. It is probable that subsurface ice facilitated the production and flowage of the debris in a manner similar to what is observed in Earth's periglacial regions.

INFLUENCE OF STRUCTURE

The role of structure in drainage development may be passive, in which case the composition of rocks and various rock discontinuities (joints, faults, and bedding) dictate the details of erosion. In this way, structure provides the boundary conditions for landscape degradation. During tectonism, such as faulting and folding, structural controls change with time, and the erosional system must adjust to changing resistances. Different structural controls also are encountered as incision of streams exposes lower units in Earth's crust.

Over the years, Russian and eastern European investigators have emphasized structural control in geomorphic analysis. I.P. Gerasimov defined structural units of the landscape called morphostructures as terrain types generated by a combination of tectonic activity and climate. Various morphostructures are produced by alternating periods of uplift (with resulting dissection) and stabilization (yielding planation surfaces). The history of a morphostructure and regional tectonism can be studied by analyses of river terraces, planation surfaces, and correlative sedimentary deposits.

Drainage Patterns

The pattern of fluvial dissection of a landscape is of considerable importance in understanding the structural influence on drainage evolution. Dendritic patterns, so called because of their similarity to branching organic forms, are most common where rocks or sediments are flat-lying and preferential zones of structural weakness are minimal. The conveyance properties of a dendritic network are analogous to blood circulation systems and tree branching. Rectangular and angular patterns occur where faults, joints, and other linear structures introduce a grain to drainage. Where a broad tilt or regional slope occurs on a surface of otherwise uniform resistance, a parallel pattern occurs. Special drainage patterns characterize belts of parallel folds (trellis pattern), domes or volcanoes (radial pattern), and other landscape types.

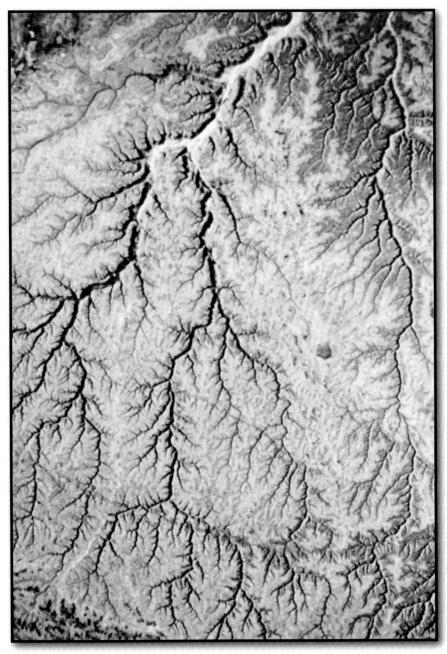

Dendritic drainage pattern developed on flat-lying limestone in central Yemen.
Courtesy of National Aeronautics and Space Administration

In a series of tilted sediments the differential erosion of softer units, such as clay and shale, results in valleys developed perpendicular to the dip or tilt of the units. These strike valleys are paralleled by ridges of the tilted sediments called cuestas. Another term for a strike stream, which parallels the structural grain, is a longitudinal stream. In contrast, transverse streams cut across structural trends. Streams flowing down the tilted sediments of the cuesta are called dip streams because they parallel the structural dip of the strata. Streams draining the cuesta scarp into longitudinal valleys flowing opposite to the structural dip are called antidip streams.

Cross-Axial Drainage

One of the most interesting anomalies that occurs in drainage evolution is the development of stream courses across the axes of structural zones (e.g., upwarps and fold belts). Some examples of cross-axial, or discordant, drainage include rivers that appear to take the most difficult routes possible through folded regions such as the Appalachian Mountains of the United States and the Zagros Mountains of Iran. The classical studies of cross-axial drainage were made during the exploration of the Colorado River system in the 19th century by the American geologist John Wesley Powell. The Colorado River and its tributaries cross great structural upwarps. Rather than flowing around domes or plunging folds, the rivers carved canyons into what appears to be paths of greatest resistance. One theory posed by Powell for such relationships is that of antecedence. According to this view, the rivers were already in their present positions when the various anticlinal folds and upwarps began to grow. A relevant analogy is a saw into which a log is being pushed. The saw represents the river and its continuing degradation, and the log represents the growing upwarp.

Another possible origin of cross-axial drainage is superimposition. According to this theory, a cover of sedimentary material must bury older structures. The river develops on this overlying sedimentary cover and subsequently imposes its pattern across the underlying structures as they are exposed by continuing degradation.

A third explanation for cross-axial drainage is that of inheritance. In this hypothesis, an erosion surface is developed across the structure zone by long-continued planation. When the streams incise, abandoning the former planation surface, they become imposed across the structures. Alternatively, the stream may actually exploit zones of weakness or minimal resistance as it downcuts from former levels. Stream capture (also called stream piracy) occurs as more aggressively eroding portions of the drainage cut through divides. In many cases, a complex combination of the above processes probably occurs to yield the final result.

Stream capture is especially common where longitudinal streams flowing on the weaker rocks of a fold belt erode into the valleys of transverse streams that must cross the resistant strata. Sections of valley abandoned after such captures are known as wind gaps. These contrast with the water gaps that still contain transverse streams. The famous water gaps of the Appalachians are excellent examples of such patterns.

INFLUENCE OF CLIMATE

The importance of climate in landscape evolution, particularly valley development, has been emphasized by many European geomorphologists. Jean Tricart and André Cailleux of France and Julius Büdel of Germany developed climatic geomorphology as a synthesis of relief-forming processes. Climatic geomorphologists define systematic morphoclimatic zones on the globe in which relief-forming mechanisms differ as a function of climate. Some of the important morphoclimatic zones are briefly outlined in the following sections.

Periglacial Zone

The term *periglacial* relates to cold-climate processes and landforms. The most important periglacial influence on valleys is frost action, which produces abundant debris by freeze-thaw action on rock and soil. During the coldest periods of the Quaternary (about the last 2.6 million years), the periglacial zone was enlarged to approximately twice its present extent. Hillslopes became mantled with frost-shattered rubble that moved downslope during cycles of freezing and thawing. The relicts of this periglacial activity characterize much of the modern humid-temperate zone—e.g., in portions of Pennsylvania and Wisconsin in the United States and England and Poland.

Arid Zone

In arid regions moisture conditions are inadequate to support abundant vegetative cover of the land surface. As a result, the land is subjected to intense fluvial, eolian, and mass-wasting processes. The importance of fluvial action may seem ironic for an arid region. Although most arid regions receive little rainfall, the amount that falls is especially effective. Rare but intense arid-region rainstorms act upon a landscape that is unprotected by vegetation. Of course, some hyperarid regions receive such infrequent rainfall that fluvial processes are indeed ineffective. Nevertheless, even the most arid places on Earth show evidence of fluvial activity, either because of wetter conditions in the past or because of very rare rainstorms.

Tropical Zone

Tropical regions are dominated by dense vegetative cover and deep weathering profiles. In continuously humid tropical zones, fluvial activity is facilitated by intense rainfall but inhibited by the protective effect of rainforests. The lateritic soils of these regions, however, do not promote deep root penetration, and the vegetative cover may be undermined by fluvial erosion or mass movement. Fluvial activity may be quite intense in the tropics, especially in tectonically active areas. In more stable cratons, however, the landscape is dominated by low-relief planation surfaces. Rivers flowing on the deeply weathered regolith of these surfaces have low stream power and transport mainly fine-grained weathering products. Thus, immense contrasts in fluvial activity exist in the tropics.

At higher tropical latitudes, the continuously humid zone of the Equator changes to a zone of seasonal rainfall. Such regions have savanna vegetation because of prolonged dry seasons. Erosion rates may be extremely high in savanna environments.

ROLE OF CLIMATIC CHANGE

Because Earth's climate has changed profoundly during the Paleogene, Neogene, and Quaternary (roughly the past 65,500,000 years), many landscapes are palimpsests — i.e., they are composed of relict elements produced under the influence of past climates and modern elements produced in the present climatic regime. The study of such landscape changes is sometimes called climato-genetic geomorphology. Some researchers in the field, notably Büdel, have maintained that little of the extant relief in humid temperate regions of Earth results from modern relief-forming processes. Rather, they believe, much of the familiar humid temperate landscape is inherited from past climatic conditions, including periglacial, arid, and tropical.

Büdel focused attention on differences in the nature of valley formation as a function of climate through the history of a landscape. He argued that very rapid valley formation accompanied periods of periglacial activity in central Europe. Modern rivers in the region seem less effective at valley incision. Most of them flow on fills within great bedrock valleys, indicating that aggradation rather than downcutting is occurring today. Prior to the Quaternary phase of valley cutting, central Europe in the early Cenozoic seems to have experienced a prolonged period of planation, resulting in low-relief plains. Büdel proposed that the remnants of these Cenozoic plains, now preserved as broad planar uplands, are inherited from a time of tropical planation. Remnants of a former tropical regolith on the uplands provide some evidence for this hypothesis.

Paleovalleys

The southwestern desert of Egypt is one of the most arid places on Earth. The region lacks surficial traces of active fluvial processes and is dominated by eolian activity. In this region, a research team headed by John F. McCauley of the U.S. Geological Survey discovered in 1982 that the local drift sand had buried an array of valleys and other relict fluvial features. The discovery was made possible by the imaging radar system of the U.S. Space Shuttle, which penetrated several metres of the extremely dry sand to reveal the previously unknown valleys. The relict valleys were probably part of Neogene river systems that drained the eastern Sahara during relatively wet climatic conditions prior to the onset of hyperaridity in the Quaternary.

A very important American paleovalley involves the complex history of the Ohio River. Prior to the glacial phases of the Quaternary, the preglacial predecessor of the

Ohio drained northwestward from the Appalachians across the Midwest, but far north of its present course. Numerous water wells in Ohio, Indiana, and Illinois are located along this paleovalley, which is called the Teays River System. The advances of Quaternary ice over the course of the Teays River eventually caused the drainage to shift from the Teays route to one roughly paralleling the glacial boundary. The modern Ohio River is the product of this heritage.

Misfit Streams

Another manifestation of the impact of climatic change is the misfit stream. Such streams are those for which some practical measure of size, most often the meander wavelength, indicates that the modern river is either too large or too small for the valley in which it flows. The former condition, known as an overfit stream, is relatively rare. An example, described below, occurs where cataclysmic glacial floods invaded valley systems formed by overland flow processes in a non-glacial climatic regime. The more common case is the underfit stream, in which valley morphology indicates a larger ancient stream.

The English-born geomorphologist George H. Dury developed a theory for the widespread phenomenon of stream underfitness. He believed that, when the larger valley forms developed, climatic change was required to reduce the channel-forming discharges from past highs to the modern shrunken channel dimensions. Dury argued that the last phase of stream shrinkage occurred at the end of the last glaciation when the global climate changed from cool and moist to warm and dry. He quantified his theory, utilizing the relationship between the wavelength of modern meandering rivers (λ) and their bank-full discharge (q_b),

$$\lambda = 54.3 \, q_b^{0.5}, \tag{9}$$

where the units of λ and q_b are metres and cubic metres per second, respectively.

Using equation 9, Dury found that since valley meanders were 5 to 10 times larger than modern river meanders, the ancient bank-full discharges must have been 25 to 100 times larger than the modern values. Such large modifications implied a phenomenal climatic change that was not accepted by the general scientific community. Numerous other factors besides climatic change play a role in the development of underfitness. These include changes in the type and amount of sediment transported by streams, the role of different rock types in shaping valley dimensions, and the role of large, rare floods (as opposed to bank-full discharge) in defining channel dimensions. The problem of underfitness remains a challenge awaiting complete geomorphological explanation.

Probably the most remarkable example of a misfitness is the channeling of the basaltic plain of eastern

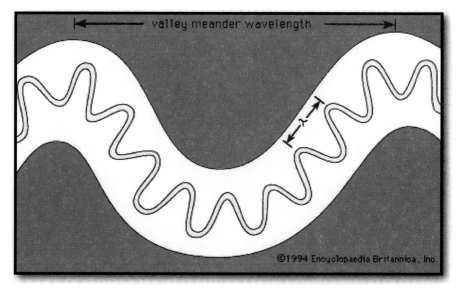

Idealized map view of a stream that is underfit in relation to its valley. The contrast between the meander wavelength λ of the modern river and that of the valley is apparent. Encyclopaedia Britannica, Inc.

Washington in the northwestern United States by cataclysmic glacial floods. The great floods emanated from glacial Lake Missoula, which was impounded between about 17,000 and 12,000 years ago by a lobe of the Cordilleran ice sheet that extended into northern Idaho. Failure of this ice dam released a lake volume of about 2,500 cubic km (600 cubic miles) at discharges of up to 2×10^7 cubic metres (7×10^8 cubic feet) per second. These immense flows completely overwhelmed the preglacial stream valleys of the Columbia Plain in eastern Washington. As the floods eroded loess and bedrock from former valley divides, a great plexus of scoured channel ways known collectively as the Channeled Scabland was formed. Because preglacial valleys were filled to overspilling, this process is really an example of stream overfitness. Numerous diagnostic landforms, including great cataracts, characterize the Channeled Scabland.

The above relationships were first described in the 1920s by the American geologist J Harlen Bretz, who contended that the Channeled Scabland could only be explained by the action of cataclysmic flooding. He encountered vehement opposition to this hypothesis but was eventually able to convince most of his critics of its validity by carefully documenting the overwhelming evidence for flood-produced landforms. Of considerable importance was the discovery of giant current ripples composed predominantly of gravel. More than 5 metres (16 feet) high and spaced 100 metres (328 feet) apart, these current ripples occurred on large bars of gravel and boulders.

The Channels of Mars

The landforms produced by large-scale fluid flow in the Channeled Scabland are remarkably similar to those in

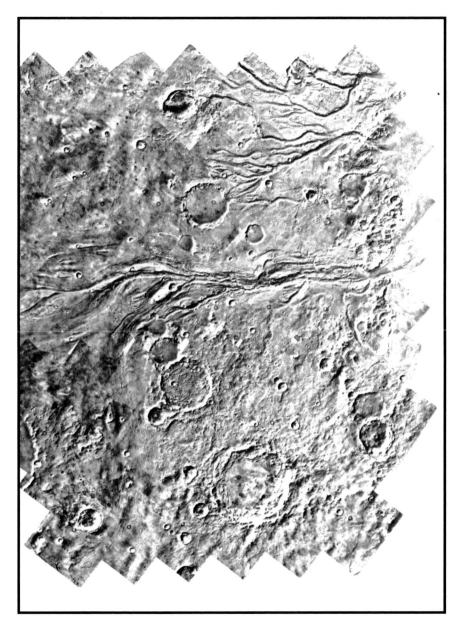

Viking photograph of the cratered plains/cratered highlands in Lunae Planum. The channels are thought to have been caused by catastrophic floods during the early history of Mars. Courtesy of the Jet Propulsion Laboratory/ National Aeronautics and Space Administration

the channeled terrains of Mars. In contrast to the Martian valley networks, the channels of the planet display evidence of large-scale fluid flows on their floors. Most Martian channels show that the erosive fluid emanated from zones of complex terrain. Apparently the fluid was derived from subsurface reservoirs, and the overlying materials collapsed as fluid was released. The channels, unlike the valley networks, probably formed over a considerable span of Martian history. The fluid for carving the channels was most likely water, perhaps with substantial amounts of entrained ice and sediment. Ground ice in Martian permafrost may have provided a source for the immense ancient floods.

CHAPTER 4
STRUCTURAL LANDFORMS

Structural landforms are topographic features that form by the differential wearing away of rocks and the deposition of the resulting debris under the influence of exogenetic geomorphic forces. Such forces operate at the interface of the planetary atmosphere, lithosphere, cryosphere, and hydrosphere. The processes generating these forces are the major agents of erosion, transport, and deposition of debris. They include fluvial, eolian, glacial, groundwater, and coastal-marine processes, as well as those associated with mass movement.

Structural landforms include caves, pediments, and sand dunes and result from forces generated by such processes interacting with the resistances imposed by rocks and sediments. For change to occur, the forces must exceed the thresholds of resistance imposed by Earth materials on which they act. The landform itself, however, may alter the forces by developing specific shapes. Sand dunes, beaches, river valleys, and glacial drumlins are all examples of landforms that modify the forces imposed upon them. Such self-regulation of landform development is a quality of landscapes that achieve equilibrium.

Although structure and lithology establish the resistance factors for structural landforms, climate defines the nature of the exogenetic geomorphological processes. In cold regions ice-related processes dominate in the development of landscapes, while in warm-wet regions fluvial processes exert primary control. Thus, a climatically controlled style of landscape development is imposed on the structurally defined surface. Moreover, process and structure interact through geologic time on an evolving landscape. As pointed out by the eminent William Morris Davis, landscape is a function of the trilogy of structure, process, and time.

CAVES

Caves, or caverns, are natural openings in Earth that are large enough for human exploration. Such a cavity is formed in many types of rock and by many processes. The largest and most common caves are those formed by chemical reaction between circulating groundwater and bedrock composed of limestone or dolomite. These caves, called solution caves, typically constitute a component of what is known as karst terrain. Named after the Karst region of the western Balkan Peninsula extending from Slovenia to Montenegro, karst terrain in general is characterized by a rough and jumbled landscape of bare bedrock ledges, deranged surface drainage, and sinkholes, as well as caves. It should be noted, however, that there is considerable variation among karst areas. Some may have dramatic surface landforms but few caves. By contrast, others may have extensive cave development with little surface expression; for example, the Guadalupe Mountains of New Mexico, the site of Carlsbad Caverns and various other caves, have very few surface karst features.

Karst landscapes are formed by the removal of bedrock (composed in most cases of limestone, dolomite, gypsum, or salt, but in some cases of such normally insoluble rocks as quartzite and granite) in solution through underground routes rather than through surface weathering and surface streams. As a result, much karst drainage is internal. Rainfall flows into closed depressions and down their drains. Further dissolution in the subsurface forms continuous conduits that serve as integrated drains for the rapid movement of underground water. The

Stalactites and stalagmites in the Queen's Chamber, Carlsbad Caverns National Park, southeastern New Mexico. NPS Photo by Peter Jones

outlets for the water-carrying conduits often are springs of majestic size. Caves are fragments of such conduit systems, and some of them provide access to active streams. These caves may be completely water-filled; others are dry passages left behind by streams that cut to lower levels. Surface streams flowing from areas underlain by insoluble rock often sink when they reach the border of a karst region. These sinking streams form tributaries of the underground drainage system.

CAVE TYPES

Not all caves are part of karst landscapes. A substantial number of relatively small caves, called volcanic caves, are formed in lava and by the mechanical movement of bedrock. Other caves are formed in glaciers by the melting of ice. Still others are created by the erosive action of water and wind or from the debris of erosive processes; these are sea caves, eolian caves, rock shelters, and talus caves.

GLACIER CAVES

These are long tunnels formed near the snouts of glaciers between the glacial ice and the underlying bedrock. Meltwater from the surface of a glacier drains downward through crevasses, which are enlarged to form shafts leading to the base of the glacier. Because the inlet water is slightly above the melting point of ice, it gradually melts the ice as it seeps along the base of the glacier.

Glacier caves may reach lengths of several kilometres. Mature caves of this sort are tubular conduits, often with intricately sculptured walls. Some of them have a branching pattern. The floors of glacier caves usually consist of rock. Most glacier caves can be explored only when the surface is frozen; at other times they are filled with water.

SEA CAVES, EOLIAN CAVES, ROCK SHELTERS, AND TALUS CAVES

Sea caves are formed by wave action on fractures or other weaknesses in the bedrock of sea cliffs along coastlines. They may be mere crevices in the cliff or roomy chambers. Some can be entered only by boat at low tide, while others, occurring along beaches, can be walked into. A sea cave may have an opening to the surface at its rear that provides access from the top of the cliff. In some cases, the ceiling entrance serves as a blowhole from which water spouts during times of high tide or rough seas. Sea caves rarely are more than a few hundred metres long.

Eolian caves are chambers scoured by wind action. They are common in desert areas where they are formed in massive sandstone cliffs. Wind sweeping around such a cavity erodes the walls, floor, and ceiling, resulting in a bottle-shaped chamber usually of greater diameter than the entrance. Eolian caves are rarely longer than a few tens of metres.

Rock shelters are produced by bedrock erosion in insoluble rocks. A common setting is where a resistant rock such as a sandstone overlies shale or some other relatively weak rock. Surface weathering or stream action wears away the shale, cutting it back into the hillside. The sandstone is left behind as a roof to the rock shelter. Rock shelters are minor features as caves, but many are important archaeological or historical sites.

Talus caves are openings formed between boulders piled up on mountain slopes. Most of them are very small both in length and in cross section. Some boulder piles, however, do have explorable interconnected "passages" of considerable length. Some of the largest talus caves occur among granite blocks in New York and New England, where integrated systems of passages between boulders have been mapped to lengths of several kilometres.

SOLUTION CAVES

As previously noted, the largest and most common caves are those formed by dissolution of limestone or dolomite. Limestone is composed mostly of calcium carbonate in the form of the mineral calcite. Dolomite rock consists of calcium magnesium carbonate, the mineral dolomite. Both these carbonate minerals are somewhat soluble in the weak acids formed by carbon dioxide dissolving in groundwater. Water seeping through soils into the bedrock, water collected by sinkholes, and surface streams sinking underground at the margins of karst areas all percolate along fractures in the bedrock and gradually create sizable passages by chemical action. Because the dissolution process takes place deep in the bedrock, it is not necessary that solution caves have entrances. Most entrances are formed by accidental processes such as the downcutting of surface valleys, the collapse of sinkholes, or the emplacement of quarries or road cuts. Accidental processes of passage collapse and passage plugging divide caves into smaller fragments. Because of this, there are many more small caves than large ones. The longest known cave is the Mammoth Cave–Flint Ridge system in south central Kentucky, which has a surveyed length of more than 555 km (345 miles).

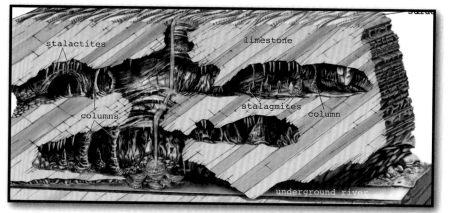

Cross section of a cave. Encyclopædia Britannica, Inc.

Most solution caves form at relatively shallow depths (from a few tens of metres to 1,000 metres [3,280 feet]) by the action of water rich in carbonic acid (H_2CO_3) derived from recent rainfall. Some solution caves, however, appear to have been formed by deep-seated waters such as oil field brines. Sources of acid other than carbonic acid (e.g., sulfuric acid from the oxidation of sulfide minerals or the oxidation of hydrogen sulfide-bearing fluids) may be the dissolving agent for such caves. According to some investigators, Carlsbad Caverns originated from dissolution with sulfuric acid.

Gypsum rock, composed primarily of calcium sulfate dihydrate (the mineral gypsum), is more soluble than limestone. Outcrops of gypsum rock are found at the land surface in arid regions such as West Texas, western Oklahoma, and eastern New Mexico. Caves formed by the dissolution of gypsum are much like limestone caves in the size, shape, and pattern of their passages. The Optimisticheskaya Cave in Ukraine is the world's longest gypsum cave, with 165 km (about 100 miles) of passage.

Caves also are formed by the dissolution of salt (the mineral halite). Because it is highly soluble in water, salt outcrops at the land surface only in extremely arid regions. Caves in salt closely resemble limestone caves in passage plan and shape. In most cases, salt caves are small, with passage lengths ranging from a few tens of metres to several hundred metres. Good examples of salt caves occur in Mount Sedom in Israel and in eastern Spain.

EVOLUTION AND DEMISE OF SOLUTION CAVES

Compared with most geologic phenomena, caves are transient features of the landscape. They form, evolve, and are destroyed over periods of time ranging from a few tens of thousands to a few million years. It is possible to sketch the "life history" of a single cave passage as the sequence from an initiation phase, a series of three critical thresholds, an enlargement phase, a stagnation phase, and a decay phase.

INITIATION PHASE

Since limestone is an impermeable rock, groundwater moves mainly through mechanical fractures—joint and bedding-plane partings. Because groundwater seeps slowly through these openings, it becomes nearly saturated with dissolved calcium carbonate, particularly deep in the rock mass. As a result, the ability of the water to further dissolve the limestone is limited, and the fractures thus enlarge very slowly. Calculations show that times on the order of 3,000 to 10,000 years are needed to enlarge a fracture from an initial width of 10 to 50 micrometres (.0004 to .002 inch) to pencil-sized openings 5 to 10 mm (0.2 to 0.4 inch) wide. When a continuous pathway from the water source to the outlet has been enlarged to 5 to 10 mm width, the initiation phase is complete.

The 5- to 10-mm size of the enlarging fracture marks a set of thresholds where new processes come into play. The slow, percolating flow of water is accelerated as the conduit becomes larger, and at the threshold size turbulence appears in the flowing water. The flow pattern is less like percolation through an aquifer and more like flow in a pipe. At the threshold size the opening is large enough and the flow velocities high enough that insoluble sediments can be transported. For the complete development of an underground drainage system, it is necessary that the water-carrying conduits also flush out the soil that washes in through sinkholes, the sediment load of sinking streams, and the insoluble weathering products from the dissolution of the limestone. Another threshold has to do with the rate at which the limestone is dissolved.

STALACTITES AND STALAGMITES

A stalactite is an elongated form made up of various minerals deposited from solution by slowly dripping water. It hangs like an icicle from the ceiling or sides of a cavern. In contrast, a stalagmite appears like an inverted stalactite, rising from the floor of a cavern.

Stalactites hanging from the ceilings of caverns commonly exhibit a central tube or the trace of a former tube whose diameter is that of a drop of water hanging by surface tension. A drop on the tip of a growing stalactite leaves a deposit only around its rim. Downward growth of the rim makes the tube. The simplest stalactite form, therefore, is a thin-walled stone straw, and these fragile forms may reach lengths of 0.5 metres (20 inches) or more where air currents have not seriously disturbed the growth. The more common form is a downward-tapering cone and is simply a thickening of the straw type by mineral deposition from a film of water descending the exterior of the pendant.

Stalagmites, on the other hand, have thicker proportions and grow up on the bottom of a cavern from the same drip-water source, the mineral from which is deposited after the water droplet falls across the open space in the rock. Not every stalactite has a complementary stalagmite, and many of the latter may have no stalactite above them. Where the paired relation exists, however, continual elongation of one or both may eventually result in a junction and the formation of a column.

Stalactites and other formations, Timpanogos Cave National Monument, Utah, U.S. Courtesy of the National Park Service

The dominant mineral in such deposits is calcite (calcium carbonate), and the largest displays are formed in caves of limestone and dolomite. Other minerals that may be deposited include other carbonates, opal, chalcedony, limonite, and some sulfides.

Conditions that favour the deposition are: (1) a source rock above the cavern; (2) downward percolation of water supplied from rain; (3) tight but continuous passageways for this water, which determine a very slow drip; and (4) adequate air space in the void to allow either evaporation or the escape of carbon dioxide from the water, which thus loses some of its solvent ability.

During the initiation phase when flow velocities are low and the water is nearly saturated, the rate at which limestone is removed is very slow. As velocities increase, unsaturated water moves deep into the bedrock, and the rate of dissolution is greatly increased. The pencil-sized threshold opening marks the boundary between the initial fracture system and the evolving conduit system.

ENLARGEMENT PHASE

Once a complete pathway has been opened to threshold size, enlargement takes place rapidly as the conduit provides an efficient route for groundwater flow. Enlargement from threshold size to a full-scale cave passage of 1 to 3 metres (about 3 to 10 feet) in diameter can be accomplished in 10,000 to 100,000 years, depending on local geology. During the enlargement phase, the conduit may become completely water-filled, in which case the growing passage takes the form of a circular or elliptical conduit as dissolution acts uniformly on the floor, walls, and ceiling. If the water source feeding the conduit is limited, a time will come when there is not enough water to fill the passage. A free air surface then develops and the dissolution of the ceiling will cease, even though the passage will continue to enlarge through dissolution of the lower walls and floor. This transition from pipe flow to open-channel flow results in a change in passage shape from that of an elliptical tube to that of a canyon. Continued solutional erosion causes the canyon to deepen, resulting in canyon passages 30 to 50 metres (about 100 to 160 feet) high and only 1 metre (about 3 feet) or less wide.

The fate of a cave passage at the end of the enlargement stage depends on what has been happening elsewhere on the land surface and in the drainage basin. If the passage lies deep below the water table, enlargement will continue until the passage becomes too wide for the ceiling bedrock to support its own weight, and the passage will ultimately collapse. During the time that the cave passage has been enlarging, surface streams have been downcutting their beds, and the position of base level and the water table is lowered. If the original water source continues to flow through the cave after the transition to canyon shape, the underground canyon can continue to deepen, keeping its gradient adjusted to the lowering surface streams. Sometimes, however, the conduit passages are simply abandoned. Veneers of insoluble sediment that accumulate on the floors of cave passages tend to protect them from solution. As surface streams downcut, the conduits are left behind and the increased hydraulic gradient causes new passages to form at lower levels. In due course, the flow is completely diverted into these new passages, and the original passages remain air-filled and dry above the descending water table.

STAGNATION AND DECAY PHASES

Segments of cave passage abandoned as surface streams downcut can survive for a long time in a stage of stagnation. Truncation of the passages by valley downcutting produces entrances. Caves in the stagnation phase are those most frequently discovered and explored by humans.

Surface erosion continues to dissect the landscape, and hilltops and plateaus are lowered. The underlying cave passages are cut into smaller and smaller fragments. Eventually the denudation of the land surface destroys the last vestiges of the passages, bringing to an end the long history of the cave conduit.

The time scales for the stagnation and decay stages are highly variable, depending on local geologic conditions. Paleomagnetic measurements of the sediments in Mammoth Cave show that the passages at the highest elevations are at least two million years old. Studies based on rates of surface weathering in the Appalachian valleys of Pennsylvania indicate that caves at the highest elevation in the residual hills may be two million to three million years old.

Larger cave systems often have complex patterns of superimposed passages that represent a long history of cave development. The oldest passages, usually but not necessarily those at the highest elevations, may have formed before the glaciations of the Quaternary. The youngest passages may be part of an integrated subsurface drainage system that exists today.

GEOMORPHIC CHARACTERISTICS OF SOLUTION CAVES

Like many other geologic features concealed beneath Earth's surface, caves are difficult to observe. One cannot really see a cave, even though one may have a point-by-point, cross-sectional view as the cave passage is illuminated during exploration. The horizontal ground plans and vertical profiles of caves must be represented by maps. These in turn are constructed from arduous station-to-station surveys by cave explorers.

Some cave-passage plans take the shape of linear, angulate, or sinuous segments of conduit. These are segments of drainage trunk without tributaries. Other cave-passage plans are branchworks. There may be a well-defined "upstream" direction, with tributary passages joining the trunk. Still other passage plans are networks in which passages are laid out in a "city-block" pattern with many intersecting passages and many closed loops. In terms of flow pattern, a single-conduit type of cave forms where much of the original catchment area was on non-karstic borderlands and the sinking stream injected large quantities of water at a single point. Branchwork caves develop where there are multiple inlets, each at the head of one of the tributary branches. Network caves are formed where flows are controlled by diffuse inlets; flow velocities remain low and solutional erosion takes place along all possible joint openings. A network cave is the underground equivalent of a swamp.

Passage cross-sectional shapes reflect the way the water flowed through the cave and the way in which the water dissolved the bedrock. Passages that formed while completely flooded are dissolved away equally on walls, ceilings, and floors. The result is an elliptical tube. In contrast, a flowing stream with a free air surface can dissolve limestone only in its bed. The result is a canyon-shaped passage. In some caves of this type, the walls are nearly vertical and may measure 30 to 50 metres (about 100 to 160 feet) high, even though the passage may only be 1 metre (about 3 feet) wide. Other cave passages are very irregular because of the meanderings of the downcutting stream. There is always competition between the hydraulics of flowing water that works to shape passages into smooth, streamlined forms and the control of passage shape by the structural arrangement of joints, fractures, and bedding-plane partings that initiated the passageway. Joint-controlled passages may be high and narrow, sometimes with irregular walls; such a configuration resulted as the passages were enlarged from the initial joint by slowly percolating water. Passages developed primarily along bedding-plane partings may be low and wide. In general, higher flow velocities favour the hydraulic forms, and slow, percolating flows tend to preserve the shapes of the initial mechanical openings.

Most passages of solution caves are nearly horizontal with gentle average slopes toward the outlet springs. If the caves were formed by pressure flow beneath the water table, the passage profile can be irregular, with both downsloping and upsloping segments. Most cave passages are not graded like surface streams. Only in some alpine environments do caves form with steeply sloping passages. Continuous lowering of the level of groundwater circulation often produces tiers of passages stacked one on top of the other, and these need not be interconnected by an explorable cave. Additional mechanisms are needed to explain the vertical arrangement of some caves that may have an internal relief from tens of metres to more than 1,000 metres (3,280 feet). Vertical integration is accomplished by some combination of the following: (1) primary vertical solution in the unsaturated zone above the water table during the same time as conduit dissolution below the water table, (2) dissolution of vertical shafts and solution chimneys in the unsaturated zone at some time after the development of the conduits, or (3) interconnection of existing dry passages by processes of breakdown and collapse.

Caves in regions of high relief are frequently developed by inputs of water that move by predominantly vertical paths through the unsaturated zone. Such caves often have a stair-step pattern, with vertical pits and shafts offset by short reaches of horizontal passage. Steeply sloping streamways are common. Some caves of the unsaturated zone are simply pits tens to hundreds of metres deep, which show little horizontal development. Others make up complicated cave systems in which many vertical infeeders join to form master streams that descend to base level as waterfalls plunging down pits. One of the largest such systems is the group of caves on the Huautla Plateau in Mexico. The greatest relief from the highest known entrance of the Sistema Huautla to the lowest point of exploration is 1,252 metres (about 4,100 feet) in a cave measuring 33.8 km (21 miles) long.

Some conduit systems such as those of the Mammoth Cave area and of the Cumberland Plateau of the Appalachian Mountains develop beneath a protective cap of sandstone, shale, and other relatively non-soluble rocks. As the caprock erodes, the underlying limestone is exposed to the runoff water that drains from the remaining area of the plateau. Such runoff water dissolves away the limestone in the unsaturated zone to form solution chimneys and vertical shafts. Solution chimneys develop along vertical fractures or along bedding planes of vertically bedded limestones. In cross section, they tend to be irregular and elongated along the controlling fracture or bedding plane. Solution chimneys follow the fracture and may be offset or descend at steep angles, depending on the pitch of the guiding fracture. Vertical shafts, by contrast, are controlled by the hydraulic forces of freely flowing water. They are often nearly perfect cylinders with circular cross sections. The walls are vertical and cut across the limestone beds with complete disregard for angle or composition of the beds. Vertical shafts and solution chimneys have no direct relation to the conduit system, especially not to the upper dry levels of the system. They sometimes are connected to present-day active horizontal conduits by drain passages. These drains usually are of small cross section and may extend from hundreds of metres or even several kilometres before connecting with the main drainage conduits. In the unsaturated zone, vertical shafts tend to shear through high-level passages as though they were not there. When vertical shafts and solution chimneys cut through several tiers of overlying horizontal passage, they provide pathways for exploration and integrate the cave system.

Cave roofs are always in a state of stress. The weight of the ceiling beds causes them to sag slightly, separating the beds along the weaker bedding planes. Each ceiling bed becomes, in effect, a fixed beam spanning the width of the cave passage. There is a strict mechanical relationship between the thickness of a beam, its density, and the width of the span. When the width of the span exceeds a certain critical value, the cave ceiling will collapse under its own weight. Processes such as solution along vertical joints cut the ceiling beams, turning them into cantilevers that have much smaller critical loads. When one ceiling bed falls, support is removed from the bed above and it also may fall. There is thus a process of upward stoping due to ceiling collapse. Upward breakdown and collapse can cause one passage to migrate up into an overlying one.

SOLUTION CAVE FEATURES

Solution caves are characterized by their sculpturings and depositional features. Scientists examine sculpturings to understand the direction and rate of flow of the underground water source. Caves are also characterized by the presence of stalactites, stalagmites, and other depositional features.

CAVE DEPOSITS

Cave deposits, or speleothems, are made up of any of the crystalline deposits that form in a solution cave after the creation of the cave itself. These deposits are generally composed of calcium carbonate dissolved from the surrounding limestone by groundwater. Carbon dioxide carried in the water is released as the water encounters the cave air; this reduces the water's capacity to hold calcite in solution and causes the calcite to be deposited. These deposits may accumulate to form stalactites, stalagmites, flowstone, helictites, cave pearls, and many other formations. Deposits formed along ceiling cracks may produce drip curtains or draperies that may then reach the floor to become walls. Speleothems may grow in pools to form the nodular encrustations of cave coral or the natural dams that continually elevate themselves through accretion of calcite. The pure white of the calcium carbonate is often tinted with hues of red, yellow, and gray and may even be translucent. The growth rate of speleothems is highly variable due to seasonal variations in the rate of flow, carbon dioxide content, and other factors. Caves owe most of their beauty and much of their interest to these secondary growths.

SOLUTIONAL SCULPTURINGS

Superimposed on the walls of cave passages are many small solutional sculpturings that record further details of water flow. Pockets of various sizes and kinds are cut back into the walls and ceiling. Some of these have ax-blade shapes and form where water seeping into the cave passage is mixed with the water already in the passage. If the seepage water and the passage water have the correct chemistry, corrosive water forms in the mixing zone and dissolves away the joint-controlled wall and ceiling pockets. Other wall and ceiling pockets are rounded kettle holes or circular cylinders that extend into the solid bedrock of the ceiling with no obvious influence from joints. The ceilings of tropical caves often contain large numbers of the cylindrical cavities, which are used as roosting places by bats. Small secondary channels are carved into the floors or ceilings by flowing water. Floor channels provide evidence of the presence of small later-stage streams that occupied the cave passage after it had been drained of its original flow. Ceiling channels are thought to be the result of upward solutional erosion by cave streams that occurred when the main channel was completely filled with clays, sand, and gravel.

Among the most significant of the solutional sculpturings are the small scooplike depressions known as scallops. Scallops vary in size from a few centimetres to more than 1 metre (about 3 feet). They are asymmetrical in cross section, having a steep wall on the upstream side and a gentler slope on the downstream side. Scallops thus provide information as to the direction of water flow in passages that have been dry for hundreds of thousands of years. The size of a scallop is inversely proportional to the flow velocity of water in the passage. As a consequence, scallops serve not only as paleo-direction indicators but also as paleo-flow meters. Scallops that are a few centimetres wide indicate flow velocities on the order of a few metres per second. The largest scallops, those that are more than one metre wide, indicate flow velocities of a few centimetres per second.

HELICTITES

These cave deposits have a branching, curved, or spiralled shape and may grow in any direction in seeming defiance of gravity. A helictite begins as a soda-straw-like tube formed as individual drops of water deposit calcium carbonate around the rim. The drops do not fall as in stalactite formation but evaporate in place. The direction of growth is thought to be determined by the chance orientation of crystal axes of the calcite carried in the water.

The flow velocity of conduit water is sufficient to transport clastic sediment through a cave system. The clastic material is derived from borderlands where it is carried into the karst by sinking streams, from overlying sandstone and shale caprock, from surface soils that are washed underground through sinkholes, and from the insoluble residue of the limestone bedrock. Some of these clastic materials are deposited in caves where they remain as clay, silt, and sand on the cave floors. Some drainage systems carry larger cobble- and boulder-sized materials that are often found in cave streambeds. Most caves have undergone several periods of deposition and excavation, and so remnant beds and pockets of sediment have been left high on cave walls and ledges. These sediments contain iron-bearing magnetic particles, which indicate the position of Earth's magnetic field at the time when the sediments were deposited. The age of the sedimentary deposits can be determined by measuring the paleomagnetic record in cave sediments and correlating it with the established geomagnetic polarity time scale. Using this method, investigators have ascertained that the age of the sediments in Mammoth Cave is more than two million years.

DEPOSITIONAL MATERIALS AND FEATURES

There are three broad categories of sedimentary material found in caves: clastic sediments carried in by streams and infiltrated from the surface; blocks, slabs, and fragments of breakdown derived from the local bedrock; and chemical sediments deposited in the cave by percolating waters. The chemical sediments are the most diverse and are responsible for the decorative beauty of many caves.

The most common of the secondary chemical sediments is calcite, calcium carbonate. There also occurs a less common form of calcium carbonate, the mineral aragonite. The second most common cave mineral is gypsum,

Giant Dome and Twin Domes, stalagmites in the Big Room of Carlsbad Cavern, one of the caves in Carlsbad Caverns National Park, southeastern New Mexico. Peter Jones/National Park Service

calcium sulfate dihydrate. Other carbonate, sulfate, and oxide minerals are occasionally found in caves as well. Many of these require that the cave be associated with ore deposits or with other special geologic environments. For this reason, of the more than 200 mineral species known to occur in caves, only about 20 are found widely.

Deposits of cave minerals occur in many forms, their shapes determined by whether they were deposited by dripping, flowing, or seeping water or in standing pools of water. Collectively, these secondary mineral forms are known as speleothems.

Water emerging from a joint in the cave ceiling hangs for a while as a pendant drop. During this time, a small amount of calcium carbonate is deposited in a ring where the drop is in contact with the ceiling. Then the drop falls, and a new drop takes its place, also depositing a small ring of calcium carbonate. In this manner, an icicle-like speleothem called a stalactite is built up. Stalactites vary in shape from thin strawlike features to massive pendants or drapery-like forms. As mentioned earlier, stalactites have a central canal that carries water from the feeder joint to the stalactite tip. When the drops fall to the floor of the cave, additional mineral matter is deposited and stalagmites are built up. Stalagmites also take on many forms, from slender broom-handle to mound- and pagoda-like shapes. Stalagmites consist of superimposed caps or layers and do not have a central canal. Stalactites may grow so large that they cannot support their own weight; the broken fragments of large stalactites are sometimes found in caves. Stalagmites are not so restricted and can reach heights of tens of metres. Water flowing along ledges and down walls leaves behind sheets of calcite, which build up a massive deposit known as a flowstone.

Most flowstone deposits are composed of calcite, though other minerals occasionally are present. The calcite is usually coarsely crystalline, densely packed, and coloured various shades of tan, orange, and brown. Some of the pigment is from iron oxides carried into the deposit by the seepage water, but the more common colouring agent is humic substances derived from overlying soils. Humic substances are the organic products of plant decay, which are also responsible for the brown colour of some soils and for the tealike colour of some swamp and lake waters. Calcite speleothems may be pure white but appear milky because of many tiny inclusions of water within the structure.

The calcite in speleothems is derived from the overlying limestone near the bedrock/soil interface. Rainwater infiltrating through the soil absorbs carbon dioxide from the carbon dioxide-rich soil and forms a dilute solution of carbonic acid. When this acid water reaches the base of the soil, it reacts with the calcite in the limestone bedrock and takes some of it into solution. The water continues its downward course through narrow joints and fractures in the unsaturated zone with little further chemical reaction. When the water emerges from the cave roof, carbon dioxide is lost into the cave atmosphere and some of the calcium carbonate is precipitated. The infiltrating water acts as a calcite pump, removing it from the top of the bedrock and redepositing it in the cave below.

Caves provide a very stable environment where temperature and relative humidity may remain constant for thousands of years. The slow growth of crystals is not interrupted, and some speleothems have shapes controlled by the forces of crystal growth rather than by the constraints of dripping and flowing water. Speleothems known as helictites are much like stalactites in that they have a central canal and grow in long tubular forms. They twist and turn in all directions, however, and are not guided by the gravitational pull on pendant water drops. Another variety of speleothem, the anthodite, is a radiating cluster of needlelike crystals. Anthodites are usually composed of aragonite, which has a different habit (i.e., shape of individual crystal grains) than the more common variety of calcium carbonate, calcite. Layered bead or corallike forms occur on cave walls, and complex arrangements of crystals are found in cave pools. Pools of water saturated with calcium carbonate have the remarkable property of surrounding themselves with rimstone dams of precipitated calcite.

Gypsum and other more water soluble sulfate minerals such as epsomite (magnesium sulfate heptahydrate) and mirabilite (sodium sulfate decahydrate) grow from seepage waters in dry caves. Deposition of the sulfate minerals is due to evaporation of the mineral-bearing solutions. These minerals occur as crusts and in the form of radiating, curving masses of fibrous crystals known as gypsum flowers. Because of their higher solubility, sulfate minerals either do not occur or are destroyed in damp or wet caves.

KARST TOPOGRAPHY

As previously noted, karst landscapes owe their existence to the removal of bedrock in solution and to the development of underground drainage without the development of surface stream valleys. Within these broad constraints, karst landscapes show much variation and are usually described in terms of a dominant landform. Most important with respect to worldwide occurrence are fluviokarst, doline karst, cone and tower karst, and pavement karst.

FLUVIOKARST

In this type of karst landscape, the pattern of surface stream channels and stream valleys are still in evidence, though much of the drainage may be underground. Tributary surface streams may sink underground, and there may be streambeds that carry water only during seasons of high flow or during extreme floods. In addition, the floors of the valleys may be dissected into a sequence of sinkholes.

Consider a normal stream valley that gradually deepens its channel until it cuts into underlying beds of limestone (or dolomite). As the valley cuts deeper and deeper into the carbonate rocks, the stream that flows through it loses water into the limestone through joints and fractures, which begin to enlarge into cave systems. At first, the cave passages will be very small and capable of carrying only a small amount of water. The stream flow on the surface will be reduced but not eliminated. As time passes, the cave passages become larger and capable of carrying more water. There will come a time when they are large enough to take the entire flow of the surface stream during periods of low flow, and during these low-flow periods — typically during summer and fall — the surface stream will run dry. With the passage of more time the cave system continues to enlarge, and more and more of the surface drainage is directed into it. The caves may become large enough to carry even the largest flood flows, and the surface channels will remain dry all year. The surface at this stage is called a dry valley, and it is no longer deepened because no more streams flow through it. Stream banks collapse, channels become overgrown with vegetation, and shallow sinkholes begin to form in the valley floor. Upstream from these "swallow holes" where surface streams are lost to the subsurface, the tributary valleys continue to deepen their channels. These evolve into so-called blind valleys, which end where a stream sinks beneath a cliff. At the top of the cliff is the abandoned floor of the dry valley. In short, fluviokarst is a landscape of active stream valleys, dry valleys, blind valleys, and deranged drainage systems. It is a common type of karst landscape where the soluble carbonate rocks are not as thick as the local relief, so that some parts of the landscape are underlain by carbonate rocks and others by such non-soluble rocks as sandstones or shales.

DOLINE KARST

Such karsts are usually rolling plains that have few surface streams and often no surface valleys. Instead, the landscape is pocked with sinkholes, often tens or hundreds of sinkholes per square kilometre. These sinkholes range from barely discernible shallow swales 1 to 2 metres (about 3 to 7 feet) wide to depressions hundreds of metres in depth and one or more kilometres in width. As the sinkholes enlarge, they coalesce to form compound sinks or valley sinks. Some sinkholes form by the dissolution of bedrock at the intersections of joints or fractures. Others result from the collapse of cave roofs, and still others form entirely within the soil. The latter, known as cover collapse sinks and cover subsidence sinks, occur where soils are thick and can be washed into the subsurface by the process of soil piping. Soil loss begins at the bedrock interface. An arched void forms, which migrates upward through the soil until finally the roof collapses abruptly to form the sinkhole. These types of sinkhole constitute a serious land-use problem in karst areas and have been responsible for much property damage when they develop beneath streets, parking lots, houses, and commercial buildings.

SINKHOLES AND CENOTES

Sinkholes, which are also known as sinks or dolines, are topographic depressions formed as underlying limestone bedrock is dissolved by groundwater. It is considered the most fundamental structure of karst topography. Sinkholes vary greatly in area and depth and may be very large. There are two main varieties, one caused by the collapse of the roof of a cavern, the other by the gradual dissolving of rock under a soil mantle. Collapsed sinkholes generally have steep rock sides and may receive streams that then flow underground. The soil-mantled sinkhole is generally shallower than the collapsed sinkhole and receives local drainage; it may become clogged with clay and hold a small lake. Some sinkholes, formed at low sea-level stages during the Pleistocene epoch, are now half-drowned and are known as cenotes.

Sinkhole near Pottstown, Pa. Comstock/Thinkstock

Cenotes (Maya: *dz'onot*) are natural wells or reservoirs that occur in the Yucatán Peninsula. They are formed when a limestone surface collapses, exposing water underneath. The major source of water in modern and ancient Yucatán, cenotes are also associated with the cult of the rain gods, or Chacs. In ancient times, notably at Chichén Itzá, precious objects, such as jade, gold, copper, and incense and also human beings, usually children, were thrown into the cenotes as offerings. A survivor was believed to bring a message from the gods about the year's crops.

CONE AND TOWER KARST

This variety of karst landscape occurs mainly in tropical areas. Thick limestones are divided into blocks by a grid of joints and fractures. Solution produces deep rugged gorges along the joints and fractures, dividing the mass of limestone into isolated blocks. Because the water dissolving the gorges drains to the subsurface, the gorges are not integrated into a valley system. In some localities, the intervening blocks are rounded into closely spaced conical hills (cone karst). In others, the deepening gorges reach a base level and begin to widen. Sufficient widening may create a lower-level plain from which the remnants of the limestone blocks stand out as isolated, near-vertical towers (tower karst). The cones and towers themselves are sculptured by solution, so that the rock surface is covered by jagged pinnacles and often punctuated by pits and crevices.

PAVEMENT KARST

This form of karst develops where bare carbonate rocks are exposed to weathering. The initiation of pavement karst is often due to glaciation, which scrapes off soil and weathered rock material to expose the bare bedrock.

Accordingly, pavement karsts occur mainly in high latitudes and alpine regions where glacial activity has been prominent. Solutional weathering of the exposed limestone or dolomite is due both to direct rainfall onto the rock surface and to meltwater derived from winter snowpack.

Pavement karst is decorated with an array of small landforms created by differential solution. These are collectively known as karren. Karren include solutionally widened joints (kluftkarren, or cleftkarren), small runnels (rinnenkarren, or runnelkarren), small residual pinnacles (spitzkarren, or pinnacle karren), and many other forms.

GEOGRAPHIC DISTRIBUTION OF KARST TERRAIN

Approximately 15 percent of Earth's land surface is karst. The distribution of karst is essentially the same as the distribution of carbonate rocks, which means that karst terrain occurs mostly in the great sedimentary basins of the world. It does not occur in the continental shields underlain by granites and related rocks or in volcanic belts, except in certain islands where massive limestones have been deposited on or around old volcanic cones.

The most extensive karst area of the United States occurs in the limestones of Mississippian age (about 325 million to 345 million years old) of the Interior Low Plateaus. Mostly doline karst with some fluviokarst is found from southern Indiana south along both the east and west flanks of the broad fold of the Cincinnati Arch through eastern and central Kentucky and into Tennessee. Karst also occurs in the limestones of Ordovician age (about 430 million to 500 million years old) that lie exposed on the inner Bluegrass structural dome in Kentucky and on the Nashville Dome in Tennessee. In south central Kentucky is the Mammoth Cave area with the world's longest known cave and many other large cave systems. The Mississippian karst of Kentucky, Tennessee, and Indiana is quite remarkable because the many long cave systems and large areas of doline karst occur in a layer of limestone slightly more than 150 metres (about 500 feet) thick. Extensive karst also is developed on the limestones that ring the Ozark Dome in Missouri and northern Arkansas. Large caves and areas of fluviokarst and doline karst are found there.

Other notable karst regions of eastern North America include the Appalachians (specifically the Valley and Ridge and Great Valley provinces as well as the Cumberland and Allegheny plateaus) and Florida, where a raised platform of carbonate rocks has large areas of doline karst and extensive internal drainage through a major limestone aquifer. Bermuda and the Bahama Islands also are underlain by young limestones that are highly "karstified." Much of this karst was drowned by rises in sea level at the end of the Pleistocene glaciation. Caves containing stalactites and stalagmites are found at depths of tens of metres below present sea level.

The southwestern United States has very diverse karst regions. For example, West Texas, western Oklahoma, and eastern New Mexico have extensive areas of doline karst in gypsum with many small caves. The Edwards Plateau in south central Texas has a subdued surface karst and numerous small caves. The Capitan reef limestone in southeastern New Mexico contains Carlsbad Caverns and other deep and large volume caves.

The Rocky Mountains have many small areas of alpine karst in Colorado, Wyoming, Utah, and Montana. These are mostly pavement karst with relatively small caves. The Rockies of Canada contain some of that country's longest and deepest caves as well as extensive areas of alpine karst.

Some of the most spectacular examples of tropical karst occur in Central America and the Caribbean. The islands of the Greater Antilles (Cuba, Jamaica, Hispaniola, and Puerto Rico) are underlain by massive limestones up to 1,000 metres (3,280 feet) thick. Regions of cone and tower karst have developed in these limestones. The karst of Mexico varies from the streamless, low-relief plain of the Yucatán Peninsula to the high plateaus of the interior with their large dolines and deep vertical caves. Cone and tower karst occurs in the southern part of Mexico and in Belize and Guatemala. Many caves have been reported in Venezuela and Colombia. Little is known of karst in the other countries of South America. Much of the continent is occupied by the Guiana Shield and the Andes Mountains.

Because of its diversity of geologic and climatic settings, Europe has many different types of karst terrain. In the south the Pyrenees exhibit spectacular alpine karst on both the Spanish and French sides. The high-altitude pavement karst contains many deep shafts. The Pierre Saint-Martin System, for example, is 1,342 metres (about 4,400 feet) deep and drains a large area of the mountain range. Southern France, notably the Grande Causse, has some of the most spectacular karst in Europe, with deep gorges, numerous caves, and much sculptured limestone. In the Alps are massive folded and faulted limestones and dolomites that underlie alpine karst terrain from France to the Balkan Peninsula. In France the Vercors Plateau is pavement karst featuring many deep caves, including the Berger Shaft—one of the deepest in Europe. The Hölloch Cave, the world's third longest at 133 km (about 83 miles), is found in the Swiss Alps. Individual limestone massifs capped with karst plateaus and abounding with deep caves occur in the Austrian Alps.

Karst is more of a local affair in northern Europe with relatively small caves in Germany and Scandinavia. Some caves have been formed since the Pleistocene glaciation in Norway, as has some high-latitude pavement karst.

England and Ireland have extensive karst areas. The karst of Wales contains the longest caves in England, while the Yorkshire karst has complex vertical caves. Many parts of Ireland are underlain by limestone, and an area called the Burren in County Clare has not only the most caves but also some of the most extensive low-altitude pavement karsts.

Most areas of eastern Europe have karst, but special attention must be paid to the Dinaric Alps along the western edge of the Balkan Peninsula. From Slovenia to Montenegro and from the Adriatic coast 50 km (31 miles) into the interior, the land surface is karst. In addition to areas of fluviokarst, doline karst, and pavement karst, the karst of the Dinaric Alps region is unique for its large number of poljes. These are closed depressions with flat and alluviated bottoms that may be as much as 60 km (37 miles) in diameter. Many of these depressions are elongate parallel to the geologic structure and to the Adriatic coastline. Although isolated poljes have been identified elsewhere, their large numbers in the karst of the Dinaric Alps are attributable to a system of active faults as well as to intense solution activity in nearly 9,000 metres (about 29,500 feet) of carbonate rock.

Much of the Mediterranean region—Greece, Turkey, Lebanon, Israel, and parts of the Arabian Peninsula—are arid karst. The region had much more rainfall during the ice ages of the Quaternary, and so karst landscapes developed. Today a combination of arid climatic conditions and overgrazing has reduced many parts of the region to bare rock, an arid-climate form of pavement karst. This is effectively a fossil karst that preserves a record of earlier climatic conditions. The karst regions extend eastward through parts of Iraq to the Zagros Mountains of Iran.

Relatively little karst has been described in Africa. Deep shafts and many caves occur in the Atlas Mountains in the northern part of the continent. Some caves have been described in Congo (Kinshasa), and caves are known in South Africa where sinkhole collapse in the Transvaal Dolomite owing to dewatering by gold mining has been a serious environmental problem.

Asia is a vast region where many types of karst occur. In Russia, important karst areas are found in the Caucasus and Ural mountains. There is an important area of gypsum karst in Ukraine, where very large network caves of gypsum occur. Karst covers about 2,000,000 square km (about 772,000 square miles) in China, but most renowned is the tower karst of Kweichow, Kwangsi, Yunnan, and Hunan provinces. The Chinese tower karst is developed on folded and faulted rocks unlike most other regions of cone and tower karst, which occur on thick horizontal strata. Isolated vertical-walled towers more than 200 metres (660 feet) high are found along river floodplains in those provinces.

Karst regions occur in the South Pacific. In Australia there are caves and some scattered sinkholes along the Nullarbor Plain. Additional karst areas occur in the eastern part of the continent. Many of the Pacific islands are coral reefs that have become karst to varying extents. Extensive cone and tower karst is found in New Guinea, Java, Borneo, and the Malay Peninsula.

VOLCANIC CAVES

Caves of various types and sizes occur where volcanic rocks are exposed. These are caves formed by flowing lava and by the effects of volcanic gases rather than by dissolution of the bedrock. Because volcanic caves form very close to the land surface, they are easily destroyed by erosional processes. As a result, such caves are usually found only in recent lava flows, those that are less than 20 million years old.

LAVA TUBES

These are the longest and most complicated of volcanic caves. They are the channels of rivers of lava that at some earlier time flowed downslope from a volcanic vent or fissure. Lava tubes develop best in highly fluid lava, notably a basaltic type known as pahoehoe. They rarely form in rough, clinkery aa flows or in the more massive block lavas. In pahoehoe flows volatile components remain in solution in the molten rock where they decrease both the rate at which the lava solidifies and its viscosity. Because of this, pahoehoe lava flows like a sticky liquid, sometimes rushing down steep slopes and forming lava falls.

Near the vent of a volcano, the overflowing lava is directed toward whatever natural channels or gullies are available. As the flow advances downslope, the sides begin to congeal, so that more and more of the flowing lava is confined to a progressively narrowing channel. At this stage, the lava flow behaves like a river moving at relatively high velocity in a narrow canyon. Gradually the surface of the flow becomes crusted over and may also be covered with solid blocks of lava that have been rafted along the flow. As more and more of the surface crusts over, the supply of fluid lava feeding the advancing front of the flow is confined to a roughly cylindrical tube beneath the surface. It is possible in the later stages of crusting to observe the lava river through the few remaining "windows" in the crust.

The development of a channel that feeds the advancing front of the lava flow represents the initial stage in the formation of a lava tube. The second stage is the draining of the original conduit. If the source of lava is cut off at the vent, the fluid lava in the tube continues to flow and the tube drains. The combustion of gases released from the lava maintains a high temperature, and the walls of the conduit may be fused to a black glaze. The draining of the tube may take place in stages, so that benches or ledges are formed along the walls. Lava dripping from the ceiling congeals to form lava stalactites, while lava dripping onto the floor gives rise to lava stalagmites. The floor of a lava tube often has a ropey pattern parallel to the flow direction, showing how the last dregs of the draining lava were frozen into place. Other features of the moving fluid such as trenchlike channels in the floor, lava falls over ledges, ponded lava, and embedded blocks may also be found frozen in place.

In their simplest form, lava tube caves are long tunnels of uniform diameter oriented down the slope of the volcano from which they had their origin. Their roofs and walls consist of solidified lava. In some cases, the floor is covered with sand or other unconsolidated material that has been washed into the cave by water. The roof of a lava tube commonly breaks down, and some caves of this type are littered with blocks of fallen ceiling material. Complete collapse of segments of the roof forms "skylights." When such openings occur at the upper end of a tube, the tube acts as a cold air trap. Many lava tubes contain ice formations—ponded ice as well as icicles and ice stalagmites where seepage water has frozen in the cold air trapped within the tubes. Some of these ice deposits persist far into the summer.

Lava tubes that have more complicated shapes also occur. Where slopes are gentle, the original lava river may branch into a distributary pattern near the toe. If these are all drained, the remaining tube branches in the downstream direction. New lava flows may override older flows and result in the formation of additional lava tubes on top of existing ones. Sometimes they are connected by younger flows falling through the roof of the older one, thus rejuvenating the older tube. Because most lava flows are thin, lava tubes form near the land surface. Portions of the roof frequently collapse, and the resulting sinkholes provide entrances to the lava tubes. The collapse process also segments the tubes, so that most lava caves have lengths of only a few hundred to a few thousand metres. Often one can line up the individual caves on maps to identify the course of the original tube. Some lava tube caves are found tens of kilometres from the vent where the flow originated.

OTHER TYPES OF LAVA CAVES

Small caves are produced in regions of active volcanism by at least three other processes. These are (1) pressure-ridge caves, (2) spatter cone chambers, and (3) blister caves.

The solidified crust of pahoehoe flows often buckles from the movement of lava underneath. The buckled crust appears as ridges several metres to a few tens of metres high, elongated perpendicular to the flow. So-called pressure-ridge caves can be formed beneath the ridges by the mechanical lifting of the roof rock. Such cavities typically measure 1 to 2 metres (about 3 to 7 feet) in height, have a roughly triangular cross section, and extend several hundred metres in length. Unlike lava tube caves that are oriented along the flow, pressure-ridge caves are oriented perpendicular to the flow.

Liquid lava can be forced upward through cracks in the congealed surface layers of the flow. When the ejected blobs of liquid freeze and weld together, they form spatter cones. If the lava subsequently drains from the feeder channel, a dome-shaped chamber is formed beneath such a cone. The depths of these spatter cone pits range from several metres to a few tens of metres.

Trapped steam or other gases can lift layers of lava while it is still in a plastic state to form small blister caves. These cavities consist of dome-shaped chambers somewhat resembling those of spatter cones. They are generally small, ranging from one to a few metres in diameter, but they often occur in great numbers in many lava flows rich in volatile components.

In the United States lava caves are found chiefly in the Pacific Northwest—northern California, Washington, Oregon, and Idaho—and in Hawaii. One of the longest (measuring 3.4 kilometres [about 2 miles]) is Ape Cave on the flank of Mount St. Helens in Washington. The cave is located on the side of the volcano opposite that involved in the catastrophic eruption of 1980 and so survived the outburst. Ape Cave is only one fragment of a series of interrelated lava tubes that mark a continuous flow path down the volcano. A large number of lava tubes also occur beneath a nearly flat plain in the Bend region of central Oregon. Many of these are related to fissure eruptions rather than to a single volcanic cone. Lava tubes are commonly found in other young volcanic regions of the world, notably in the Canary Islands, on Iceland, along the East African Rift Valley, and in parts of Australia.

TECTONIC CAVES

Tectonic caves are formed by a mass movement of the bedrock. The rocks separate along joints or fractures, and are pulled apart mechanically. The resulting cave is usually a high, narrow fissure that has nearly planar walls with matching patterns on opposite sides of the passage. The ceiling is often a flat bed of rock that did not move or that moved along some different fracture. The floor of a tectonic cave may consist of massive bedrock or of a rubble of fallen blocks, or it may be covered with soil and other material washed in from the surface.

Because tectonic caves are formed by mechanical processes, the most important characteristic of the bedrock is that it be mechanically strong. Massive, brittle rocks such as sandstones and granites are the best host rocks for tectonic caves.

Although tectonic caves can be formed by any geologic force that causes rocks to move apart, the key mechanism is gravity sliding. The optimum setting for the development of tectonic caves occurs where massive rocks dip gently to the sides of ridges or mountains. The presence of shale layers between beds of massive sandstone can act as a lubricating layer and facilitate mechanical slippage. Gravity causes the massive rocks to slip and separate along vertical fractures, which then become tectonic caves. The amount of slippage must be small for the cave to maintain its roof. Too much slippage and consequent roof collapse will form an open canyon. Still more slippage can result in a landslide.

Tectonic caves occur in many geologic settings and in great numbers, since they are produced by minor slippages in outcrops of massive sandstones, granites, basalts, and even limestone. Tectonic caves are among the most common caves, but they are rarely noticed or catalogued. They contain few, if any, features that attract attention and usually are quite small. Most such caves measure from several metres to a few hundred metres in length. Many of them consist of a single passage that extends into hillsides along major fractures. Some of the larger tectonic caves have a grid or network pattern that matches the pattern of the fractures or joints.

PEDIMENTS

Pediments are any relatively flat surface of bedrock (exposed or veneered with alluvial soil or gravel) that occurs at the base of a mountain or as a plain having no associated mountain. They are sometimes mistaken for groups of merged alluvial fans and are most conspicuous in basin-and-range-type desert areas throughout the world.

The angle of a pediment's slope is generally from $0.5°$ to $7°$. Its form is slightly concave, and it is typically found at the base of hills in arid regions where rainfall is spasmodic and intense for brief periods of time. There is frequently a sharp break of slope between the pediment and the steeper hillside above it. Water passes across the pediment by laminar sheet flow, but if this is disturbed, the flow becomes turbulent and gullies develop.

Though features characteristic of pediments attain their fullest development in arid regions, beveled bedrock surfaces also occur in humid areas. In the tropics, for example, the surfaces tend to be mantled with soils and obscured by vegetation. Many tropical towns sited on pediments (which offer easier building sites than the steep hillsides above or the river marshes below) show severe gullying where the water flow has been concentrated between walls and buildings.

SAND DUNES

Sand dunes are structural landforms that are composed of accumulations of sand grains. These features are shaped into a mound or ridge by the wind under the influence of gravity. Sand dunes are comparable to other forms that appear when a fluid moves over a loose bed, such as subaqueous "dunes" on the beds of rivers and tidal estuaries and sand waves on the continental shelves beneath shallow seas. Dunes are found wherever loose sand is windblown: in deserts, on beaches, and even on some eroded and abandoned farm fields in semiarid regions, such as northwest India and parts of the southwestern United States. Images of Mars returned by the U.S. Mariner 9 and Viking spacecrafts have shown that dunes are widely distributed on that planet both in craters and in a sand sea surrounding the north polar ice cap.

True dunes must be distinguished from dunes formed in conjunction with vegetation. The latter cover relatively small areas on quiet humid coastlands and also occur on the semiarid margins of deserts. True dunes cover much more extensive areas — up to several hundred square kilometres — primarily in great sand seas (ergs), some of which are as big as France or Texas. They also occur, however, as small isolated dunes on hard desert surfaces, covering an area of as little as 10 square metres (107 square feet). Areas of gently undulating sandy surfaces with low relief are classified as sand sheets. They commonly have a nearly flat or rippled surface of coarse sand grains and are only a few centimetres to metres thick. Minor sand sheets cover only a few square kilometres around the margins of dune fields. A few, such as the Selima Sand Sheet in southwestern Egypt and the northwestern Sudan, are probably almost as extensive as some of the great sand seas.

During the last 2 million years or so the conditions of very low rainfall under which true dunes form expanded beyond the margins of the Sahara and other present-day arid regions into areas that are now more humid. The best evidence for these changes is the presence of sand seas that are immobilized by vegetation. Dunes formed under similar climates in the geologic past and at certain times occupied deserts as extensive as modern ones. Rocks formed by the solidification of ancient sand seas occur, for example, in the walls of the Grand Canyon in the southwestern United States, in the west Midlands of England, and in southern Brazil.

GEOMORPHIC CHARACTERISTICS

An understanding of sand dunes requires a basic knowledge of their sands, the winds, and the interactions of these main elements. These factors will be treated in turn in the following sections.

SANDS

Dunes are almost invariably built of particles of sand size. Clay particles are not usually picked up by the wind because of their mutual coherence, and if they are picked up they tend to be lifted high into the air. Only where clays are aggregated into particles of sand size, as on the Gulf Coast of Texas, will they be formed into dunes. Silt is more easily picked up by the wind but is carried away faster than sand, and there are few signs of dunelike bed forms where silt is deposited, for instance as sheets of loess. Particles coarser than sands, such as small pebbles, only form dunelike features when there are strong and persistent winds, as in coastal Peru, and these coarse-grained features are generally known as granule ripples rather than dunes. Larger particles, such as small boulders, can be moved by the wind only on slippery surfaces (e.g., ice or wet saline mud) and never form into dunes.

Common dune sands have median grain diameters between 0.02 and 0.04 cm (0.008 and 0.016 inch). The maximum common range is between 0.01 and 0.07 cm (0.004 and 0.03 inch). Most dune sands are well sorted, and a sample of sand from a dune will usually have particles all of very similar size. The sand on sand sheets, however, is poorly sorted and often bimodal—i.e., it is a mixture of coarse sands, often about 0.06 cm (0.024 inch) in diameter, and much finer sands, as well as particles of intermediate size. Windblown sands, especially the coarser particles, are often rounded and minutely pitted, the latter giving the grains a frosted appearance when seen under a microscope.

Most windblown sand on Earth is composed of quartz. Quartz exists in large quantities in many igneous and metamorphic rocks in crystals of sand size. It tends to accumulate when these rocks are weathered away because it resists chemical breakdown better than most minerals, which are taken away in solution. Most of the great sand seas occur in continental interiors that have been losing soluble material for millions of years; as a consequence, quartzose sandstones are common. These sandstones are eroded by rainwash and stream runoff, processes that are spasmodic but violent in deserts. The eroded products are transported to great interior basins where they

Gypsum dunes at White Sands National Monument, New Mexico. Jeremy Woodhouse/Getty Images

are deposited. Such alluvial deposits are the sources of most windblown sand. Quartz also predominates in most coastal dune sands, but there usually are considerable mixtures of other minerals in dunes of this kind.

Dune sands not composed of quartz are rarer but not unknown. Near volcanic eruptions in Hawaii, some western states of the continental United States, and Tanzania, for example, dunes are built of volcanic ash particles. In many arid areas, gypsum crystals of sand size are deposited on the floors of ephemeral lakes as the water dries out; they are then blown like sand to form gypsum dunes. Gypsum dunes occur in the White Sands National Monument in New Mexico, as well as in northern Algeria and southwestern Australia.

WINDS

Winds have three sources of variation that are important—namely, direction, velocity, and turbulence. Most of the great deserts are found in the subtropical areas of high atmospheric pressure, where the winds circulate in a clockwise direction in the Northern Hemisphere and a counterclockwise direction in the Southern Hemisphere. The high-pressure systems tend to dip down to the east so that winds are stronger there, a pattern mirrored by the dunes. Poleward of these circulation systems are the zones of eastward moving depressions in which there are generally westerly winds that mold the dunes of the North American and Central Asian deserts and of the northern Sahara. The boundaries between these two circulation systems migrate back and forth seasonally, so that complicated dune patterns are found in the zones of overlap. Only a few deserts, notably the Thar Desert of India and the Sonoran Desert of the American Southwest, are affected by monsoonal wind systems. Some dunes are built by sea breezes and local winds, as in coastal Peru.

The direction of the wind at any one place in the desert is affected by a number of local factors. Winds are particularly channeled around topographical features, such as the Tibesti Massif in the Sahara, so that dunes are affected by different winds on different sides of the obstruction. Winds also can be channeled around the dunes themselves, thereby developing patterns of secondary flow that modify the shapes of the dunes.

The pattern of wind velocity also is important. Like many natural phenomena, wind velocities have a log-normal distribution: there are a large number of moderate breezes and a diminishing number of increasingly more violent winds. The greatest volumes of sand are probably moved by unusually strong winds, because the amount of sand moved by wind is a power function (exponential factor) of the wind speed. For example, a 10-km- (6-mile-) per-hour wind carries 13 grams per hour (0.39 ounce per hour), a 20-km- (12-mile-) per-hour wind carries 274 grams (about 10 ounces) per hour, and a 30-km- (19-mile-) per-hour wind carries 1,179 grams (about 2.6 pounds) per hour. A wind of a particular velocity will move fewer larger than smaller grains. Strong winds often blow from a particular direction, as in the southern Sahara, where the intense winds of sandstorms come predominantly from one direction. Such winds are responsible for the undulations of the sand sheets, because they alone can move coarse sands. Lighter winds blow from several different directions, and the dunes, being of finer sand, are therefore affected by several winds.

The wind is retarded near the surface by friction. Above the ground the wind velocity increases rapidly. The near-surface velocity must rise above a certain threshold value before sand will be picked up, the value depending on the size of the sand grains; for example, a wind of 12 km (about 8 miles) per hour measured at a height of 10 metres (about 33 feet) is required to move sands 0.02 cm (0.008 inch) in diameter, and a 21-km- (13-mile-) per-hour wind is required to move 0.06-cm (0.02-inch) sands. Once sand movement has been initiated by wind of such velocity, it can be maintained by winds blowing at lower speeds. Because instantaneous wind speeds in eddies can rise well above the average velocity, turbulence also is important, but it is difficult to measure.

FORMATION AND GROWTH OF DUNES

The dune-forming process is complex, particularly where many thousands of dunes have grown side-by-side in sand seas. Yet, an introductory account can be given based on the example of a single dune on a hard desert surface.

Most of the sand carried by the wind moves as a mass of jumping (saltating) grains; coarser particles move slowly along the surface as creep and are kept in motion partly by the bombardment of the saltating grains. Saltating sand bounces more easily off hard surfaces than off soft ones, with the result that more sand can be moved over a pebbly desert surface than over a smooth or soft one. Slight hollows or smoother patches reduce the amount of sand that the wind can carry, and a small sand patch will be initiated. If it is large enough, this patch will attract more sand.

The wind adjusts its velocity gradient on reaching the sand patch; winds above a certain speed decrease their near-surface velocity and deposit sand on the patch. This adjustment takes place over several metres, the sand being deposited over this distance, and a dune is built up. The growth of this dune cannot continue indefinitely. The windward slope is eventually adjusted, so that there is an increase in the near-surface velocity up its face to compensate for the drag imposed by the sandy surface. When this happens, the dune stops growing and there is no net gain or loss of sand.

As the dune grows, the smooth leeward slope steepens until the wind cannot be deflected down sharply enough to follow it. The wind then separates from the surface leaving a "dead zone" in the lee into which falls the sand brought up the windward slope. When this depositional slope is steepened to the angle of repose of dry sand (about 32°), this angle is maintained and the added sand slips down the slope or slip face. When this happens, the dune form is in equilibrium, and the dune moves forward as a whole, sand being eroded from the windward side and deposited on the lee.

If the regional rate of sand flow can be calculated from measurements of wind speed and direction, and if it is assumed that the dune has a simple cross section that migrates forward without change of form, a formula for the rate of movement of a dune that agrees with actual measurements can be derived. In Peru dunes have been observed to move at 30 metres (about 100 feet) per year; in California rates of 25 metres (about 80 feet) per year have been measured; and in the al-Khārijah Oases (or Kharga Depression) in southern Egypt dunes have been reported to move 20 to 100 metres (about 65 to 330 feet) per year, depending on dune size (in general, small dunes move faster than large dunes because their smaller cross-sectional area requires less sand to be transported to reconstitute their form one dune-length downwind).

DUNE AND SHEET PATTERNS

If the wind were a homogeneous stream of air blowing from one constant direction, long straight dune ridges oriented at right angles to the wind would result. Most dunes, however, are neither straight nor at right angles to the wind, and this indicates that the winds are not a uniform stream or that they blow from different directions. The fairly uniform geometric shapes of several basic types of dunes can be recognized from desert to desert on Earth, and some of the same types have been identified on Mars as well.

Barchan dunes are common to both Earth and Mars. These small crescent-shaped sand bodies occur in areas where the regional wind blows consistently from one direction. Their crescentic shape must be due to spatial variations in wind velocity, and the regular repetition of dune shapes and spacings when they are close together indicate that the variations in the wind are also regular. This is a property common to all bed forms. It is thought that the flow of a fluid arranges itself in long spiral vortices parallel to the direction of flow, which, with zones of faster and slower velocities arranged transverse to the flow, gives a regular sinuous pattern on the bed.

Where there is a continuous sand cover, a varied dune pattern results from the pattern of flow. The main forms are transverse ridges composed of alternating crescentic elements, like barchans, facing downwind, and other crescentic elements facing upwind. These enclose between them a regular pattern of small hollows. Superimposed on this are small straight ridges parallel with the flow. These elements form a network pattern that is extremely common in the great sand seas. The dunes commonly reach a height of nearly 200 metres (about 660 feet) and are spaced hundreds of metres to more than 2 km (about 1 mile) apart.

One of the important features of sandy terrains is that their forms occur in a number of distinct sizes. Large features are covered with smaller ones, and the smaller ones are covered with ripples. In most of the larger sand seas there is usually a network pattern of very large dunes known as compound dunes, mega-dunes, or *draa*. These are sometimes arranged parallel to the apparent flow, in long ridges, and occasionally transverse to it in great sand waves. The compound dunes are usually covered with a smaller, secondary dune pattern, and the smaller dunes with ordinary sand ripples in most cases. Within each of the size groups of the hierarchy (ripples, dunes, or compound dunes) there are variations in size depending on the grain size of the sand and wind velocity; for example, whereas most ripples are spaced only a few centimetres apart, "mega-ripples," built in very coarse sand, are spaced almost as far apart as small dunes; and whereas most dunes are about 100 metres (about 330 feet) apart, the low undulations of coarse sand on sand sheets are up to 500 metres (1,640 feet) apart. The relation between sand grain size and the shape of a dune is not, however, one of simple cause and effect, for the relation is not constant in all dunes of a given shape or in all localities.

Some dune forms can be related to variations in the overall wind direction, usually on a seasonal cycle. In some areas, winds from opposed directions blow during different seasons, so that "reversing dunes" are formed, in which the slip faces face first in one direction and then in the other. Distinct dunes are formed around topographic obstructions and in sheltered zones on the lee of small hills into which the sand migrates. If the wind meets a high scarp or large hill massif, a so-called echo dune is deposited on the upwind side separated from the scarp by a rolling eddy of air that keeps a corridor free of sand. Many oases and routeways are found in this kind of corridor. Echo dunes are among the largest dunes in the desert, sometimes reaching a height of more than 400 metres (about 1,300 feet).

FIXED DUNES IN SEMIARID REGIONS

Dunes also form around plants in the desert where ground-water is available for vegetation. The usual dune forms that occur in such instances are isolated mounds around individual plants. These forms are known as coppice dunes, or *nebkha*. Further, in many regions that are now subhumid or humid, one finds areas of older dunes fixed by vegetation, providing undeniable evidence that these regions were once more arid than they are today. On the North American high plains, in Hungary, and in Mongolia, the fixed sands have a cover of rich grassland. In Poland they are covered with coniferous forests. The dune patterns on these fixed sands bear a close resemblance to those in active sand seas, except that their forms are rounded and subdued.

CHAPTER 5
COASTAL LANDFORMS

C oastal landforms, which appear as any of the relief features present along any coast, differ from continental and structural types because they are the result of a combination of coastal processes, sediments, and the geology of the coast itself.

The coastal environment of the world is made up of a wide variety of landforms manifested in a spectrum of sizes and shapes ranging from gently sloping beaches to high cliffs, yet coastal landforms are best considered in two broad categories: erosional and depositional. In fact, the overall nature of any coast may be described in terms of one or the other of these categories. It should be noted, however, that each of the two major landform types may occur on any given reach of coast.

FACTORS AND FORCES IN THE FORMATION OF COASTAL FEATURES

The landforms that develop and persist along the coast are the result of a combination of processes acting upon the sediments and rocks present in the coastal zone. The most prominent of these processes involves waves and the currents that they generate, along with tides. Other factors that significantly affect coastal morphology are climate and gravity.

WAVES

The most obvious of all coastal processes is the continual motion of the waves moving toward the beach. Waves vary considerably in size over time at any given location and also vary markedly from place to place. Waves interact with the ocean bottom as they travel into shallow water; as a result, they cause sediment to become temporarily suspended and available for movement by coastal currents. The larger the wave, the deeper the water in which this process takes place and the larger the particle that can be moved. Even small waves that are only a few tens of centimetres high can pick up sand as they reach the shore. Larger waves can move cobbles and rock material as large as boulders.

Generally, small waves cause sediment—usually sand—to be transported toward the coast and to become deposited on the beach. Larger waves, typically during storms, are responsible for the removal of sediment from the coast and its conveyance out into relatively deep water.

The Mediterranean-washed pebble beach at Nice on the French Riviera. © Nedra Westwater/Black Star

Waves erode the bedrock along the coast largely by abrasion. The suspended sediment particles in waves, especially pebbles and larger rock debris, have much the same effect on a surface as sandpaper does. Waves have considerable force and so may break up bedrock simply by impact.

LONGSHORE CURRENTS

Waves usually approach the coast at some acute angle rather than exactly parallel to it. Because of this, the waves are bent (or refracted) as they enter shallow water, which in turn generates a current along the shore and parallel to it. Such a current is called a longshore current, and it extends from the shoreline out through the zone of breaking waves. The speed of the current is related to the size of the waves and to their angle of approach. Under rather quiescent conditions, longshore currents move only about 10–30 cm (4–12 inches) per second; however, under stormy conditions they may exceed 1 metre (about 3 feet) per second. The combination of waves and longshore current acts to transport large quantities of sediment along the shallow zone adjacent to the shoreline.

Because longshore currents are caused by the approaching and refracting waves, they may move in either direction along the coast, depending on the direction of wave approach. This direction of approach is a result of the wind direction, which is therefore the ultimate factor in determining the direction of longshore currents and the transport of sediment along the shoreline.

Although a longshore current can entrain sediment if it moves fast enough, waves typically cause sediment to be picked up from the bottom, and the longshore current transports it along the coast. In some locations there is quite a large volume of net sediment transport along the coast because of a dominance of one wind direction—and therefore wave direction—over another. This volume may be on the order of 100,000 cubic metres (about 3.5 million cubic feet) per year. Other locations may experience more of a balance in wave approach, which causes the longshore current and sediment transport in one direction to be nearly balanced by the same process in the other direction.

RIP CURRENTS

Another type of coastal current caused by wave activity is the rip current (incorrectly called rip tide in popular usage). As waves move toward the beach, there is some net shoreward transport of water. This leads to a slight but important upward slope of the water level (setup), so that the absolute water level at the shoreline is a few centimetres higher than it is beyond the surf zone. This situation is an unstable one, and water moves seaward through the surf zone in an effort to relieve the instability of the sloping water. The seaward movement is typically confined to narrow pathways. In most cases, rip currents are regularly spaced and flow at speeds of up to several tens of centimetres per second. They can carry sediment and often are recognized by the plume of suspended sediment moving out through the surf zone. In some localities rip currents persist for months at the same site, whereas in others they are quite ephemeral.

TIDES

The rise and fall of sea level caused by astronomical conditions is regular and predictable. There is a great range in the magnitude of this daily or semi-daily change in water level. Along some coasts the tidal range is less than 0.5 metre (1.6 feet), whereas in the Bay of Fundy in southeastern Canada the maximum tidal range is just over 16 metres (about 50 feet). A simple but useful classification of coasts is based solely on tidal range without regard to any other variable. Three categories have been established: micro-tidal (less than 2 metres [about 7 feet]), meso-tidal (2 to 4 metres [about 7 to 13 feet]), and macro-tidal (more than 4 metres). Micro-tidal coasts constitute the largest percentage of the world's coasts, but the other two categories also are widespread.

The role of tides in molding coastal landforms is twofold: (1) tidal currents transport large quantities of sediment and may erode bedrock, and (2) the rise and fall of the tide distributes wave energy across a shore zone by changing the depth of water and the position of the shoreline.

Tidal currents transport sediment in the same way that longshore currents do. The speeds necessary to transport the sediment (typically sand) are generated only under certain conditions—usually in inlets, at the mouths of estuaries, or any other place where there is a constriction in the coast through which tidal exchange must take place. Tidal currents on the open coast, such as along a beach or rocky coast, are not swift enough to transport sediment. The speed of tidal currents in constricted areas, however, may exceed 2 metres (about 7 feet) per second, especially in inlets located on a barrier island complex. The speed of these tidal currents is dictated by the volume of water that must pass through the inlet during a given flood or ebb-tide cycle. This may be either six or 12 hours in duration, depending on whether the local situation is semidiurnal (12-hour cycle) or diurnal (24-hour cycle). The volume of water involved, called the tidal prism, is the product of the tidal range and the area of the coastal bay being served by the inlet. This means that though there may be a direct relationship between tidal range and tidal-current speed, it is also possible to have very swift tidal currents on a coast where the tidal range is low if the bay being served by the inlet is quite large. This is a very common situation along the coast of the Gulf of Mexico where the range is typically less than 1 metre (about 3 feet) but where there are many large coastal bays.

The rise and fall of the tide along the open coast has an indirect effect on sediment transport, even though currents capable of moving sediment are not present. As the tide comes in and then retreats along a beach or on a rocky coast, it causes the shoreline to move accordingly. This movement of the shoreline changes the zone where waves and longshore currents can do their work.

TIDAL FLATS

Level muddy surfaces bordering estuaries are called tidal flats. These features are alternately submerged and exposed to the air by changing tidal levels. The tidal waters enter and leave a tidal flat through fairly straight major channels, with minor channels serving as tributaries as well as distributaries. The minor channels meander and migrate considerably over periods of several years.

In addition to the alternating submergence and exposure, the varying influences of fresh river water and saline marine waters cause physical conditions, principally temperature, salinity, and acidity, to vary more widely than in any other marine environment. Waves are generally very small because of the shallow bottom and short fetch. The mud of a tidal flat is characteristically rich in dissolved nutrients, plankton, and organic debris, and it supports large numbers of smaller mobile and burrowing animals, notably crabs, pelecypods, gastropods, and worms. Vegetation is generally sparse; if wave erosion is minimal, however, felts and mats of blue or blue-green algae may be present.

Tidal range in combination with the topography of the coast is quite important in this situation. The greater the tidal range, the more effect this phenomenon has on the coast. The slope of a beach or other coastal landform also is important, however, because a steep cliff provides only a nominal change in the area over which waves and currents can do their work even in a macro-tidal environment. On the other hand, a broad, gently sloping beach or tidal flat may experience a change in the shoreline of as much as 1 km (0.6 mile) during a tidal cycle in a macro-tidal setting. Examples of this situation occur in the Bay of Fundy and along the West German coast of the North Sea.

OTHER FACTORS AND PROCESSES

Climate is an extremely important factor in the development of coastal landforms. The elements of climate include rainfall, temperature, and wind.

Rainfall is important because it provides runoff in the form of streams and also is a factor in producing and transporting sediment to the coast. This fact gives rise to a marked contrast between the volume and type of sediment carried to the coast in a tropical environment and those in a desert environment.

Temperature is important for two quite different reasons. It is a factor in the physical weathering of sediments and rocks along the coast and in the adjacent drainage basins. This is particularly significant in cold regions where the freezing of water within cracks in rocks causes the rocks to fragment and thereby yield sediment. Some temperate and arctic regions have shore ice up to several months each year. Under these conditions there is no wave impact, and the coast becomes essentially static until the ice thaws or breaks up during severe storms. Such conditions prevail for three to four months along much of the coast of the Great Lakes in North America.

Wind is important primarily because of its relationship to waves. Coasts that experience prolonged and intense winds also experience high wave-energy conditions. Seasonal patterns in both wind direction and intensity can be translated directly into wave conditions. Wind also can be a key factor in directly forming coastal landforms, particularly coastal dunes. The persistence of onshore winds throughout much of the world's coast gives rise to sand dunes in all places where enough sediment is available and where there is a place for it to accumulate.

Gravity, too, plays a major role in coastal processes. Not only is it indirectly involved in processes associated with wind and waves but it also is directly involved through downslope movement of sediment and rock as well. This role is particularly evident along shoreline cliffs where waves attack the base of the cliffs and undercut the slope, resulting in the eventual collapse of rocks into the sea or their accumulation as debris at the base of the cliffs.

LANDFORMS OF EROSIONAL COASTS

There are two major types of coastal morphology: one is dominated by erosion and the other by deposition. They exhibit distinctly different landforms, though each type may contain some features of the other. In general, erosional coasts are those with little or no sediment, whereas depositional coasts are characterized by abundant sediment accumulation over the long term. Both temporal and geographic variations may occur in each of these coastal types.

Erosional coasts typically exhibit high relief and rugged topography. They tend to occur on the leading edge of lithospheric plates, the west coasts of both North and South America being excellent examples. Glacial activity also may give rise to erosional coasts, as in northern New England and in the Scandinavian countries. Typically, these coasts are dominated by exposed bedrock with steep slopes and high elevations adjacent to the shore. Although these coasts are erosional, the rate of shoreline retreat is slow due to the resistance of bedrock to erosion. The type of rock and its lithification are important factors in the rate of erosion.

SEA CLIFFS

The most widespread landforms of erosional coasts are sea cliffs. These very steep to vertical bedrock cliffs range from only a few metres high to hundreds of metres above sea level. Their vertical nature is the result of wave-induced erosion near sea level and the subsequent collapse of rocks at higher elevation. Cliffs that extend to the shoreline commonly have a notch cut into them where waves have battered the bedrock surface.

At many coastal locations there is a thin, narrow veneer of sediment forming a beach along the base of sea cliffs. This sediment may consist of sand, but it is more commonly composed of coarse material—cobbles or boulders. Beaches of this kind usually accumulate during relatively low wave-energy conditions and are removed during the stormy season when waves are larger. The coasts of California and Oregon contain many places where this situation prevails. The presence of even a narrow beach along a rocky coast provides the cliffs protection against direct wave attack and slows the rate of erosion.

WAVE-CUT PLATFORMS

At the base of most cliffs along a rocky coast one finds a flat surface at about the mid-tide elevation. This is a benchlike feature called a wave-cut platform, or wave-cut bench. Such surfaces may measure from a few metres to hundreds of metres wide and extend to the base of the adjacent cliff. They are formed by wave action on the bedrock along the coast. The formation process can take a long time, depending on the type of rock present. The existence of extensive wave-cut platforms thus implies that sea level did not fluctuate during the periods of formation. Multiple platforms of this type along a given reach of coast indicate various positions of sea level.

SEA STACKS

Erosion along rocky coasts occurs at various rates and is dependent both on the rock type and on the wave energy at a particular site. As a result of the above-mentioned conditions, wave-cut platforms may be incomplete, with erosional remnants on the horizontal wave-cut surface. These remnants are called sea stacks, and they provide a spectacular type of coastal landform. Some are many metres high and form isolated pinnacles on the otherwise smooth wave-cut surface. Because erosion is a continual process, these features are not permanent and will eventually be eroded, leaving no trace of their existence.

SEA ARCHES

Another spectacular type of erosional landform is the sea arch, which forms as the result of different rates of erosion typically due to the varied resistence of bedrock. These archways may have an arcuate or rectangular shape, with the opening extending below water level. The height of an arch can be up to tens of metres above sea level.

It is common for sea arches to form when a rocky coast undergoes erosion and a wave-cut platform develops.

Continued erosion can result in the collapse of an arch, leaving an isolated sea stack on the platform. Still further erosion removes the stack, and eventually only the wave-cut platform remains adjacent to the eroding coastal cliff.

LANDFORMS OF DEPOSITIONAL COASTS

Coasts adjacent to the trailing edge of lithospheric plates tend to have widespread coastal plains and low relief. The Atlantic and Gulf coasts of the United States are representative. Such coasts may have numerous estuaries and lagoons with barrier islands or may develop river deltas. They are characterized by an accumulation of a wide range of sediment types and by many varied coastal environments. The sediment is dominated by mud and sand; however, some gravel may be present, especially in the form of shell material.

Depositional coasts may experience erosion at certain times and places due to such factors as storms, depletion of sediment supply, and rising sea level. The latter is a continuing problem as the mean annual temperature of Earth rises and the ice caps melt. Nevertheless, the overall, long-range tendency along these coasts is that of sediment deposition.

All of the processes discussed at the beginning of this section are in evidence along depositional coasts. Waves, wave-generated currents, and tides significantly influence the development of depositional landforms. In general, waves exert energy that is distributed along the coast essentially parallel to it. This is accomplished by the waves themselves as they strike the shore and also by the long-shore currents that move along it. In contrast, tides tend to exert their influence perpendicular to the coast as they flood and ebb. The result is that the landforms that develop along some coasts are due primarily to wave processes while along other coasts they may be due mainly to tidal processes. Some coasts are the result of near equal balance between tide and wave processes. As a consequence, investigators speak of wave-dominated coasts, tide-dominated coasts, and mixed coasts.

A wave-dominated coast is one that is characterized by well-developed sand beaches typically formed on long barrier islands with a few widely spaced tidal inlets. The barrier islands tend to be narrow and rather low in elevation. Longshore transport is extensive, and the inlets are often small and unstable. Jetties are commonly placed along the inlet mouths to stabilize them and keep them open for navigation. The Texas and North Carolina coasts of the United States are excellent examples of this coastal type.

Tide-dominated coasts are not as widespread as those dominated by waves. They tend to develop where tidal range is high or where wave energy is low. The result is a coastal morphology that is dominated by funnel-shaped embayments and long sediment bodies oriented essentially perpendicular to the overall coastal trend. Tidal flats, salt marshes, and tidal creeks are extensive. The West German coast of the North Sea is a good example of such a coast.

Mixed coasts are those where both tidal and wave processes exert considerable influence. These coasts characteristically have short stubby barrier islands and numerous tidal inlets. The barriers commonly are wide at one end and narrow at the other. Inlets are fairly stable and have large sediment bodies on both their landward and seaward sides. The Georgia and South Carolina coasts of the United States typify a mixed coast.

JETTIES

Jetties are engineering structures connected with river, harbour, and coastal works. Regardless of their structural components and shape, all jetties are designed to influence the current or tide or to protect a harbour or beach from waves (breakwater). The two principal kinds of jetties are those constructed at river mouths and other coastal entrances and those used for the berthing of ships in harbours and offshore where harbour facilities are not available. Jettylike structures may be built out at intervals from the banks of rivers where a wide channel must be narrowed to concentrate the current and thus help maintain a navigable channel. These structures—variously termed spurs, spur dikes, and groins—may also be projected from the concave side of a river to retard bank erosion.

Jetties of open-pile or impervious-masonry construction may be built on each side of a navigation channel immediately outside the entrances to docks that must be entered through locks. These structures, sometimes called lead-in jetties, form a funnel-shaped entrance to or exit from the lock. They serve to protect vessels from river or tidal currents and to provide temporary mooring facilities; if of solid construction, they may serve also as breakwaters.

Entrance jetties are built at bay inlets, at entrances to harbours of the lagoon type, and at the mouths of rivers. They are also referred to as training jetties, because they "train," or confine and direct, the currents so as to maintain the channel by promoting scour and extend farther into deep water where currents slacken and deposit silt and other transported material; they also protect such entrances from the disturbing effects of littoral currents, sand drift, and wave action. Entrance jetties are usually constructed in pairs, either parallel or converging toward the seaward ends, and are of several structural types.

GENERAL COASTAL MORPHOLOGY

Depositional coasts can be described in terms of three primary large-scale types: (1) deltas, (2) barrier island/estuarine systems, and (3) strand-plain coasts. The latter two have numerous features in common.

DELTAS

An accumulation of sediment at the mouth of a river extending beyond the trend of the adjacent coast is called a delta. Deltas vary greatly in both size and shape, but they all require that more sediment is deposited at the river mouth than can be carried away by coastal processes. A delta also requires a shallow site for accumulation — namely, a gently sloping continental shelf.

The size of a delta is typically related to the size of the river, specifically to its discharge. The shape of a delta, on the other hand, is a result of the interaction of the river with tidal and wave processes along the coast.

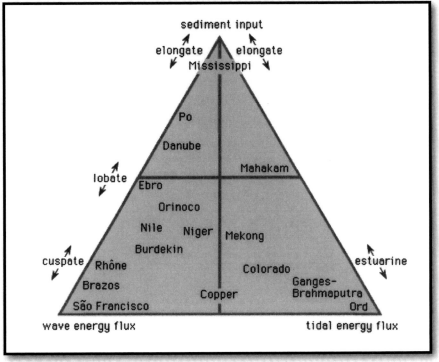

Classification of river deltas based on the three dominant processes that control delta morphology (see text). From W.E. Galloway, *Deltas, Models for Exploration* (1975); Houston Geological Society

A classification utilizing each of these three factors as end members provides a good way of considering the variation in delta morphology. River-dominated deltas are those where both wave and tidal current energy on the coast is low and the discharge of water and sediment are little affected by them. The result is an irregularly shaped delta with numerous digitate distributaries. The Mississippi Delta is a good example of a river-dominated delta.

Waves may remove much of the fine deltaic sediment and smooth the outer margin of the delta landform as well. This results in a smooth, cuspate delta that has few distributaries. The São Francisco Delta in Brazil is such a delta. Some wave-dominated deltas are strongly affected by longshore currents, and the river mouth is diverted markedly along the coast. The Sénégal Delta on the west coast of Africa is an example.

Tide-dominated deltas tend to be developed in wide, funnel-shaped configurations with long sand bodies that fan out from the coast. These sand bodies are oriented with the strong tidal currents of the delta. Tidal flats and salt marshes also are common. The Ord Delta in northern Australia and the Ganges-Brahmaputra Delta in Bangladesh are representative of such a deltaic type.

BARRIER ISLAND/ ESTUARINE SYSTEMS

Many depositional coasts display a complex of environments and landforms that typically occur together. Irregular coasts have numerous embayments, many of which are fed by streams. Such embayments are called estuaries, and they receive much sediment due to runoff from an adjacent coastal plain. Seaward of the estuaries are elongate barrier islands that generally parallel the shore. Consisting mostly of sand, they are formed primarily by waves and longshore currents. These barrier islands are typically separated from the mainland and may have lagoons, which are long, narrow, coastal bodies of water situated between the barrier and the mainland.

Most barrier islands contain a well-developed beach, coastal dunes, and various environments on their landward side, including tidal flats, marshes, or washover fans. Such coastal barriers are typically interrupted by tidal inlets, which provide circulation between the various coastal bays and the open marine environment. These inlets also are important pathways for organisms that migrate between coastal and open marine areas as well as for pleasure and commercial boat traffic.

STRAND-PLAIN COASTS

Some wave-dominated coasts do not contain estuaries and have no barrier island system. These coasts, however, do have beaches and dunes, and may even have coastal marshes. The term *strand plain* has been applied to coasts of this sort. Examples include parts of western Louisiana and eastern Texas. In most respects, they are similar in morphology to barrier islands but lack inlets.

BEACHES AND COASTAL DUNES

There are several specific landforms representative of coastal environments that are common to each of the three major categories described above. Especially prominent among these are beaches and dunes. They are the primary landforms on barrier islands, strand-plain coasts, and many deltas, particularly the wave-dominated variety.

BEACHES

Beaches are areas made up of sediments that accumulate along the sea or lake shores. The configuration and contours of a beach depends on the action of coastal processes, the kinds of sediment involved, and the rate of delivery of this sediment. There are three different kinds of beaches. The first occurs as a sediment strip bordering a rocky or cliffy coast; the second is the outer margin of a plain of marine or fluvial accumulation (free beaches); and the third, of fairly peculiar character, consists of the narrow sediment barriers stretching for dozens or even hundreds of kilometres parallel to the general direction of the coast. These barriers separate lagoons from the open sea and generally are dissected by some tidal inlets. Certain sediment forelands, such as spits, points, and tombolos (which connect an island with a mainland), also occasionally are called beaches.

The profile of an active beach varies greatly. Its form and dimensions depend on a number of factors, such as wave parameters, tide height, and sediment composition and distribution. The following, however, constitute some of the profile elements that commonly occur. At the upper part, above high sea level, a beach terrace is located, and there may be a series of beach ridges or berms created by

Tree-lined beach, Oahu, Hawaii. © Corbis

the waves of a previous major storm. This terrace surface is inclined seaward. The next element is a steeper, frontal beach slope or face, and beneath it a low-tide terrace may be developed. If the tides are high enough (more than 2 metres [6.6 feet]), the frontal slope may be more than 1 km (0.6 mile) in width in regions with abundant sand and a shallow bottom. In some areas the low-tide terrace terminates with another inclined shoreface, if the nearshore sea zone is rather deep. Finally, one or several parallel, submarine, long-shore bars with intervening troughs may exist along sandy shores; if present, these bars constitute the last profile element.

Some minor relief forms are usually present on the surface of sand beaches. These include oscillation ripples, swash or rill furrows, and the well-known beach cusps (concave seaward) at the beach margin.

In many countries the wind strongly affects the dynamics of the beach. The beach is exposed to the sea wind, and sand is usually blown off to the rear parts of the beach, where it forms small hummocks. As these join together, foredunes are being built, and, if the beach is well-supplied with sand in the right area, several rows of dunes will be formed. When the sand is abundant, dunes will shift to adjacent low-lying plains and may bury fertile soils, woods, and buildings.

If sand is no longer delivered to the region of developed dunes, gaps will form in the ridges parallel to the shore. In such zones, parabolic dunes with their summits coastward are created. After long stabilization, the summits of the parabolas may be broken through by the wind, thus gradually forming a series of ridges parallel to the prevailing winds.

Beach sands in temperate latitudes consist mainly of quartz, some feldspars, and a small percentage of heavy minerals. In the tropics, however, calcareous beaches composed of skeletal remnants of marine organisms and precipitated particles, such as oolites, are widespread.

BEACH PROFILE

A consideration of the beach must also include the seaward adjacent nearshore environment because the two are intimately related. The nearshore environment extends from the outer limit of the longshore bars that are usually present to the low-tide line. In areas where longshore bars are absent, it can be regarded as coincident with the surf zone. The beach extends from the low-tide line to the distinct change in slope and/or material landward of the unvegetated and active zone of sediment accumulation. It may consist of sand, gravel, or even mud, though sand is the most common beach material.

The beach profile typically can be divided into two distinct parts: (1) the seaward and relatively steep sloping foreshore, which is essentially the intertidal beach, and (2) the landward, nearly horizontal backshore. Beach profiles take on two different appearances, depending on conditions at any given time. During quiescent wave conditions, the beach is said to be accretional, and both the foreshore and backshore are present. During storm conditions, however, the beach experiences erosion, and the result is typically a profile that shows only the seaward sloping foreshore. Because the beach tends to repair itself during nonstorm periods, a cyclic pattern of profile shapes is common.

The nearshore zone is where waves steepen and break, and then re-form in their passage to the beach, where they break for the last time and surge up the foreshore. Much sediment is transported in this zone, both along the shore and perpendicular to it. During storms the waves tend to be steep, and erosion of the beach occurs with sediment transported offshore. The intervening calmer conditions permit sediment to be transported landward and rebuild the beach. Because wave conditions may change daily, the nature of the profile and the sediment on the foreshore portion of the beach may also change daily. This is the zone of continual change on the beach.

The backshore of the beach is not subjected to wave activity except during storm conditions. It is actually in the supra-tidal zone—i.e., the zone above high tide where inundation by water is caused not by regular astronomical tides but rather by storm-generated tides. During non-storm conditions the back-beach is relatively inactive except for wind action, which may move sediment. In most cases, there is an onshore component to the wind, and sediment is carried from the back-beach landward, typically forming dunes. Any obstruction on the back-beach, such as vegetation, pieces of driftwood, fences, or even trash discarded by people, results in wind-blown sand accumulation.

There are variations in beach forms along the shore as well as in those perpendicular to the shore. Most common is the rhythmic topography that is seen along the foreshore. A close look at the shoreline along most beaches will show that it is not straight or gently curved but rather that it displays a regularly undulating surface much like a low-amplitude sine curve. This is seen both on the plan view of the shoreline and the topography of the foreshore. The spacing is regular along a given reach of coast, but it may vary from place to place or from time to time at a given place. At some locations, concentrations of gravel or shells may develop, forming beach cusps (more or less triangular deposits that point seaward) during some wave conditions.

Although there is a common trend to the beach profile, some variation exists both because of energy conditions and because of the material making up the beach. Generally speaking, a beach that is accumulating sediment and experiencing low-energy conditions tends to have a steep foreshore, whereas the same beach would have a relatively gentle foreshore during storm conditions when erosion is prevalent. The grain size of beach sediment also is an important factor in the slope of the foreshore. In general, the coarser the constituent grains, the steeper the foreshore. Examples include the gravel beaches of New England, as contrasted to the gently sloping sand beaches of the Texas coast.

COASTAL DUNES

Immediately landward of the beach are commonly found large, linear accumulations of sand known as dunes. They form as the wind carries sediment from the beach in a landward direction and deposits it wherever an obstruction hinders further transport. Sediment supply is the key limiting factor in dune development and is the primary reason why some coastal dunes, such as those on the west Florida peninsula, are quite small, whereas others in such areas as the Texas coast and the Florida panhandle have large dunes.

Small wind-shadow dunes, or coppice mounds, actually may form on the backshore of the beach. If sediment continues to be supplied and beach erosion does not destroy them, these small sand accumulations will become foredunes, the seaward-most line of coastal dunes. It is in this fashion that a coast progrades, or grows seaward. Many barrier-island or strand-plain coasts exhibit numerous, essentially parallel dune ridges testifying to this type of growth.

The sediment in dunes tends to be fine to medium sand that is quite well sorted. Shell debris or other material is uncommon unless it is the same size or mass as the dune sand. There are various types of vegetation that grow on the dune surface and stabilize it. These grasses and vines often can be seen on the backshore portion of beaches as well. Dunes lacking vegetation are usually active and exhibit various signs of sand mobility. Most widespread are the nearly ubiquitous ripples that cover the dune surface. Large lobes of sand or even an entire dune may also move as wind blows across the dune. This activity results in cross stratification of the dune in large sweeping patterns of wedge-shaped packages of sand.

CHAPTER 6
GLACIAL LANDFORMS

G lacial landforms are made up of any product of flow-ing ice and meltwater. Such landforms are being produced today in glaciated areas, such as Greenland, Antarctica, and many of the world's higher mountain ranges. In addition, large expansions of present-day gla-ciers have recurred during the course of Earth's history. At the maximum of the last ice age, which ended about 20,000 to 15,000 years ago, more than 30 percent of Earth's land surface was covered by ice. Consequently, if they have not been obliterated by other landscape-modifying processes since that time, glacial landforms may still exist in regions that were once glaciated but are now devoid of glaciers.

Periglacial (near glacial) features , which form indepen-dently of glaciers, are nonetheless a product of the same cold climate that favours the development of glaciers, and so are treated here as well.

GENERAL CONSIDERATIONS

Before describing the different landforms produced by glaciers and their meltwater, the glacial environment and the processes responsible for the formation of such land-forms is briefly discussed.

TYPES OF GLACIERS

There are numerous types of glaciers, but it is sufficient here to focus on two broad classes: mountain, or valley, glaciers and continental glaciers, or ice sheets, (including ice caps).

Generally, ice sheets are larger than valley glaciers. The main difference between the two classes, however, is their relationship to the underlying topography. Valley glaciers are rivers of ice usually found in mountainous regions, and their flow patterns are controlled by the high relief in those areas. In map view, many large valley glacier systems, which have numerous tributary glaciers that join to form a large "trunk glacier," resemble the roots of a plant. Pancakelike ice sheets, on the other hand, are continuous over extensive areas and completely bury the underlying landscape beneath hundreds or thousands of metres of ice. Within continental ice sheets, the flow is directed more or less from the centre outward. At the periphery, however, where ice sheets are much thinner, they may be controlled by any substantial relief existing in the area. In this case, their borders may be lobate on a scale of a few kilometres, with tonguelike protrusions called outlet glaciers. Viewed by themselves, these are nearly indistinguishable from the lower reaches of a large valley glacier system. Consequently, many of the landforms produced by valley glaciers and continental ice sheets are similar or virtually identical, though they often differ in magnitude. Nonetheless, each type of glacier produces characteristic features and thus warrants separate discussion.

GLACIAL EROSION

Two processes, internal deformation and basal sliding, are responsible for the movement of glaciers under the influence of gravity. The temperature of glacier ice is a critical condition that affects these processes. For this reason, glaciers are classified into two main types, temperate and polar, according to their temperature regime. Temperate

A glacier at Denali National Park in Alaska.. DEA/M. Santini/De Agostini/Getty Images

glaciers are also called isothermal glaciers, because they exist at the pressure-melting point (the melting temperature of ice at a given pressure) throughout their mass. The ice in polar, or cold glaciers, in contrast, is below the pressure-melting point. Some glaciers have an intermediate thermal character. For example, subpolar glaciers are temperate in their interior parts, but their margins are cold-based. This classification is a broad generalization, however, because the thermal condition of a glacier may show wide variations in both space and time.

Internal deformation, or strain, in glacier ice is a response to shear stresses arising from the weight of the ice (ice thickness) and the degree of slope of the glacier surface. Internal deformation occurs by movement within and between individual ice crystals (slow creep) and by brittle failure (fracture), which arises when the mass of ice cannot adjust its shape rapidly enough by the creep process to take up the stresses affecting it. The relative importance of these two processes is greatly influenced by the temperature of the ice. Thus, fractures due to brittle failure under tension, known as crevasses, are usually much deeper in polar ice than they are in temperate ice.

The temperature of the basal ice is an important influence upon a glacier's ability to erode its bed. When basal temperatures are below the pressure-melting point, the ability of the ice mass to slide on the bed (basal sliding) is inhibited by the adhesion of the basal ice to the frozen bed beneath. Basal sliding is also diminished by the greater rigidity of polar ice: this reduces the rate of creep, which, in turn, reduces the ability of the more rigid ice to deform around obstacles on the glacier bed. Thus, the flow of cold-based glaciers is predominantly controlled by internal deformation, with proportionately low rates of basal sliding. For this reason, rates of abrasion are commonly low beneath polar glaciers, and slow rates of erosion commonly result. Equally, the volume of meltwater is frequently very low, so that the extent of sediments and landforms derived from polar glaciers is limited.

Temperate glaciers, being at the pressure-meeting point, move by both mechanisms, with basal sliding being the more important. It is this sliding that enables temperate glaciers to erode their beds and carve landforms so effectively. Ice is, however, much softer and has a much lower shear strength than most rocks, and pure ice alone is not capable of substantially eroding anything other than unconsolidated sediments. Most temperate glaciers have a basal debris zone from several centimetres to a few metres thick that contains varying amounts of rock debris in transit. In this respect, glaciers act rather like sheets of sandpaper; while the paper itself is too soft to sand wood, the adherent hard grains make it a powerful abrasive system. The analogy ends here, however, for the rock debris found in glaciers is of widely varying sizes—from the finest rock particles to large boulders—and also generally of varied types as it includes the different rocks that a glacier is overriding. For this reason, a glacially abraded surface usually bears many different "tool-marks," from microscopic scratches to gouges centimetres deep and tens of metres long. Over thousands of years glaciers may erode their substrate to a depth of several tens of metres by this mechanism, producing a variety of streamlined landforms typical of glaciated landscapes.

Several other processes of glacial erosion are generally included under the terms *glacial plucking* or *quarrying*. This process involves the removal of larger pieces of rock from the glacier bed. Various explanations for this phenomenon have been proposed. Some of the mechanisms suggested are based on differential stresses in the rock caused by ice being forced to flow around bedrock obstacles. High stress gradients are particularly important, and the resultant tensile stresses can pull the rock apart along pre-existing joints or crack systems. These pressures have been shown to be sufficient to fracture solid rock, thus making it available for removal by the ice flowing above it. Other possibilities include the forcing apart of rock by the pressure of crystallization produced beneath the glacier as water derived from the ice refreezes (regelation) or because of temperature fluctuations in cavities under the glacier. Still another possible mechanism involves hydraulic pressures of flowing water known to be present, at least temporarily, under nearly all temperate glaciers. It is hard to determine which process is dominant because access to the base of active glaciers is rarely possible. Nonetheless, investigators know that larger pieces of rock are plucked from the glacier bed and contribute to the number of abrasive "tools" available to the glacier at its base. Other sources for the rock debris in glacier ice may include rockfalls from steep slopes bordering a glacier or unconsolidated sediments overridden as a glacier advances.

GLACIAL DEPOSITION

Debris in the glacial environment may be deposited directly by the ice (till) or, after reworking, by meltwater streams (outwash). The resulting deposits are termed glacial drift.

As the ice in a valley glacier moves from the area of accumulation to that of ablation, it acts like a conveyor belt, transporting debris located beneath, within, and above the glacier toward its terminus or, in the case of an ice sheet, toward the outer margin. Near the glacier margin where the ice velocity decreases greatly is the zone of deposition. As the ice melts away, the debris that was originally frozen into the ice commonly forms a rocky and/or muddy blanket over the glacier margin. This layer often

slides off the ice in the form of mudflows. The resulting deposit is called a flow-till by some authors. On the
other hand, the debris may be laid down more or less in
place as the ice melts away around and beneath it. Such
deposits are referred to as melt-out till and sometimes as
ablation till. In many cases, the material located between
a moving glacier and its bedrock bed is severely sheared,
compressed, and "over-compacted." This type of deposit
is called lodgment till. By definition, till is any material
laid down directly or reworked by a glacier. Typically, it is
a mixture of rock fragments and boulders in a fine-grained
sandy or muddy matrix (non-stratified drift). The exact
composition of any particular till, however, depends on the
materials available to the glacier at the time of deposition.
Thus, some tills are made entirely of lake clays deformed
by an overriding glacier. Other tills are composed of river
gravels and sands that have been "bulldozed" and striated
during a glacial advance. Tills often contain some of the
tools that glaciers use to abrade their bed. These rocks and
boulders bear striations, grooves, and facets, and characteristic till-stones are commonly shaped like bullets or
flat-irons. Till-boulders of a rock type different from the
bedrock on which they are deposited are dubbed "erratics." In some cases, erratics with distinctive lithologies
can be traced back to their source, enabling investigators
to ascertain the direction of ice movement of ice sheets in
areas where striations either are absent or are covered by
till or vegetation.

Meltwater deposits, also called glacial outwash, are
formed in channels directly beneath the glacier or in
lakes and streams in front of its margin. In contrast to
till, outwash is generally bedded or laminated (stratified
drift), and the individual layers are relatively well sorted
according to grain size. In most cases, gravels and boulders in outwash are rounded and do not bear striations or

grooves on their surfaces, since these tend to wear off rapidly during stream transport. The grain size of individual deposits depends not only on the availability of different sizes of debris but also on the velocity of the depositing current and the distance from the head of the stream. Larger boulders are deposited by rapidly flowing creeks and rivers close to the glacier margin. Grain size of deposited material decreases with increasing distance from the glacier. The finest fractions, such as clay and silt, may be deposited in glacial lakes or ponds or transported all the way to the ocean.

Finally, it must be stressed that most glacier margins are constantly changing chaotic masses of ice, water, mud, and rocks. Ice-marginal deposits thus are of a highly variable nature over short distances, as is much the case with till and outwash as well.

EROSIONAL LANDFORMS

Glacial erosion is caused by two different processes: abrasion and plucking. Evidence of both processes appears in valley and continental glaciers. Even though these processes are at work across an entire glaciated valley or across large whole landscapes, abrasion and plucking can occur at smaller scales in the form of rock polish, striations, p-forms, and glacial grooves.

SMALL-SCALE FEATURES OF GLACIAL EROSION

Nearly all glacially scoured erosional landforms bear the tool-marks of glacial abrasion provided that they have not been removed by subsequent weathering. Even though these marks are not large enough to be called landforms, they constitute an integral part of any glacial landscape and thus warrant description here. The type of mark produced on a surface during glacial erosion depends on the size and shape of the gravel or rock that forms the tool, the pressure being applied to it, and the relative hardnesses of the tool and the substrate.

ROCK POLISH

The finest abrasive available to a glacier is the so-called rock flour produced by the constant grinding at the base of the ice. Rock flour acts like jewelers' rouge and produces microscopic scratches, which with time smooth and polish rock surfaces, often to a high lustre.

STRIATIONS

These are scratches visible to the naked eye, ranging in size from fractions of a millimetre to a few millimetres deep and a few millimetres to centimetres long. Large striations produced by a single tool may be several centimetres deep and wide and tens of metres long.

Because the striation-cutting tool was dragged across the rock surface by the ice, the long axis of a striation indicates the direction of ice movement in the immediate vicinity of that striation. Determination of the regional direction of movement of former ice sheets, however, requires measuring hundreds of striation directions over an extended area because ice moving close to the base of a glacier is often locally deflected by bedrock obstacles. Even when such a regional study is conducted, additional information is frequently needed in low-relief areas to determine which end of the striations points down-ice toward the former outer margin of the glacier. On an outcrop scale, such information can be gathered by studying "chatter marks." These crescentic gouges and lunate fractures are caused by the glacier dragging a rock or boulder over a hard and brittle rock surface and forming a series of sickle-shaped gouges. Such depressions in the bedrock are steep-sided on their "up-glacier" face and have a lower slope on their down-ice side. Depending on whether the horns of the sickles point up the glacier or down it, the chatter marks are designated crescentic gouges or lunate fractures. Another small-scale feature that allows absolute determination of the direction in which the ice moved is what is termed knob-and-tail. A knob-and-tail is formed during glacial abrasion of rocks that locally contain spots more resistant than the surrounding rock, as is the case, for example, with silicified fossils in limestone. After abrasion has been active for some time, the harder parts of the rock form protruding knobs as the softer rock is preferentially eroded away around them. During further erosion, these protrusions protect the softer rock on their lee side and a tail forms there, pointing from the knob to the margin of the glacier. The scale of these features depends primarily on the size of the inhomogeneities in the rock and ranges from fractions of millimetres to metres.

P-FORMS AND GLACIAL GROOVES

These features, which extend several to tens of metres in length, are of uncertain origin. P-forms (P for plastically molded) are smooth-walled, linear depressions which may be straight, curved, or sometimes hairpin-shaped and measure tens of centimetres to metres in width and depth. Their cross sections are often semicircular to parabolic, and their walls are commonly striated parallel to their long axis, indicating that ice once flowed in them. Straight P-forms are frequently called glacial grooves, even though the term is also applied to large striations, which, unlike the P-forms, were cut by a single tool. Some researchers believe that P-forms were not carved directly by the ice but rather were eroded by pressurized mud slurries flowing beneath the glacier.

EROSIONAL LANDFORMS OF VALLEY GLACIERS

Many of the world's higher mountain ranges—e.g., the Alps, the North and South American Cordilleras, the Himalayas, and the Southern Alps in New Zealand, as well as the mountains of Norway, including those of Spitsbergen—are partly glaciated today. During periods of the Pleistocene, such glaciers were greatly enlarged and filled most of the valleys with ice, even reaching far beyond the mountain front in certain places. Most scenic alpine landscapes featuring sharp mountain peaks, steep-sided valleys, and innumerable lakes and waterfalls are a product of several periods of glaciation.

Erosion is generally greater than deposition in the upper reaches of a valley glacier, whereas deposition exceeds erosion closer to the terminus. Accordingly, erosional landforms dominate the landscape in the high areas of glaciated mountain ranges.

CIRQUES, TARNS, U-SHAPED VALLEYS, ARÊTES, AND HORNS

The heads of most glacial valleys are occupied by one or several cirques (or corries). A cirque is an amphitheatre-shaped hollow with the open end facing down-valley. The back is formed by an arcuate cliff called the headwall. In an ideal cirque, the headwall is semicircular in plan view. This situation, however, is generally found only in cirques cut into flat plateaus. More common are headwalls angular in map view due to irregularities in height along their perimeter. The bottom of many cirques is a shallow basin, which may contain a lake. This basin and the base of the adjoining headwall usually show signs of extensive glacial abrasion and plucking. Even though the exact process of cirque formation is not entirely understood, it seems that the part of the headwall above the glacier retreats by frost shattering and ice wedging. The rock debris then falls either onto the surface of the glacier or into the randkluft or bergschrund. Both names describe the crevasse between the ice at the head of the glacier and the cirque headwall. The rocks on the surface of the glacier are successively buried by snow and incorporated into the ice of the glacier. Because of a downward velocity component in the ice in the accumulation zone, the rocks are eventually moved to the base of the glacier. At that point, these rocks, in addition to the rock debris from the bergschrund, become the tools with which the glacier erodes, striates, and polishes the base of the headwall and the bottom of the cirque.

During the initial growth and final retreat of a valley glacier, the ice often does not extend beyond the cirque. Such a cirque glacier is probably the main cause for the formation of the basin scoured into the bedrock bottom of many cirques. Sometimes these basins are "over-deepened" several tens of metres and contain lakes called tarns.

In contrast to the situation in a stream valley, all debris falling or sliding off the sides and the headwalls of a glaciated valley is immediately removed by the flowing ice. Moreover, glaciers are generally in contact with a much larger percentage of a valley's cross section than equivalent rivers or creeks. Thus glaciers tend to erode the bases of the valley walls to a much greater extent than do streams, whereas a stream erodes an extremely narrow line along the lowest part of a valley. The slope of the adjacent valley walls depends on the stability of the bedrock and the angle of repose of the weathered rock debris accumulating at the base of and on the valley walls. For this reason, rivers tend to form V-shaped valleys. Glaciers, which inherit V-shaped stream valleys, reshape them drastically by first removing all loose debris along the base of the valley walls and then preferentially eroding the bedrock along the base and lower sidewalls of the valley. In this way, glaciated valleys assume a characteristic parabolic or U-shaped cross profile, with relatively wide and flat bottoms and steep, even vertical sidewalls. By the same process, glaciers tend to narrow the bedrock divides between the upper reaches of neighbouring parallel valleys to jagged, knife-edge ridges known as arêtes. Arêtes also form between two cirques facing in opposite directions. The low spot, or saddle, in the arête between two cirques is called a col. A higher mountain often has three or more cirques arranged in a radial pattern on its flanks. Headward erosion of these cirques finally leaves only a sharp peak flanked by nearly vertical headwall cliffs, which are separated by arêtes. Such glacially eroded mountains are termed horns, the most widely known of which is the Matterhorn in the Swiss Alps.

HANGING VALLEYS

Large valley glacier systems consist of numerous cirques and smaller valley glaciers that feed ice into a large trunk glacier. Because of its greater ice discharge, the trunk glacier has greater erosive capability in its middle and lower reaches than smaller tributary glaciers that join it there. The main valley is therefore eroded more rapidly than the side valleys. With time, the bottom of the main valley becomes lower than the elevation of the tributary valleys. When the ice has retreated, the tributary valleys are left joining the main valley at elevations substantially higher than its bottom. Tributary valleys with such unequal or discordant junctions are called hanging valleys. In extreme cases where a tributary joins the main valley high up in the steep part of the U-shaped trough wall, waterfalls may form after deglaciation, as in Yosemite and Yellowstone national parks in the western United States.

PATERNOSTER LAKES

Some glacial valleys have an irregular, longitudinal bedrock profile, with alternating short, steep steps and longer, relatively flat portions. Even though attempts have been made to explain this feature in terms of some inherent characteristic of glacial flow, it seems more likely that differential erodibility of the underlying bedrock is the real cause of the phenomenon. Thus the steps are probably formed by harder or less fractured bedrock, whereas the flatter portions between the steps are underlain by softer or more fractured rocks. In some cases, these softer areas have been excavated by a glacier to form shallow bedrock basins. If several of these basins are occupied by lakes along one glacial trough in a pattern similar to beads on a string, they are called paternoster (Latin: "our father") lakes by analogy with a string of rosary beads.

DRUMLINS

A drumlin is an oval or elongated hill believed to have been formed by the streamlined movement of glacial ice sheets across rock debris, or till. The name is derived from the Gaelic word *druim* ("rounded hill," or "mound") and first appeared in 1833.

Drumlins are generally found in broad lowland regions, with their long axes roughly parallel to the path of glacial flow. Although they come in a variety of shapes, the glacier side is always high and steep, while the lee side is smooth and tapers gently in the direction of ice movement. Drumlins can vary widely in size, with lengths from 1 to 2 km (0.6 to 1.2 miles), heights from 15 to 30 metres (50 to 100 feet), and widths from 400 to 600 metres (1,300 feet to 1,970 feet).

ROCHES MOUTONNÉES

These structures are bedrock knobs or hills that have a gently inclined, glacially abraded, and streamlined stoss side (i.e., one that faces the direction from which the overriding glacier impinged) and a steep, glacially plucked lee side. They are generally found where jointing or fracturing in the bedrock allows the glacier to pluck the lee side of the obstacle. In plan view, their long axes are often, but not always, aligned with the general direction of ice movement. Both roches moutonnées and rock drumlins range in length from several metres to several kilometres and in height from tens of centimetres to hundreds of metres. They are typical of both valley and continental glaciers. The larger ones, however, are restricted to areas of continental glaciation.

Most drumlins are composed of till, but they may vary greatly in their composition. Some contain significant amounts of gravels, whereas others are made up of rock underlying the surface till (rock drumlins). Drumlins are often associated with smaller, glacially streamlined bedrock forms known as roches moutonnées.

Drumlins are commonly found in clusters numbering in the thousands. Often arranged in belts, they disrupt drainage so that small lakes and swamps may form between them. Large drumlin fields are located in central Wisconsin and in central New York; in northwestern Canada; in southwestern Nova Scotia; and in Ireland.

EROSIONAL LANDFORMS OF CONTINENTAL GLACIERS

In contrast to valley glaciers, which form exclusively in areas of high altitude and relief, continental glaciers, including the great ice sheets of the past, occur in high and middle latitudes in both hemispheres, covering landscapes that range from high alpine mountains to low-lying areas with negligible relief. Therefore, the landforms produced by continental glaciers are more diverse and widespread. Yet, just like valley glaciers, they have an area where erosion is the dominant process and an area close to their margins where net deposition generally occurs. The capacity of a continental glacier to erode its substrate has been a subject of intense debate. All of the areas formerly covered by ice sheets show evidence of areally extensive glacial scouring. The average depth of glacial erosion during the Pleistocene probably did not exceed a few tens of metres, however. This is much less than the deepening of glacial valleys during mountain glaciation. One of the reasons for the apparent limited erosional capacity of continental ice sheets in areas of low relief may be the scarcity of tools available to them in these regions. Rocks cannot fall onto a continental ice sheet in the accumulation zone, because the entire landscape is buried. Thus, all tools must be quarried by the glacier from the underlying bedrock. With time, this task becomes increasingly difficult as bedrock obstacles are abraded and streamlined. Nonetheless, the figure for depth of glacial erosion during the Pleistocene cited above is an average value, and locally several hundreds of metres of bedrock were apparently removed by the great ice sheets. Such enhanced erosion seems concentrated at points where the glaciers flowed from hard, resistant bedrock onto softer rocks or where glacial flow was channelized into outlet glaciers.

As a continental glacier expands, it strips the underlying landscape of the soil and debris accumulated at the preglacial surface as a result of weathering. The freshly exposed harder bedrock is then eroded by abrasion and plucking. During this process, bedrock obstacles are shaped into streamlined "whaleback" forms, such as roches moutonnées and rock drumlins. The adjoining valleys are scoured into rock-floored basins with the tools plucked from the lee sides of roches moutonnées. The long axes of the hills and valleys are often preferentially oriented in the direction of ice flow. An area totally composed of smooth whaleback forms and basins is called a streamlined landscape.

Streams cannot erode deep basins because water cannot flow uphill. Glaciers, on the other hand, can flow uphill over obstacles at their base as long as there is a sufficient slope on the upper ice surface pointing in that particular direction. Therefore the great majority of the innumerable lake basins and small depressions in formerly glaciated areas can only be a result of glacial erosion. Many of these lakes, such as the Finger Lakes in the U.S. state of New York, are aligned parallel to the direction of regional ice flow. Other basins seem to be controlled by preglacial drainage systems. Yet, other depressions follow the structure of the bedrock, having been preferentially scoured out of areas underlain by softer or more fractured rock.

A number of the largest freshwater lake basins in the world (e.g., the Great Lakes or the Great Slave Lake and Great Bear Lake in Canada) are situated along the margins of the Precambrian shield of North America. Many researchers believe that glacial erosion was especially effective at these locations because the glaciers could easily abrade the relatively soft sedimentary rocks to the south with hard, resistant crystalline rocks brought from the shield areas that lie to the north. Nonetheless, further research is necessary to determine how much of the deepening of these features can be ascribed to glacial erosion, as opposed to other processes such as tectonic activity or preglacial stream erosion.

FJORDS

Fjords are long narrow arms of the sea. Fjords are found along some steep, high-relief coastlines where continental glaciers formerly flowed into the sea. They are deep, narrow valleys with U-shaped cross sections that often extend inland for tens or hundreds of kilometres and are now partially drowned by the ocean. These troughs are typical of the Norwegian coast, but they also are found in Canada, Alaska, Iceland, Greenland, Antarctica, New Zealand, and southernmost Chile.

Fjords commonly are deeper in their middle and upper reaches than at the seaward end. This results from the greater erosive power of the glaciers closer to their source, where they are moving most actively and vigorously. Because of the comparatively shallow thresholds of fjords, the bottoms of many have stagnant water and are rich in black mud containing hydrogen sulfide. The floor and steep walls of fjords show ample evidence of glacial erosion. The long profile of many fjords, including alternating basins and steps, is very similar to that of glaciated valleys. Toward the mouth, fjords may reach great depths, as in the case of Sogn Fjord in southern Norway where the maximum water depth exceeds 1,300 metres (about 4,300 feet). At the mouth of a fjord itself, however, the floor rises steeply to create a rock threshold, and water depths decrease markedly. At Sogn Fjord the water at this "threshold" is only 150 metres (about 500 feet) deep, and in many fjords the rock platform is covered by only a few metres of water.

The exact origin of fjords is still a matter of debate. While some scientists favour a glacial origin, others believe that much of the relief of fjords is a result of tectonic activity and that glaciers only slightly modified preexisting large valleys. In order to erode Sogn Fjord to its present depth, the glacier occupying it during the maximum of the Pleistocene must have been 1,800 to 1,900 metres (5,900 to 6,200 feet) thick. Such an ice thickness may seem extreme, but even now, during an interglacial period, the Skelton Glacier in Antarctica has a maximum thickness of about 1,450 metres (about 4,700 feet). This outlet glacier of the Antarctic ice sheet occupies a trough, which in places is more than 1 km (0.6 mile) below sea level and would become a fjord in the event of a large glacial retreat.

Glacial erosion produces U-shaped valleys, and fjords are characteristically so shaped. Because the lower (and more horizontally inclined) part of the U is far underwater, the visible walls of fjords may rise vertically for hundreds of feet from the water's edge, and close to the shore the water may be many hundreds of feet deep. In some fjords small streams plunge hundreds of feet over the edge of the fjord; some of the world's highest waterfalls are of this type. Fjords commonly have winding channels and occasional sharp corners. In many cases the valley, floored with glacial debris, extends inland into the mountains; sometimes a small glacier remains at the valley's head. The river

Scenic fjord, or sea inlet, winding deep into the mountainous coast of western Norway. Bob and Ira Spring

that formed the original valley commonly reestablishes itself on the upper valley floor after the disappearance of the ice and begins to build a delta at the fjord's head. Often this delta is the only place on the fjord where villages and farms can be established.

DEPOSITIONAL LANDFORMS

Glacial landforms can also be created by deposition. Moving ice can pick up and transport material, sometimes forcibly removing bits of rock from the sides of mountains. Advancing glacial ice pushes soil and other material before it. At the fringes of the glacier, this mass of till forms moraines. The movement of tremendous amounts of ice across Earth's surface scours exposed bedrock and alters the shapes of hills during its passage over them. Meltwater flowing from glaciers also transports sediment and other debris. In addition, when temperatures increase as a result of seasonal cycles or long-term changes in climate, pockets of ice that melt in low-lying areas may form glacial lakes and streams.

DEPOSITIONAL LANDFORMS OF VALLEY GLACIERS

The depositional landforms that result from the movement of valley glaciers are very similar to those produced by continental glaciers. The landforms resulting from continental glaciers, however, tend to be larger. In valleys, moraines and flutes are among the most common glacial landforms.

MORAINES

As a glacier moves along a valley, it picks up rock debris from the valley walls and floor, transporting it in, on, or under the ice. As this material reaches the lower parts of the glacier where ablation is dominant, it is concentrated along the glacier margins as more and more debris melts out of the ice. If the position of the glacier margin is constant for an extended amount of time, larger accumulations of glacial debris (till) will form at the glacier margin. In addition, a great deal of material is rapidly flushed through and out of the glacier by meltwater streams flowing under, within, on, and next to the glacier. Part of this streamload is deposited in front of the glacier close to its snout. There, it may mix with material brought by, and melting out from, the glacier as well as with material washed in from other, nonglaciated tributary valleys. If the glacier then advances or readvances after a time of retreat, it will "bulldoze" all the loose material in front of it into a ridge of chaotic debris that closely hugs the shape of the glacier snout. Any such accumulation of till melted out directly from the glacier or piled into a ridge by the glacier is a moraine. Large valley glaciers are capable of forming moraines a few hundred metres high and many hundreds of metres wide. Linear accumulations of till formed immediately in front of or on the lower end of the glacier are end moraines. The moraines formed along the valley slopes next to the side margins of the glacier are termed lateral moraines. During a single glaciation, a glacier may form many such moraine arcs, but all the smaller moraines, which may have been produced during standstills or short advances while the glacier moved forward to its outermost ice position, are generally destroyed as the glacier resumes its advance. The end moraine of largest extent formed by the glacier (which may not be as extensive as the largest ice advance) during a given glaciation is called the terminal moraine of that glaciation. Successively smaller moraines formed during standstills or small readvances as the glacier retreats from the terminal moraine position are recessional moraines.

KAMES

Kames are moundlike hills of poorly sorted drift, mostly sand and gravel, deposited at or near the terminus of a glacier. A kame may be produced either as a delta of a meltwater stream or as an accumulation of debris let down onto the ground surface by the melting glacier. A group of closely associated kames is called a kame field, or kame complex, and may be interspersed with kettles or kettle lakes. A kame terrace is produced when a meltwater stream deposits its sediments between the ice mass and the valley wall. In small areas, kames may form the terminal moraine.

FLUTES

The depositional equivalent of erosional knob-and-tail structures are known as flutes. Close to the lower margin, some glaciers accumulate so much debris beneath them that they actually glide on a bed of pressurized muddy till. As basal ice flows around a pronounced bedrock knob or a boulder lodged in the substrate, a cavity often forms in the ice on the lee side of the obstacle because of the high viscosity of the ice. Any pressurized muddy paste present under the glacier may then be injected into this cavity and deposited as an elongate tail of till, or flute. The size depends mainly on the size of the obstacle and on the availability of subglacial debris. Flutes vary in height from a few centimetres to tens of metres and in length from tens of centimetres to kilometres, even though very large flutes are generally limited to continental ice sheets.

DEPOSITIONAL LANDFORMS OF CONTINENTAL GLACIERS

Many of the deposits of continental ice sheets are very similar to those of valley glaciers. Terminal, end, and recessional moraines are formed by the same process as with valley glaciers, but they can be much larger. Morainic ridges may be laterally continuous for hundreds of kilometres, hundreds of metres high, and several kilometres wide. Since each moraine forms at a discreet position of the ice margin, plots of end moraines on a map of suitable scale allow the reconstruction of ice sheets at varying stages during their retreat.

In addition to linear accumulations of glacial debris, continental glaciers often deposit a more or less continuous, thin (less than 10 metres [about 33 feet]) sheet of till over large areas, which is called ground moraine. This type of moraine generally has a "hummocky" topography of low relief, with alternating small till mounds and depressions. Swamps or lakes typically occupy the low-lying areas. Flutes are a common feature found in areas covered by ground moraine.

Another depositional landform associated with continental glaciation is the drumlin, a streamlined, elongate mound of sediment. Such structures often occur in groups of tens or hundreds, which are called drumlin fields. The long axis of individual drumlins is usually aligned parallel to the direction of regional ice flow. In long profile, the stoss side of a drumlin is steeper than the lee side. Some drumlins consist entirely of till, while others have bedrock cores draped with till. The till in many drumlins has been shown to have a "fabric" in which the long axes of the individual rocks and sand grains are aligned parallel to the ice flow over the drumlin. Even though the details of the process are not fully understood, drumlins seem to form subglacially close to the edge of an ice sheet, often directly down-ice from large lake basins overridden by the ice during an advance. The difference between a rock drumlin and a drumlin is that the former is an erosional bedrock knob, whereas the latter is a depositional till feature.

KETTLES

A depression in a glacial outwash drift made by the melting of a detached mass of glacial ice that became wholly or partly buried is called a kettle, or kettle hole. The occurrence of these stranded ice masses is thought to be the result of gradual accumulation of outwash atop the irregular glacier terminus. Kettles may range in size from 5 m (15 feet) to 13 km (8 miles) in diameter and up to 45 metres (147 feet) in depth. When filled with water they are called kettle lakes. Most kettles are circular in shape because melting blocks of ice tend to become rounded; distorted or branching depressions may result from extremely irregular ice masses.

Two types of kettles are recognized: a depression formed from a partially buried ice mass by the sliding of unsupported sediment into the space left by the ice and a depression formed from a completely buried ice mass by the collapse of overlying sediment. By either process, small kettles may be formed from ice blocks that were not left as the glacier retreated but rather were later floated into place by shallow meltwater streams. Kettles may occur singly or in groups; when large numbers are found together, the terrain appears as mounds and basins and is called kettle and kame topography.

MELTWATER DEPOSITS

Much of the debris in the glacial environment of both valley and continental glaciers is transported, reworked, and laid down by water. Whereas glaciofluvial deposits are formed by meltwater streams, glaciolacustrine sediments accumulate at the margins and bottoms of glacial lakes and ponds.

GLACIOFLUVIAL DEPOSITS

The discharge of glacial streams is highly variable, depending on the season, time of day, and cloud cover. Maximum discharges occur during the afternoon on warm, sunny summer days and minima on cold winter mornings. Beneath or within a glacier, the water flows in tunnels and is generally pressurized during periods of high discharge. In addition to debris washed in from unglaciated highlands adjacent to the glacier, a glacial stream can pick up large amounts of debris along its path at the base of the glacier. For this reason, meltwater streams issuing forth at the snout of a valley glacier or along the margin of an ice sheet are generally laden to transporting capacity with debris. Beyond the glacier margin, the water, which is no longer confined by the walls of the ice tunnel, spreads out and loses some of its velocity. Because of the decreased velocity, the stream must deposit some of its load. As a result, the original stream channel is choked with sediments, and the stream is forced to change its course around the obstacles, often breaking up into many winding and shifting channels separated by sand and gravel bars. The highly variable nature of the sediments laid down by such a braided stream reflects the unstable environment in which they form. Lenses of fine-grained, cross-bedded sands are often interbedded laterally and vertically with stringers of coarse, bouldery gravel. Since the amount of sediment laid down generally decreases with distance from the ice margin, the deposit is often wedge-shaped in cross section, ideally gently sloping off the end moraine formed at that ice position and thinning downstream. The outwash is then said to be "graded to" that particular moraine. In map view, the shape of the deposit depends on the surrounding topography. Where the valleys are deep enough not to be buried by the glaciofluvial sediments, as in most mountainous regions, the resulting elongate, planar deposits are termed valley trains. On the other hand, in low-relief areas the deposits of several ice-marginal streams may merge to form a wide outwash plain, or sandur.

If the ice margin stabilizes at a recessional position during glacial retreat, another valley train or sandur may be formed inside of the original one. Because of the downstream thinning of the outwash at any one point in the valley, the recessional deposit will be lower than and inset into the outer, slightly older outwash plain. Flat-topped remnants of the older plain may be left along the valley sides; these are called terraces. Ideally each recessional ice margin has a terrace graded to it, and these structures can be used in addition to moraines to reconstruct the positions of ice margins through time. In some cases where the glacier either never formed moraines or where the moraines were obliterated by the outwash or postglacial erosion, terraces are the only means of ice margin reconstruction.

Streams that flow over the terminus of a glacier often deposit stratified drift in their channels and in depressions on the ice surface. As the ice melts away, this ice-contact stratified drift slumps and partially collapses to form stagnant ice deposits. Isolated mounds of bedded sands and gravels deposited in this manner are called kames. Kame terraces form in a similar manner but between the lateral margin of a glacier and the valley wall. Glacial geologists sometimes employ the term *kame moraine* to describe deposits of stratified drift laid down at an ice margin in the arcuate shape of a moraine. Some researchers, however, object to the use of the term moraine in this context because the deposit is not composed of till.

In some cases, streams deposit stratified drift in subglacial or englacial tunnels. As the ice melts away, these sinuous channel deposits may be left as long linear gravel ridges called eskers. Some eskers deposited by the great ice sheets of the Pleistocene can be traced for hundreds of kilometres, even though most esker segments are only a few hundred metres to kilometres long and a few to tens of metres high.

ESKERS

Long, narrow, winding ridges composed of stratified sand and gravel deposited by a subglacial or englacial meltwater stream are called eskers. Eskers may range from 5 to 50 metres (16 to 160 feet in height, from 500 metres (160 to 1,600 feet) in width, and a few hundred feet to tens of miles in length. They may occur unbroken or as detached segments. The sediment is sorted according to grain size, and cross-laminations that show only one flow direction commonly occur. Thus

eskers are considered to be channel deposits (left by streams that flowed through tunnels in and below the ice) that were let down onto the ground surface as the glacier retreated. Esker formation presumably takes place after a glacier stagnates, because movement of the ice would likely spread the material and produce ground moraine. Notable areas of eskers are found in Maine, U.S.; Canada; Ireland; and Sweden. Because of ease of access, esker deposits often are quarried for their sand and gravel for construction purposes.

Eskers, narrow ridges of gravel and sand left by a retreating glacier, winding through western Nunavut, Canada, near the Thelon River. © Richard Alexander Cooke III

Kettles, potholes, or ice pits are steep-sided depressions typical of many glacial and glaciofluvial deposits. Kettles form when till or outwash is deposited around ice blocks that have become separated from the active glacier by ablation. Such "stagnant" ice blocks may persist insulated under a mantle of debris for hundreds of years. When they finally melt, depressions remain in their place, bordered by slumped masses of the surrounding glacial deposits. Many of the lakes in areas of glacial deposition are water-filled kettles and so are called kettle lakes. If a sandur or valley train contains many kettles, it is referred to as a pitted outwash plain.

GLACIOLACUSTRINE DEPOSITS

Glacial and proglacial lakes are found in a variety of environments and in considerable numbers. Erosional lake basins have already been mentioned, but many lakes are formed as streams are dammed by the ice itself, by glacial deposits, or by a combination of these factors. Any lake that remains at a stable level for an extended period of time (e.g., hundreds or thousands of years) tends to form a perfectly horizontal, flat, terracelike feature along its beach. Such a bench may be formed by wave erosion of the bedrock or glacial sediments that form the margin of the lake, and it is called a wave-cut bench. On the other hand, it may be formed by deposition of sand and gravel from long-shore currents along the margin of the lake, in which case it is referred to as a beach ridge. The width of these shorelines varies from a few metres to several hundred metres. As the lake level is lowered due to the opening of another outlet or downcutting of the spillway, new, lower shorelines may be formed. Most former or existing glacial lakes (e.g., the Great Salt Lake and the Great Lakes in North America) have several such shorelines that can be used both to determine the former size and depth of now-extinct or shrunken lakes and to determine the amount of differential postglacial uplift because they are now tilted slightly from their original horizontal position.

Where a stream enters a standing body of water, it is forced to deposit its bedload. The coarser gravel and sand are laid down directly at the mouth of the stream as successive, steeply inclined foreset beds. The finer, suspended silt and clay can drift a bit farther into the lake, where they are deposited as almost flat-lying bottomset beds. As the sediment builds out farther into the lake (or ocean), the river deposits a thin veneer of subhorizontal gravelly topset beds over the foreset units. Because the foreset–topset complex often has the shape of a triangle with the mouth of the stream at one apex, such a body of sediment is called a delta. Many gravel and sand pits are located in deltas of former glacial lakes.

The flat-lying, fine-grained bottomset beds of many large former glacial lakes filled in and buried all of the pre-existing relief and are now exposed, forming perfectly flat lake plains. Cuts into these sediments often reveal rhythmically interbedded silts and clays. Some of these so-called rhythmites have been shown to be the result of seasonal changes in the proglacial environment. During the warmer summer months, the meltwater streams carry silt and clay into the lakes, and the silt settles out of suspension more rapidly than the clay. A thicker, silty summer layer is thus deposited. During the winter, as the surface of the lake freezes and the meltwater discharge into it ceases, the clays contained in the lake water slowly settle out of suspension to form a thin winter clay layer. Such lacustrine deposits with annual silt and clay "couplets" are known as varves.

PERIGLACIAL LANDFORMS

In the cold, or periglacial (near-glacial), areas adjacent to and beyond the limit of glaciers, a zone of intense freeze-thaw activity produces periglacial features and landforms. This happens because of the unique behaviour of water as it changes from the liquid to the solid state. As water freezes, its volume increases about 9 percent. This is often combined with the process of differential ice growth, which traps air, resulting in an even greater increase in volume. If confined in a crack or pore space, such ice and air mixtures can exert pressures of about 200,000 kilopascals (29,000 pounds per square inch). This is enough to break the enclosing rock. Thus freezing water can be a powerful agent of physical weathering. If multiple freeze-and-thaw cycles occur, the growth of ice crystals fractures and moves material by means of frost shattering and frost heaving, respectively. In addition, in permafrost regions where the ground remains frozen all year, characteristic landforms are formed by perennial ice.

FELSENMEERS, TALUS, AND ROCK GLACIERS

In nature, the tensional strength of most rocks is exceeded by the pressure of water crystallizing in cracks. Thus, repeated freezing and thawing not only forms potholes in poorly constructed roads but also is capable of reducing exposed bedrock outcrops to rubble. Many high peaks are covered with frost-shattered angular rock fragments. A larger area blanketed with such debris is called a felsenmeer, from the German for "sea of rocks." The rock fragments can be transported downslope by flowing water or frost-induced surface creep, or they may fall off the cliff from which they were wedged by the ice. Accumulations of this angular debris at the base of steep slopes are known as talus. Owing to the steepness of the valley sides of many glacial troughs, talus is commonly found in formerly glaciated mountain regions. Talus cones are formed when the debris coming from above is channelized on its way to the base of the cliff in rock chutes. As the talus cones of neighbouring chutes grow over time, they may coalesce to form a composite talus apron.

In higher mountain regions, the interior of thick accumulations of talus may remain at temperatures below freezing all year. Rain or meltwater percolating into the interstices between the rocks freezes over time, filling the entire pore space. In some cases, enough ice forms to enable the entire mass of rock and ice to move downhill like a glacier. The resulting massive, lobate, mobile feature is called a rock glacier. Some rock glaciers have been shown to contain pure ice under a thick layer of talus with some interstitial ice. These features may be the final retreat stages of valley glaciers buried under talus.

PERMAFROST, PATTERNED GROUND, SOLIFLUCTION DEPOSITS, AND PINGOS

Permafrost is ground that remains perennially frozen. It covers about 20–25 percent of Earth's land surface today. The "active layer" of soil close to the surface of permafrost regions undergoes many seasonal and daily freeze-thaw cycles. The constant change in the volume of water tends to move the coarser particles in the soil to the surface. Further frost heaving arranges the stones and rocks according to their sizes to produce patterned ground. Circular arrangements of the larger rocks are termed stone rings. When neighbouring stone rings coalesce, they form polygonal stone nets. On steeper slopes, stone rings and stone nets are often stretched into stone stripes by slow downhill motion of the soggy active layer of the permafrost. In other areas, patterned ground is formed by vertical or subvertical polygonal cracks, which are initiated in the soil by contraction during extremely cold winters. During the spring thaw of the active layer, water flows into these cracks, freezes, and expands. This process is repeated year after year, and the ice-filled cracks increase in size. The resulting ice wedges are often several metres deep and a few tens of centimetres wide at the top. Along the sides of ice wedges, the soil is deformed and compressed. Because of this disturbance and sediment that may be washed into the crack as the ice melts, relict patterned ground may be preserved during a period of warmer climate long after the permafrost has thawed. Today, relict patterned ground that formed during the last ice age exists more than 1,000 km (about 620 miles) to the south of the present limit of permafrost.

When the active layer of permafrost moves under the influence of gravity, the process is termed gelifluction. The soft flowing layer is often folded and draped on hillsides and at the base of slopes as solifluction, or gelifluction, lobes.

In some permafrost areas, a locally abundant groundwater supply present at a relatively shallow depth may cause the exceptional growth of ice within a confined area. The sustained supply of liquid water results in the expansion of an increasingly large, lens-shaped ice body. These conical mounds, or pingos, may be several tens of metres high and hundreds of metres in diameter.

CHAPTER 7
TECTONIC LANDFORMS AND METEORITE CRATERS

As mentioned earlier, tectonic landforms are relief features that are produced chiefly by uplift or subsidence of Earth's crust or by upward magmatic movements. They include mountains, plateaus, and rift valleys.

Virtually all large-scale landforms are the result of both tectonic processes that built the large differences in elevation and erosional processes that sculpted the relief of such areas into their individual shapes. Thus, it might be said that tectonic processes built the Alps, but erosional processes gave the Matterhorn its unique profile. In all cases, erosion acts to reduce differences in elevation, but when the rate of erosion is not too rapid, landforms created by tectonic processes can persist for hundreds of millions of years after the processes have ceased to operate.

Despite the ubiquity of landforms arising from tectonic and erosional processes, extraterrestrial impacts also play a part in landform evolution. On Earth the initial craters and other landforms created by extraterrestrial impacts are later altered by other processes, such as erosion, glacial scouring, and plate tectonics. Meteorite crater formation is arguably the most important geologic process in the solar system, as meteorite craters cover most solid-surface bodies, Earth being a notable exception. Meteorite craters can be found not only on rocky surfaces like that of the Moon but also on the surfaces of comets and ice-covered moons of the outer planets.

TECTONIC LANDFORMS

Whereas erosion shapes landforms, their origins lie in tectonic processes that build the major structures of Earth. The word *tectonic* is derived from the Greek word *tekton*, which means "builder." Tectonic processes build landforms mainly by causing the uplift or subsidence of rock material—blocks, layers, or slices of Earth's crust, molten lavas, and even large masses that include the entire crust and uppermost part of the planet's mantle. In some areas, these processes create and maintain high elevations such as mountains and plateaus. In others, they produce topographic depressions, as exemplified by Death Valley in the western United States, the Dead Sea in the Middle East, or the Turfan Depression in western China. Virtually all areas below sea level have been formed by tectonic processes.

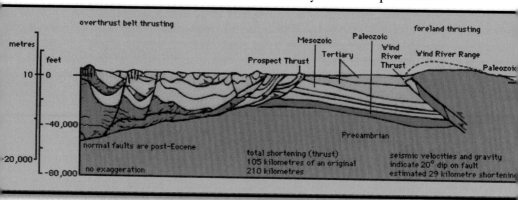

East–west cross section of the fold and thrust belt in eastern Idaho (left) *and the block-faulted uplift of the Wind River Range in Wyoming* (right). Adapted from Robbie Gries, "Oil and Gas Prospecting Beneath Precambrian of Foreland Thrust Plates in Rocky Mountains," *The American Association of Petroleum Geologists Bulletin,* vol. 67, no. 1 (January 1983); © copyright 1983, The American Association of Petroleum Geologists, all rights reserved

Mountain ranges and plateaus result either from the uplift of Earth's surface or from the emplacement of volcanic rock onto the surface. Many mountain ranges consist of chains of volcanoes that are made up of rocks derived from depths of tens of kilometres below the surface. Some plateaus are created by huge outpourings of lavas over vast areas. In addition, the intrusion of molten rock into the crust from below can raise the surface. Many other mountain ranges have been formed by the overthrusting of one terrain or block of crust over an adjacent one, which is another mechanism that uplifts the surface. Similarly, the folding of rocks at the surface creates the ridges and valleys that define some mountain chains. These processes of overthrusting (or underthrusting) and folding result from horizontal forces that cause crustal shortening (in its horizontal dimension) and crustal thickening. Finally, heating and thermal expansion of the outer 100 to 200 km (about 60 to 125 miles) of Earth can uplift broad areas into either mountain ranges or plateaus.

Similarly, tectonic valleys, basins, and depressions of smaller size can form by the reverse of two of the processes mentioned above. Crustal extension (in its horizontal dimension) and crustal thinning occur where two blocks

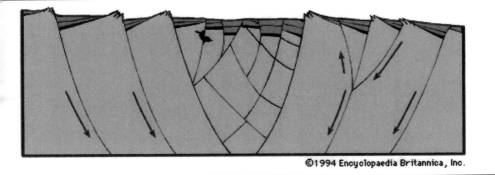

©1994 Encyclopaedia Britannica, Inc.

Idealized cross section of a tectonic valley showing the subsidence and rotation of blocks along curved faults. Encyclopaedia Britannica, Inc.

of crust move apart; a valley or basin forms between such blocks where the intervening segment of crust has been thinned and its top surface subsides. Likewise, subsidence of Earth's surface can occur by the cooling and the thermal contraction of the outer 100 km of the planet. Plateaus and entire mountain ranges can subside by this mechanism to form large basins in some areas.

SALT DOMES

Salt domes are largely subsurface geologic structures that consist of a vertical cylinder of salt (including halite and other evaporites) 1 km (0.6 mile) or more in diameter. These structures are embedded in horizontal or inclined strata. In the broadest sense, the term includes both the core of salt and the strata that surround and are "domed" by the core. Similar geologic structures in which salt is the main component are salt pillows and salt walls, which are related genetically to salt domes, and salt anticlines, which are essentially folded rocks pierced by upward migrating salt. Other material, such as gypsum and shale, form the cores of similar geologic structures, and all such structures, including salt domes, are known as diapiric structures, or diapirs, from the Greek word *diapeirein*, "to pierce." The embedded material in all instances appears to have pierced surrounding rocks. Upward flow is believed to have been caused by the following: gravity forces, in situations where relatively light rocks are overlain by relatively heavy rocks and the light rocks rise like cream to the surface; tectonic (earth-deformation) forces, in situations where mobile material (not necessarily lighter) is literally squeezed by lateral stress through less mobile material; or a combination of both gravity and tectonic forces.

"Classic" salt domes develop directly from bedded salt by gravitational stress alone. Salt domes also may develop

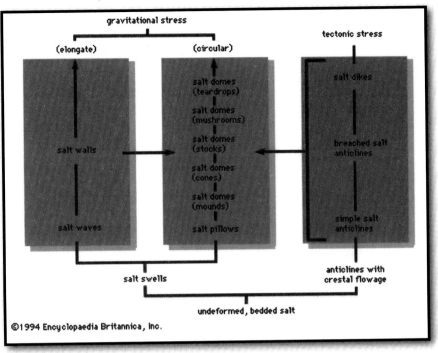

Interrelationships of salt structures. Encyclopaedia Britannica, Inc.

from salt walls and salt anticlines, however. In the latter case, the development of the domes results from superposition of gravitational stress on salt masses that initially developed due to tectonic stress.

PHYSICAL CHARACTERISTICS

A salt dome consists of a core of salt and an envelope of surrounding strata. In some areas, the core may contain "cap rock" and "sheath" in addition to salt.

The size of typical salt domes (including cap rock and sheath) varies considerably. In most cases, the diameter is 1 km (0.6 mile) or more and may range up to more than 10 km (about 6 miles). The typical salt dome is at least 2 km (about 1 mile) high (in the subsurface), and some are known to be higher than 10 km.

The cores of salt domes of the North American Gulf Coast consist virtually of pure halite (sodium chloride) with minor amounts of anhydrite (calcium sulfate) and traces of other minerals. Layers of white pure halite are interbedded with layers of black halite and anhydrite. German salt dome cores contain halite, sylvite, and other potash minerals. In Iranian salt domes, halite is mixed with anhydrite and marl (argillaceous limestone) and large blocks of limestone and igneous rock.

The interbedded salt–anhydrite and salt–potash layers are complexly folded; folds are vertical and more complex at the outer edge of the salt. In German domes, when relative age of the internal layers can be deciphered, older material is generally in the centre of the salt mass and younger at the edges. Study of halite grains in some Gulf Coast salt domes indicates a complex pattern of orientation that varies both vertically and horizontally in the domes. Mineral grains in the centre of a Caspian salt dome are vertical; those at its edge are horizontal.

Cap rock is a cap of limestone–anhydrite, characteristically 100 metres (328 feet) thick but ranging from 0 to 300 metres (0 to 980 feet). In many cases, particularly on Gulf Coast salt domes, the cap can be divided into three zones, more or less horizontally, namely, an upper calcite zone, a middle transitional zone characterized by the presence of gypsum and sulfur, and a lower anhydrite zone. These zones are irregular and generally are gradational with each other, although in some instances the contact between gypsum and anhydrite is quite abrupt. Cap rock is generally believed to develop from solution of salt from the top of the salt core; this leaves a residue of insoluble anhydrite that is later altered to gypsum, calcite, and sulfur. Presumably, solution takes place in the circulating (shallow) water zone; deeply buried domes with cap rock must have been shallow at some former time and subsequently buried.

Shale sheath is a feature that is common to many Gulf Coast salt domes. In shape, it may completely encase the salt (like a sheath), or it may be limited to the lower portions of the salt. It is most common on the deeper portions of salt domes whose tops are near the surface or on deeply buried salt domes. The fluid pressure within the shale is significantly greater than that within the surrounding rocks, and the stratification (bedding planes) of the shale is distorted. Fossils in the shale are older than in surrounding sediments, indicating that the shale came from an older, and therefore deeper, layer.

The strata around salt cores can be affected in three ways: they can be uplifted, they can be lowered, or they can be left unaffected while surrounding strata subside relatively. Uplifted strata have the structural features of domes or anticlines; characteristically they are domed over or around (or both) the core (including cap and sheath if present) and dip down into the surrounding synclines. The domed strata are generally broken by faults that radiate out from the salt on circular domes but that may be more linear on elongate domes or anticlines with one fault or set of faults predominant. Lowered strata develop into synclines, and a circular depression called a rim syncline may encircle or nearly encircle the domal uplift. Unaffected strata develop into highs surrounded by low areas. These highs, called remnant highs or turtleback highs, do not have as much vertical relief as the salt domes among which they are interspersed. Present-day structure of strata around salt domes may not in every instance coincide with the present-day position of the salt. This offset relationship suggests that late uplift of the salt dome shifted its centre compared with early uplift.

ORIGIN

In general, salt structures associated with folds have been linked with the same forces that caused the folding. Salt structures in areas without any apparent folding, however, puzzled early geologists and gave rise to a bewildering series of hypotheses. It is now generally agreed that salt structures (and diapiric or piercement structures) develop as the result of gravitational forces, tectonic forces, or some combination of these forces, at the same time or with one force following the other. Whatever the precise circumstance, development of diapiric structures requires a rock that flows.

Although rock flow is difficult to visualize because of slow rates of movement, its results can be clearly seen: stonework that sags, mine and tunnel openings that flow shut, and glaciers of rock salt that move down mountainsides with all the features of glaciers of ice. Given very long periods of time and the relatively high temperature and pressure due to depth of burial, considerable movement of a relatively plastic material such as salt can result. A movement of 1 mm (0.039 inch) a year, for example, over a period of 1 million years would produce a net movement of 1,000 metres (3,280 feet). The most common rocks that flow are halite, sylvite, gypsum, and high-pressure shale. These rocks also have densities that are lower than consolidated rock such as sandstone, and if buried by sandstone they would be gravitationally unstable. All of them are deposited by normal processes of sedimentation and are widespread in sedimentary strata.

Study of models and natural salt structures have led to a reconstruction of the sequence of events in the development of salt domes. First, thick salt is deposited and buried by denser sedimentary strata. The salt and overlying strata become unstable and salt begins to flow from an

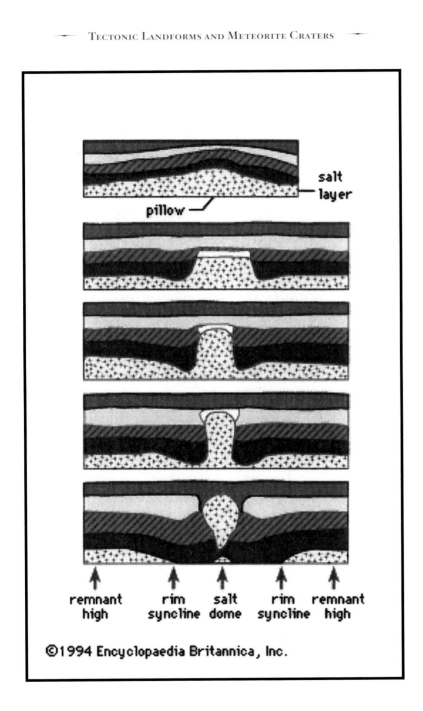

Stages in the development of shallow piercement salt dome; initial stage at left.
Encyclopaedia Britannica, Inc.

undeformed bed to a rounded salt pillow. Flow continues into the centre of the pillow, doming the overlying strata; at the same time the area from which the salt flowed subsides, forming a rim syncline. The strata overlying the salt, because they are literally spread apart, are subject to tension, and fractures (faults) develop. Eventually, the salt breaks through the centre of the domed area, giving rise to a plug-shaped salt mass in the centre of domed, upturned, and pierced strata. Upward growth of the salt continues apace with deposition of additional strata, and the salt mass tends to maintain its position at or near the surface. If the salt supply to the growing dome is exhausted during growth, development ceases at whatever stage the dome has reached, and the dome is buried.

DISTRIBUTION

Salt structures develop in any sedimentary basin in which thick salt deposits were later covered with thick sedimentary strata or tectonically deformed or both. With the exception of the shield areas, salt structures are widespread. By their very nature, the classic salt domes generated by gravitational instability alone are limited to areas that have not been subject to significant tectonic stress. Some salt domes do, however, occur in regions that were subject to tectonic stress. Three of the many areas of salt structures in the world are representative of all; these are the Gulf of Mexico region of North America, the North German–North Sea area of Europe, and the Iraq–Iran–Arabian Peninsula of the Middle East.

ECONOMIC SIGNIFICANCE

Salt domes make excellent traps for hydrocarbons because surrounding sedimentary strata are domed upward and blocked off. Major accumulations of oil and natural gas are associated with domes in the United States, Mexico, the North Sea, Germany, and Romania. In the Gulf Coastal Plain of Texas and Louisiana, salt domes will be a significant source of hydrocarbons for some years to come. Huge supplies of oil have been found in salt dome areas off the coast of Louisiana. Some individual salt domes in this region are believed to have reserves of more than 500,000,000 barrels of oil. Salt domes in northern Germany have produced oil for many years. Exploration for salt dome oil in the North Sea has extended production offshore.

The cap rock of shallow salt domes in the Gulf Coast contains large quantities of elemental sulfur. Salt domes are major sources of salt and potash in the Gulf Coast and Germany; halite and sylvite are extracted from domes by underground mining and by brine recovery.

Salt domes have also been utilized for underground storage of liquefied propane gas. Storage "bottles" are made by drilling into the salt and then forming a cavity by subsequent solution. Such cavities, because of their impermeability, also have been considered as sites for disposal of radioactive wastes.

TECTONIC BASINS AND RIFT VALLEYS

These landforms are characterized by relatively steep, mountainous sides and flat floors. The steep sides are created by displacement on faults such that the valley floor moves down relative to the surrounding margins, or, conversely, the margins move up relative to the floor. Differences in the elevations of valley floors and surrounding mountains or plateaus range from only several hundred metres to more than 2,000 metres (about 6,560 feet) in major rift valleys. The widths of tectonic valleys and basins vary from as little as 10 km (about 6 miles) to more than 100 km (about 60 miles). Their lengths typically are hundreds of kilometres, but range from a few tens to thousands of kilometres.

The vast majority of tectonic basins and valleys are produced by an extension of Earth's crust and the subsequent dropping of a block of crust into the space created by the divergence of large crustal blocks or lithospheric plates. The extension of the brittle crust causes it to fracture, and as the adjoining crustal blocks or plates move apart, a smaller block slides down into the resulting gap. The down-dropping of this block between the surrounding fault blocks, which commonly rise during an episode of crustal extension, creates a rift valley or tectonic basin. The geologic term for this type of tectonic depression is "graben," the German word for "ditch" or "trough."

Tectonic depressions also can be produced by horizontal compression of the crust—i.e., by crustal shortening. Two types of compressional tectonic valleys and basins can be recognized: ramp valleys and foreland basins. A ramp valley is analogous to a rift valley but is formed by the margins of the valley being pushed over its floor. A foreland basin, on the other hand, results from a gentle downward bending or flexing of the entire lithosphere.

RIFT VALLEYS

In the simplest case, a rift valley forms when a block of crust, tens of kilometres wide and hundreds of kilometres long, drops down between two diverging lithospheric plates, much as the keystone in an arch will fall if the walls of the arch move apart. This process is responsible for the relatively symmetrical cross sections of most parts of the East African Rift System, where the valley floor lies 1,000 metres (3,280 feet) or more below the higher plateaus of Ethiopia and Kenya. In some places, the sides of the rift valley make single, steep walls as high as 1,000 metres.

Lake Tanganyika, in the centre of the East African Rift System. As the Nubian and Somalian plates continue to diverge from one another, the depth of Lake Tanganyika increases. Kay Honkanen/Ostman Agency

In others, the edges of the valleys consist of steps or tiers with each small inner block dropping with respect to its neighbouring outer block. Thus the deepest part of the rift valley is not always at its centre.

Volcanoes mark the axes of some, but by no means all, rift valleys. Where the lithospheric plates separate and the crust is thinned, the underlying parts of the lithosphere in the mantle also must diverge, allowing hot material from the asthenosphere to rise to shallow depths. Some such material from the asthenosphere has erupted at volcanoes within the eastern rift of the East African Rift System in Ethiopia and Kenya and within a small section of the western rift in Congo (Kinshasa). Most of the western rift, which extends from Uganda through Lake Tanganyika and Lake Nyasa (Malawi), however, has no volcanoes.

Many rift valleys are asymmetrical with one steep wall and one gentle side. The steep wall is formed by slip on one or two major faults; however, unlike the simple grabens described above, no major fault bounds the other side of the rift valley. Instead, the other side is formed by a flexing of the lithosphere and by a tilting of the surface. Small faults are common, but over all there is a relatively gentle slope into the rift valley. Death Valley, in California, has a very steep eastern margin and a gentler western edge. The floor of Death Valley is moving down along a fault along its eastern margin and is rotating about an axis west of the valley. Thus, the most rapid sinking is along the valley's eastern edge, where the lowest point in the Western Hemisphere, Badwater, lies 86 metres (about 280 feet) below sea level. Similarly, the Baikal Rift in Siberia, which contains the deepest lake in the world, Lake Baikal, has a very steep northwestern edge and a gentler southeastern margin.

Within some rift valleys are narrow ridges (10 to 20 kilometres [about 6 to 12 miles] wide) that are bounded by steep sides, separating the ridges from neighbouring parts of the valleys. A ridge of this kind is called a horst, a block of crust bounded by faults such that the flanks of the range have dropped with respect to it. A horst is the opposite of a graben. The third highest mountain in Africa, Margherita Peak of the Ruwenzori Range (located along the border of Uganda and Congo) marks the highest point on a horst within the western rift of the East African Rift System.

Horsts can be found in most rift valleys, but unlike the Ruwenzori, they rarely dominate the landscape. The floors of most rift valleys have dropped relative to the surrounding landscape, but the tops of horsts rarely stand higher than the surface outside the valleys. Thus most horsts are merely blocks that have remained at nearly the same height as the unbroken crust outside of the rift valleys. Most horsts exist because rift valleys formed adjacent to them, not because they were elevated.

Some rift valleys, such as the East African Rift Valley in Ethiopia and Kenya, have formed over large domes. Upwelling of hot material within the underlying asthenosphere not only pushes the overlying lithosphere up but heats it as well, causing it to expand. To some extent the upward bulging of the lithosphere causes it to stretch, and this stretching manifests itself as a rift valley. Rift valleys that have formed in this way are commonly associated with extensive volcanism.

Certain rift valleys seem to be created by distant forces acting upon the lithosphere. These valleys cannot be associated with large domes, and in general volcanism is rare or absent. The Baikal Rift, for example, seems to be associated with the same forces that are pushing India into the rest of Eurasia. Moreover, though the elevations of the flanks are high (more than 3,000 metres [9,850 feet] in some places), the overall elevation decreases rapidly to only a couple of hundred metres at distances of just 50 to 100 km (about 30 to 60 miles) northwest of Lake Baikal. Thus, a broad dome is not present.

BASINS AND RANGES

Some areas, such as the Basin and Range Province of the western United States (Utah, Nevada, and California), contain an extensive network of relatively small tectonic depressions closely akin to rift valleys. The topography consists of basins 10 to 30 km (about 6 to 19 miles) wide and 50 to 200 km (about 30 to 125 miles) long, separated by ranges of similar dimensions. The basins contain young sediment derived from the neighbouring ranges and are quite flat. The sides of the basins can be steep or gentle. Where a major fault separates a basin from a range, the edge of the basin is often steep. Where the edge of the basin is produced by the tilting of the basin down and of the range up, the flank is gentle, with average slopes ranging up to 15°.

These tilted, gently dipping slopes are particularly apparent wherever lavas, resistant to erosion in dry climates, had flowed onto the surfaces before they were tilted. Such tilted lava-capped surfaces are known as louderbacks. In sum, the tectonic basins of the Basin and Range Province are similar to rift valleys, but their dimensions are smaller, and the ranges are tilted blocks or horsts.

Networks of basins and ranges exist in several other high plateaus. Northerly trending basins lace the Tibetan Plateau; however, unlike those of the western United States, they are more widely spaced, occurring hundreds of kilometres apart. Moreover, a single northerly trending range in Tibet does not in general separate neighbouring basins from one another. The development of a basin and range morphology in Tibet is at a much earlier geologic stage than that of the western United States. The landscape of western Turkey likewise is cut by easterly trending basins and neighbouring ranges that were formed by crustal extension in its north–south dimension. This morphology of basins and ranges extends westward beneath the Aegean Sea. Many of the islands in the Aegean are ranges between basins that stand high enough to poke above sea level. Thus, whereas the dominant feature in a rift valley is the deep wide valley itself, the ranges and valleys are of comparable importance in basin and range topography.

PULL-APART BASINS

Some tectonic valleys are rectangular or rhomb-shaped basins, bounded by as many as four steep sides. The Dead Sea, the lowest place on Earth, lies 396 metres (1,300 feet) below sea level at the bottom of just such a basin. Another is the Imperial Valley of southern California, most of which also lies below sea level. These tectonic valleys are closely related to major strike-slip faults—nearly vertical faults along which material on one side moves horizontally with respect to that on the other.

In regions such as the Dead Sea or southern California, nearly parallel strike-slip faults bound two sides of the tectonic valley and end at the valley. Slip on the overlapping segments of the strike-slip faults results in crustal extension in the region between the two faults. Thus two sides of the tectonic valley are bounded by faults with primarily horizontal displacement, and the other two sides are bounded by faults with vertical components of slip. These basins are called pull-apart basins because the crust is literally pulled apart in the section between the two strike-slip faults.

RAMP VALLEYS

As previously noted, these depressions are similar to rift valleys, but they have been formed by the opposite process — crustal shortening. A ramp valley develops when blocks of crust are thrust toward one another and up onto an intervening crustal block. The latter is forced down by the weight of this material, resulting in the formation of the valley. The thrusting of the material onto the intervening crustal block creates high mountains adjacent to the valley.

Ramp valleys are characterized by steep sides tens of kilometres apart, and flat floors, which contain debris eroded from the neighbouring mountains. Escarpments on the edges of ramp valleys are not as sharply defined as for simple rift valleys, but the surrounding mountains can be higher than those that bound the latter. To a casual observer, the landscapes of ramp and rift valleys are very similar. In fact, early theories for rift valleys incorrectly attributed their origin to that of ramp valleys.

The most spectacular example of a ramp valley is the Turfan Depression, the second lowest place on Earth (154 metres [about 500 feet] below sea level), which lies within the Tien Shan of western China and along the northern margin of the Gobi. In general, the rapid filling of ramp valleys in all but the most arid climates makes them ephemeral features; however, small, young ramp valleys can be found in the South Island of New Zealand east of the Southern Alps, and remnants of ramp valleys lie within the Rocky Mountains of the western United States.

FORELAND BASINS

These lie in front of major mountain ranges—e.g., south of the Himalayas, north of the Alps, and east of the Canadian Rocky Mountains. Most basins of this kind are subsurface features, filled with sediment eroded from the adjacent mountain ranges; thus, they are not easily recognized in the flat landscape that is visible. Foreland basins are formed because the overthrusting of the mountains onto a neighbouring lithospheric plate places a heavy load on the plate and flexes it down, much as a diving board is flexed down by the weight of the diver. Foreland basins are deepest and young sediments are thickest next to the mountain range, and the thickness of material decreases gradually and smoothly away from the mountains. The rapid deposition of sediment from the mountains makes a nearly flat surface, such as the Indo-Gangetic Plain of northern Pakistan and India where the Indus and Ganges rivers flow south of the Himalayas. Foreland basins can be important sites of oil and gas reserves.

METEORITE CRATERS AS MEASURES OF GEOLOGIC ACTIVITY

Meteorite craters, which appear as depressions in Earth's surface, result from the impact of a natural object from interplanetary space with Earth or with other comparatively large solid bodies such as the Moon, other planets

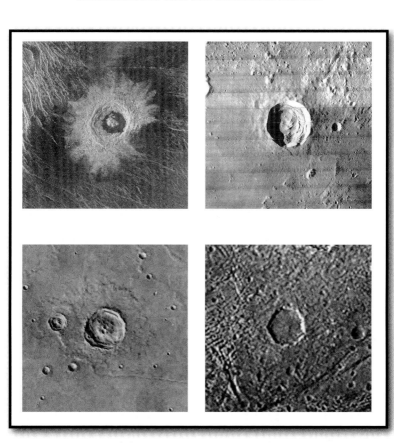

Four impact craters of the same size (30 km [20 miles] in diameter) imaged by spacecraft on different solid bodies of the solar system and reproduced at the same scale. They are (clockwise from upper left) *Golubkhina crater on Venus, Kepler crater on the Moon, an unnamed crater on Jupiter's moon Ganymede, and an unnamed crater on Mars. The images are oriented such that the craters appear illuminated from the left; the Venusian crater is imaged in radar wavelengths, the others in visible light.* (Venus and Moon) Robert Herrick/Lunar and Planetary Institute; (Mars) Calvin Hamilton/Los Alamos National Laboratory; (Ganymede) Paul Schenk/Lunar and Planetary Institute

and their satellites, or larger asteroids and comets. For this discussion, the term *meteorite crater* is considered to be synonymous with *impact crater*. As such, the colliding objects are not restricted by size to meteorites as they are found on Earth, where the largest known meteorite is a nickel-iron object less than 3 metres (10 feet) across. Rather, they include chunks of solid material of the same nature as comets or asteroids and in a wide range of sizes—from small meteoroids up to comets and asteroids themselves.

The formation of the solar system left countless pieces of debris in the form of asteroids and comets and their fragments. Gravitational interactions with other objects routinely send this debris on a collision course with planets and their moons. The resulting impact from a piece of debris produces a surface depression many times larger than the original object. Although all meteorite craters are grossly similar, their appearance varies substantially with both size and the body on which they occur. If no other geologic processes have occurred on a planet or moon, its entire surface is covered with craters as a result of the impacts sustained over the past 4.6 billion years since the major bodies of the solar system formed. On the other hand, the absence or sparseness of craters on a body's surface, as is the case for Earth's surface, is an indicator of some other geologic process (e.g., erosion or surface melting) occurring during the body's history that is eliminating the craters.

THE IMPACT-CRATERING PROCESS

When an asteroidal or cometary object strikes a planetary surface, it is traveling typically at several tens of kilometres per second—many times the speed of sound. A collision at such extreme speeds is called a hypervelocity impact. Although the resulting depression may bear some resemblance to the hole that results from throwing a pebble into a sandbox, the physical process that occurs is actually much closer to that of an atomic bomb explosion. A large meteorite impact releases an enormous amount of kinetic energy in a small area over a short time. Planetary scientists' knowledge of the crater-formation process is derived from field studies of nuclear and chemical explosions and of rocket missile impacts, from laboratory simulations of impacts using gun-impelled high-velocity projectiles, from computer models of the sequence of crater formation, and from observations of meteorite craters themselves. A generally accepted model of impact cratering postulates the following sequence of events, which for purposes of illustration refers to a planet as the impacted body.

Immediately after a meteorite strikes the surface of the planet, shock waves are imparted both to the surface material and to the meteorite itself. As the shock waves expand into the planet and the meteorite, they dissipate energy and form zones of vaporized, melted, and crushed material outward from a point below the planet's surface that is roughly as deep as the meteorite's diameter. The meteorite is usually vaporized completely by the released energy. Within the planet, the expanding shock wave is closely followed by a second wave, called a rarefaction, or release, wave, generated by the reflection of the original wave from the free surface of the planet. The dissipation of these two waves sets up large pressure gradients within the planet. The pressure gradients generate a subsurface flow that projects material upward and outward from the point of impact. The material being excavated resembles an outward-slanted curtain moving away from the point of impact.

The depression that is produced has the form of an upward-facing parabolic bowl about four times as wide as it is deep. The diameter of the crater relative to that of the meteorite depends on several factors, but it is thought for most craters to be about 10 to 1. Excavated material surrounds the crater, causing its rim to be elevated above the surrounding terrain. The height of the rim accounts for about 5 percent of the total crater depth. The excavated

Moltke crater, a simple crater on the Moon photographed by Apollo 10 astronauts in 1969. The depression, about 7 km (4.3 miles) in diameter, is parabolic in shape, and the excavated material forms a raised rim and a surrounding ejecta blanket. NASA

material outside the crater is called the ejecta blanket. The elevation of the ejecta blanket is highest at the rim and falls off rapidly with distance.

When the crater is relatively small, its formation ends when excavation stops. The resulting landform is called a simple crater. The smallest craters require no more than a few seconds to form completely, whereas craters that are tens of kilometres wide probably form in a few minutes.

As meteorite craters become larger, however, the formation process does not cease with excavation. For such craters the parabolic hole is apparently too large to support itself, and it collapses in a process that generates a variety of features. This collapse process is called the modification stage, and the final depression is known as a complex crater. The modification stage of complex crater formation is poorly understood because the process is

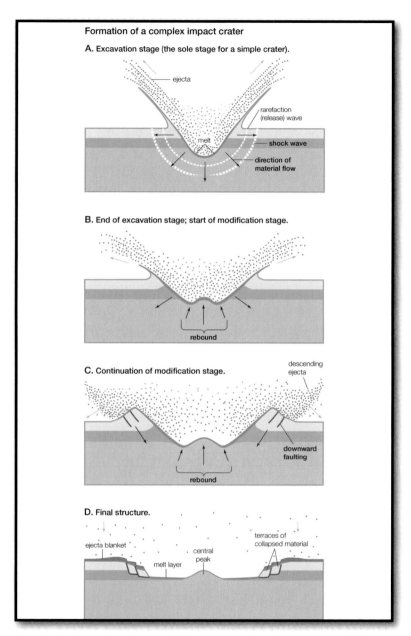

Formation of a complex impact crater

A. Excavation stage (the sole stage for a simple crater).

ejecta

rarefaction (release) wave

melt

shock wave

direction of material flow

B. End of excavation stage; start of modification stage.

rebound

C. Continuation of modification stage.

descending ejecta

downward faulting

rebound

D. Final structure.

ejecta blanket

melt layer

central peak

terraces of collapsed material

Steps in the formation of a complex impact crater. During excavation (A) material thrown out of the bowl-shaped depression resembles an outward-moving curtain. As formation of a larger crater progresses (B–D), the depression is unable to support itself. The centre of the depression rebounds upward, and the edges collapse to form terraces. Encyclopædia Britannica, Inc.

mostly beyond current technological capability to model or simulate and because explosion craters on Earth are too small to produce true complex crater landforms. Although conceptually the modification stage is considered to occur after excavation, it may be that collapse begins before excavation is complete. The current state of knowledge of complex crater formation relies primarily on inferences drawn from field observations of Earth's impact structures and spacecraft imagery of impact craters on other solid bodies in the solar system.

Features associated with complex craters are generally attributed to material moving back toward the point of impact. Smaller complex craters have a flat floor caused by a rebound of material below the crater after excavation. This same rebound causes large complex craters to have a

Orientale Basin, or Mare Orientale, a multiringed impact basin on the Moon, in an image made in 1967 by the Lunar Orbiter 4 spacecraft. Two widely spaced ring structures, which are inward-facing faults called megaterraces, surround the initial excavation cavity (partially flooded with lava). The outer megaterrace, named the Cordillera Mountains, is 930 km (580 miles) in diameter. NASA/Lunar Planetary Institute

central peak; even-larger craters have a raised circular ring within the crater. Analogues to the central peak and ring are the back splash and outward ripple that are seen briefly when a pebble is dropped into water. Also associated with the modification stage is downward faulting, which forms terraces of large blocks of material along the inner rim of the initial cavity. In the case of very large craters, discrete, inward-facing, widely spaced faults called megaterraces form well outside the initial excavation cavity. Craters with megaterraces are called impact basins.

VARIATIONS IN CRATERS ACROSS THE SOLAR SYSTEM

Although impact craters on all the solid bodies of the solar system are grossly similar, their appearances from body to body can vary dramatically. The most-notable differences are a result of variations among the bodies in surface gravity and crustal properties. A higher surface gravitational acceleration creates a greater pressure difference between the floor of the crater and the surface surrounding the crater. That pressure difference is thought to play a large role in driving the collapse process that forms complex craters, the effect being that the smallest complex craters seen on higher-gravity bodies are smaller than those on lower-gravity bodies. For example, the diameters of the smallest craters with central peaks on the Moon, Mercury, and Venus decrease in inverse proportion to the bodies' surface gravities; Mercury's surface gravity is more than twice that of the Moon, whereas Venus's gravity is more than five times that of the Moon.

The inherent strength of the impacted surface has an effect similar to that of surface gravity in that it is easier for craters to collapse on bodies with weaker near-surface materials. For example, the presence of water in the near-surface materials of Mars, a condition thought to be likely, would help explain why the smallest complex craters there are smaller than on Mercury, which has a similar surface gravity. Layering in a body's near-surface material in which weak material overlies stronger strata is thought to modify the excavation process and contribute to the presence of craters with flat floors that contain a central pit. Such craters are particularly prominent on Ganymede, the largest moon of Jupiter.

Observations of the solid planets show clearly that the presence of an atmosphere changes the appearance of impact craters, but details of how the cratering process is altered are poorly understood. Comparison of craters on planets with and without an atmosphere shows no obvious evidence that an atmosphere does more than minimally affect the excavation of the cavity and any subsequent collapse. It does show, however, that an atmosphere strongly affects emplacement of the ejecta blanket. On an airless body the particles of excavated material follow ballistic trajectories. In the presence of an atmosphere most of this material mixes with the atmosphere and creates a surface-hugging fluid flow away from the crater that is analogous to volcanic pyroclastic flow on Earth. On an airless body an ejecta blanket shows a steady decrease in thickness away from the crater, but on a planet with an atmosphere the fluid flow of excavated material lays down a blanket that is relatively constant in thickness away from the crater and that ends abruptly at the outer edge of the flow. The well-preserved ejecta blankets around Venusian craters show this flow emplacement, and field observations of Earth's impact structures indicate that much of their ejecta were emplaced as flows. On Mars most of the ejecta blankets also appear to have been emplaced as flows, but many of these are probably mudflows caused by abundant water near the Martian surface.

TEKTITES

Tektites have been the subject of intense scientific scrutiny throughout much of the 20th century owing to their unknown and possibly extraterrestrial origins, but they are now recognized as having formed from the melting and rapid cooling of terrestrial rocks that have been vaporized by the high-energy impacts of large meteorites, comets, or asteroids upon Earth's surface. The extremely high temperatures and enormous pressures generated by such impacts melted the rocks at the site, producing clouds of molten silicate droplets that quickly cooled to a glassy form before falling back to Earth. The term is derived from the Greek word *tēktos*, meaning "melted," or "molten."

Tektites range in size from a few tens of micrometres to about 10 cm (4 inches) in diameter. Those larger than a few millimetres are all rich in silica; they are somewhat like terrestrial obsidians but differ from them and other terrestrial volcanic glasses by their lower water content. Chemically, tektites are further distinguished from acid igneous (granitic) rocks by their lower content of soda and potash and their higher content of lime, magnesia, and iron. Under the microscope, tektites are seen to lack the small crystals (microlites) characteristic of terrestrial volcanic glasses.

Tektites are of varied colour, shape, and surface sculpture. In colour they range from green or dark brown to black. Some are lustrous and others have a delicate sheen from minute alternating ridges and furrows that swirl over the entire surface. The younger, less-corroded tektites include those with spherical, elliptical, lenticular, teardrop, dumbbell, disk, and button shapes.

Microtektites of millimetre and smaller size, first discovered in 1968, exhibit wider variation in composition than the large tektites; e.g., their silica content can be as low as 50 percent, similar to that of terrestrial basalts. Microtektites have been found so far only in deep-sea sediments, probably because of the difficulty of distinguishing them in the more abundant and coarser land sediments. They are distinguished from volcanic ash by their rounded shapes and composition, which is identical with that of the large tektites.

METEORITE CRATERS AS MEASURES
OF GEOLOGIC ACTIVITY

A common misconception is that Earth has very few impact craters on its surface because its atmosphere is an effective shield against meteoroids. Earth's atmosphere certainly slows and prevents typical asteroidal fragments up to a few tens of metres across from reaching the surface and forming a true hypervelocity impact crater, but kilometre-scale objects of the kind that created the smallest telescopically visible craters on the Moon are not significantly slowed by Earth's atmosphere. The Moon and Earth certainly experienced similar numbers of these larger impact events, but on Earth subsequent geologic processes (e.g., volcanism and plate tectonic processes) completely eliminated or severely degraded the craters. The dominant role of erosion as a geologic process that destroys craters is unique to Earth among the solid bodies that have been well-studied. Erosional processes may be important in eliminating craters on Titan, Saturn's largest moon, if methane proves to play the role there that water does in Earth's hydrologic cycle. Elsewhere only volcanic and tectonic processes are capable of eliminating large meteorite craters.

An absence or sparseness of craters in a given region of a large solid body indicates that relatively recent geologic activity has resurfaced it or otherwise greatly altered its surface appearance. For example, on the Moon the dark mare regions are much less heavily cratered than the light highland areas because the mare were flooded by basaltic volcanic flows about one billion years after formation of the highland areas. From simple counts of the craters larger than a given size per unit area for different regions of a body, it is possible to determine relative surface ages of different regions in order to gain insight into a body's geologic history. For the Moon absolute ages can be assigned to regions with different numbers of craters per unit area because surface samples from several regions were collected during Apollo lunar landing missions and dated in laboratories on Earth. For other large bodies, assigning absolute ages to given regions based on the number of craters is based on estimates of asteroidal and cometary impact rates, the size range of those objects, and the size of the crater that forms from a given impacting object. Very little data exist as a basis for these estimates, particularly for impact rates. Absolute ages determined for planetary surfaces other than the Moon consequently have large uncertainties relative to the age of the solar system.

CONCLUSION

Some of the most interesting and beautiful parts of the natural world are mountains, valleys, drumlins, and other landforms. Formed by tectonic forces, erosion, extraterrestrial impacts, and the movement of water or glaciers, landforms range from large features, such as mountain ranges, that run the length of a continent to smaller singular structures, such as a small hill, a mountain valley, a cave, or an individual beach. Beyond their roles as influencers of weather and climate and as habitats for living things, landforms frame scenic vistas or provide the vantage points from which bodies of water, forested landscapes, and even cities can be viewed.

When one classifies landforms, one finds a great deal of overlap between the different categories. Given enough time, some landforms fall into many of the categories discussed in this book. For example, mountain ranges are products of plate tectonics, but they are also large continental features. Mountain ranges can be classified as structural landforms, because they are affected by erosional processes. If mountain ranges occur along the coast, some geomorphologists may even classify them as coastal features.

Such limitations in this classification highlight the fact that all landforms are constantly changing. The actions of wind, water, and ice are among the most noticeable forces that alter the appearance of mountains, river valleys, beaches, and other features. Change is also apparent within caves, as stalactites slowly accumulate minerals carried by drops of water. However, over millions of years, seismic activity and volcanism—along with long-term climate changes and sea-level fluctuations—have the power to remake entire continents.

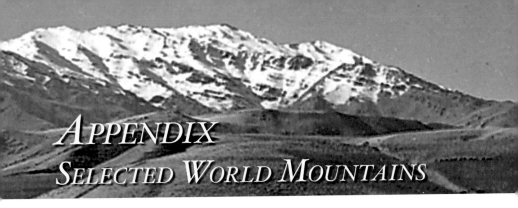

APPENDIX
SELECTED WORLD MOUNTAINS

NAME	RANGE	LOCATION	HEIGHT		YEAR FIRST CLIMBED
			FT	M	
Africa					
Kilimanjaro (Kibo peak)		Tanzania	19,340	5,895	1889
Mt. Kenya (Batian peak)		Kenya	17,058	5,199	1899
Margherita	Ruwenzori	Congo (Dem. Rep.)-Uganda	16,795	5,119	1906
Antarctica					
Vinson Massif	Sentinel Range	Ellsworth Mtns.	16,066	4,897	1966
Tyree	Sentinel Range	Ellsworth Mtns.	15,919	4,852	1967
Shinn	Sentinel Range	Ellsworth Mtns.	15,751	4,801	1966
Asia					
Everest (Chomol-ungma)	Himalayas	Nepal-Tibet, China	29,028	8,848	1953

| NAME | RANGE | LOCATION | HEIGHT | | YEAR FIRST CLIMBED |
			FT	M	
K2 (God-win Austen; Chogori)	Kara-koram	Pakistan-Xinjiang, China	28,251	8,611	1954
Kanchenjunga (Gangch-hendzonga)	Himalayas	Nepal-India	28,169	8,586	1955
Lhotse I	Himalayas	Nepal-Tibet, China	27,940	8,516	1956
Caucasus					
Elbrus	Caucasus	Russia	18,510	5,642	1874
Dykh-Tau	Caucasus	Russia	17,073	5,204	1888
Koshtan-Tau	Caucasus	Russia	16,900	5,151	1889
Europe					
Mont Blanc	Alps	France-Italy	15,771	4,807	1786
Dufourspitze (Monte Rosa)	Alps	Switzer-land-Italy	15,203	4,634	1855
Dom (Mischabel)	Alps	Switzer-land	14,911	4,545	1858
North America					
McKinley	Alaska	Alaska, U.S.	20,320	6,194	1913
Logan	St. Elias Mtns.	Yukon, Can.	19,524	5,951	1925
Citlaltépetl (Orizaba)	Cordillera Neo-Volcánica	Mexico	18,406	5,610	1848

NAME	RANGE	LOCATION	HEIGHT		YEAR FIRST CLIMBED
			FT	M	
Oceania					
Jaya (Sukarno, Carstensz)	Sudirman	Indonesia	16,500	5,030	1962
Pilimsit (Idenburg)	Sudirman	Indonesia	15,750	4,800	1962
Trikora (Wilhelmina)	Jayawijaya	Indonesia	15,580	4,750	1912
South America					
Aconcagua	Andes	Argentina-Chile	22,831	6,959	1897
Ojos del Salado	Andes	Argentina-Chile	22,615	6,893	1937
Bonete	Andes	Argentina	22,546	6,872	1913

Conversions rounded to nearest 10 feet.

GLOSSARY

aggradation A modification of Earth's surface in the direction of uniformity of grade by deposition.

allotropy the existence of a substance, especially an element, in two or more different forms (as of crystals), usually in the same phase.

alluvial fan Sedimentary deposit that accumulates at the mouth of a mountain canyon because of the reduction or cessation of sediment transport by the issuing stream.

anthropomorphic Ascribing human characteristics to nonhuman things.

arcuate Curved like a bow.

bajadas A broad slope of debris spread along the lower slopes of mountains by descending streams, usually found in arid or semiarid climates.

craton A stable, relatively immobile area of Earth's crust that forms the mass of a continent or the central basin of an ocean.

cordillera a system of mountain ranges often consisting of a number of more or less parallel chains.

débouché a point of emergence.

eolian borne, produced, or eroded by the wind.

endogenic Of or relating to metamorphism taking place within a planet or moon.

epeirogenic The deformation of Earth's crust by which the broader features of relief are produced.

epicontinental Lying upon a continent or a continental shelf.

escarpment A long cliff or steep slope separating two comparatively level or more gently sloping surfaces and resulting from erosion or faulting.

fluvial Of, relating to, or living in a stream or river, or produced by the action of a stream.

hydraulic Operated, moved, or effected by means of water.

hydrographic Of or relating to the characteristic features (as flow or depth) of bodies of water.

inselberg An isolated hill standing above plains, especially one that is left behind after other material erodes. The name is derived from the German term for "island mountains."

isostatic General equilibrium in Earth's crust maintained by a yielding flow of rock material beneath the surface under the stress of gravity.

lee The side of an area that is sheltered from the wind.

lithosphere The outer part of the solid Earth composed of rock essentially like that exposed at the surface, consisting of the crust and outermost layer of the mantle, and usually considered to be about 100 km (60 miles) in thickness.

meanders A winding path or course of a stream or river.

morphology Structure or form. More specifically, the external structure of rocks in relation to the development of erosional forms or topographic features.

orogeny the process of mountain formation especially by folding of Earth's crust.

outwash Debris in the glacial environment deposited directly by the ice (till) or, after reworking, by meltwater streams (outwash).

pans A natural basin or depression in land .

pediment A broad gently sloping bedrock surface with low relief that is situated at the base of a steeper slope and is usually thinly covered with alluvial gravel and sand.

peneplain A land surface of considerable area and slight relief shaped by erosion.

planation The condition or process of becoming flattened.

subaerial Situated on or immediately adjacent to Earth's surface.

tectonism The process of deformation that produces continents, ocean basins, plateaus, mountains, folds of strata, and faults in Earth's crust.

till Material laid down directly or reworked by a glacier. Typically, it is a mixture of rock fragments and boulders in a fine-grained sandy or muddy matrix.

topography The configuration of a surface including its relief and the position of its natural and man-made features.

uniformitarianism In geology, the doctrine that existing processes acting in the same manner and with essentially the same intensity as at present are sufficient to account for all geologic change.

wash The dry bed of a stream.

CONTINENTAL LANDFORMS

General overviews of geomorphology and the development of continental landforms are provided in Robert S. Anderson and Suzanne P. Anderson, *Geomorphology: The Mechanics and Chemistry of Landscapes* (2010); Dale F. Ritter, R. Craig Kochel, and Jerry R. Miller, *Process Geomorphology*, 4th ed. (2010); and Doug Burbank and Robert Anderson, *Tectonic Geomorphology* (2000). The seminal works of William Morris Davis, especially his 1899 essay "The Geographical Cycle" and his 1905 essay "The Geographical Cycle in an Arid Climate," both reprinted in *Geographical Essays* (1909, reprinted 1954), paved the way for Walther Penck, *Morphological Analysis of Land Forms: A Contribution to Physical Geology* (1953, reprinted 1972; originally published in German, 1924); and for Lester C. King, "Canons of Landscape Evolution," *Bulletin of the Geological Society of America*, 64:721–752 (1953).

MOUNTAINS AND VALLEYS

General treatments of mountains are provided in Philip N. Owens and Olav Slaymaker, *Mountain Geomorphology* (2004); William B. Bull, *Tectonic Geomorphology* (2007); and David R. Butler, Stephen J. Walsh, and George P. Malanson (eds.), *Mountain Geomorphology: Integrating Earth Systems* (2003).

Introductions to fluvial geomorphology and the development of landforms in valleys are found in Ro Charlton, *Fundamentals of Fluvial Geomorphology* (2007); and John

S. Bridge, *Rivers and Floodplains: Forms, Processes, and Sedimentary Record* (2003). Descriptions of valleys can be found in geomorphology textbooks, including M.J. Selby, *Earth's Changing Surface: An Introduction to Geomorphology* (1986); and Arthur L. Bloom, *Geomorphology: A Systematic Analysis of Late Cenozoic Landforms* (1978). The relevant fluvial phenomena are treated in David Knighton, *Fluvial Forms and Processes: A New Perspective* (1998); and the relevant hillslope phenomena in M.J. Selby and A.P.W. Hodder, *Hillslope Materials and Processes*, 2nd ed. (1993).

CAVES AND SAND DUNES

Two introductory texts are Arthur N. Palmer, *Cave Geology* (2007); and Derek C. Ford and Paul Williams, *Karst Hydrogeology and Geomorphology* (2007). A discussion of cave geology, hydrology, mineralogy, and biology can be found in T.D. Ford and C.H.D. Cullingford (eds.), *The Science of Speleology* (1976), with a good chapter on volcanic caves. Carol A. Hill and Paolo Forti, *Cave Minerals of the World*, 2nd ed. (1997), is a systematic description of minerals and speleothems. M.M. Sweeting, *Karst in China* (1995), examines the Chinese experience of karst research, focusing on the evaluation and analysis of Chinese research methods.

Dune geomorphology is described in Nicholas Lancaster, *Geomorphology of Desert Dunes* (1995). Descriptions and geographic distribution of forms produced by wind deposition are provided in a still-useful classic text, R.A. Bagnold, *The Physics of Blown Sand and Desert Dunes* (1941, reprinted 2005). More information is given in *A Study of Global Sand Seas* (1979); Carol S. Breed et al., "Eolian (Wind-Formed) Landforms," in Terah L. Smiley et al. (eds.), *Landscapes of Arizona: The Geological Story* (1984), pp. 359–413; and Ronald Greeley and James D. Iversen, *Wind as a Geological Process: On Earth, Mars, Venus, and Titan* (1985).

COASTAL LANDFORMS

An introduction to coastal geomorphology is provided in Eric Bird, *Coastal Geomorphology: An Introduction*, 2nd ed. (2008); and Gerhard Masselink and Michael Hughes, *Introduction to Coastal Processes and Geomorphology* (2003); and Robin Davidson-Arnott, *Introduction to Coastal Processes and Geomorphology* (2010). Other useful texts include Paul D. Komar, *Beach Processes and Sedimentation*, 2nd ed. (1997); Richard A. Davis, Jr., and Duncan Fitzgerald, *Beaches and Coasts* (2004); and Richard A. Davis, Jr., *Coastal Sedimentary Environments*, 2nd rev. and expanded ed. (1985). Alan S. Trenhaile, *The Geomorphology of Rock Coasts* (1987), is an advanced treatment that describes various coastal landforms and the physical and chemical processes contributing to their development.

GLACIAL LANDFORMS

Introductions to glacial landforms and processes are provided in Matthew M. Bennett and Neil F. Glasser (eds.), *Glacial Geology: Ice Sheets and Landforms*, 2nd ed. (2010); and I. Peter Martini, Michael E. Brookfield, and Steven Sadura, *Principles of Glacial Geomorphology and Geology* (2001). The classic text on glacial geology is Richard Foster Flint, *Glacial and Quaternary Geology* (1971); it provides encyclopaedic coverage, including an extensive bibliography. Hypotheses and observations on glacial erosion and deposition are included in David Drewry, *Glacial Geologic Processes* (1986), even though the coverage of glacial landforms is not complete. David E. Sugden and Brian S. John, *Glaciers and Landscape: A Geomorphological Approach* (1976, reprinted 1984), is an excellent detailed introduction to glacial landforms and the processes that shaped them. The most comprehensive and up-to-date account of glacial geomorphology and sedimentology is Douglas I. Benn and

David J.A. Evans, *Glaciers and Glaciation* (1998). A detailed discussion of the formation of permafrost can be found in Stuart A. Harris, *The Permafrost Environment* (1986), and in Peter J. Williams and Michael W. Smith, *The Frozen Earth: Fundamentals of Geocryology* (1989).

TECTONIC LANDFORMS

General descriptions of landforms created by tectonic forces occur in David M. Ferrari and Antonio R. Guiseppi (eds.), *Geomorphology and Plate Tectonics* (2009); Doug Burbank and Robert Anderson, *Tectonic Geomorphology* (2000); and Michael A. Summerfield, *Global Geomorphology* (1991). An excellent introduction to geology, somewhat dated but very well illustrated, is Arthur Holmes, *Principles of Physical Geology*, 2nd rev. ed. (1965), with a particularly good treatment of rift valleys. William J. Perry, Dietrich H. Roder, and David R. Lageson (comps.), *North American Thrust-Faulted Terranes* (1984), is a collection of technical papers describing segments of folded and thrusted mountain belts in North America and the mechanics of such deformation. Introductory articles on volcanism at hot spots and island arcs include K. Burke and T. Wilson, "Hot Spots on Earth's Surface," *Scientific American*, 235(2):46–57 (August 1976); and Bruce D. Marsh, "Island-Arc Volcanism," *American Scientist*, 67(2):161–172 (March-April 1979). A discussion of the forces that support mountain ranges and how some ranges are constructed can be found in Peter Molnar, "The Structure of Mountain Ranges," *Scientific American*, 255(1):70–79 (July 1986).

PLAYAS

A survey of the flora of North American playas is provided in David A. Haukos and Loren M. Smith, *Common*

Flora of the Playa Lakes (1997). A valuable review is the chapter by P.A. Shaw and David S.G. Thomas on pans, playas, and salt lakes in David S.G. Thomas (ed.), *Arid Zone Geomorphology: Process, Form, and Change in Drylands*, 2nd ed. (1997).

TECTONIC BASINS AND RIFT VALLEYS

A stunning treatment of Africa's rift valley is provided in Pavitt Nigel, *Africa's Great Rift Valley* (2001). B.H. Baker, P.A. Mohr, and L.A.J. Williams, *Geology of the Eastern Rift System of Africa* (1972), provides a summary of the eastern branch of the East African Rift System. More specific treatment is found in B.H. Baker and J. Wohlenberg, "Structure and Evolution of the Kenya Rift Valley," *Nature*, 229(5286):538–542 (Feb. 19, 1971). Also, a useful series of reviews can be found in G. Pàlmason (ed.), *Continental and Oceanic Rifts* (1982).

METEORITE CRATERS

Overviews of the study of meteorite craters can be found in Bevan M. French, *Traces of Catastrophe: A Handbook of Shock-Metamorphic Effects in Terrestrial Meteorite Impact Structures* (1998); and Henry J. Melosh, *Impact Cratering: A Geologic Process* (1989). An overview of the formation of impact basins and their appearance throughout the solar system is Paul D. Spudis, *The Geology of Multi-Ring Impact Basins: The Moon and Other Planets* (1993). Important collections of scientific papers on impact craters include Burkhard O. Dressler and Virgil L. Sharpton (eds.), *Large Meteorite Impacts and Planetary Evolution II* (1999); and Lawrence T. Silver and Peter H. Schultz (eds.), *Geological Implications of Impacts of Large Asteroids and Comets on Earth*

INDEX